# Teaching
# Learning

When Sid Jacobson invited me to preview his new book, Teaching Learning, I was delighted as I know how knowledgeable he is; and how good a writer as well. THIS BOOK IS GREAT!

Sid has written what may be the definitive guide for parents (and teachers, counselors, therapists, coaches and anyone else who works with children). He literally covers it all: how to prepare yourself, the most important things you need to pay attention to when you are working with children to help them succeed, motivation, strategies, interventions. He has addressed more things than I could think of that will help your child to enjoy the process of learning.

I know Sid as a Master NLP Trainer and he's translated what could be incomprehensible to the average person into a virtual step-by-step guide book to what it takes to make sure your child succeeds. If you apply even one quarter of what Sid covers in Teaching Learning you're child will be on the way to be a master learner of anything they put their attention on, now and for the rest of their lives.

By the time you've read through Teaching Learning you will be more informed about how children learn and what it takes to insure they are successful than most educators you will ever meet. While Sid has covered all the theory you would ever hope to know about how people learn (not just children, but adults as well), this is most definitely a "how-to" book with examples, exercises and a series of interesting, innovative, exciting and educational "experiments" for you to master the material he includes.

I read several hundred books a year and seldom rave about any, however Teaching Learning is one of the few books I'm raving about. As proof of how important I think this book is I'm planning on buying many copies and giving them out to literally everyone I know and care about who has children, regardless of their age or where they are in their schooling experience. I'm even including those who have "grown" children who are well beyond their schooling years. It's never too late to learn when you know how to do it well, and this book is a gift to anyone who wants to know how, or help someone else get it.

—Joseph Riggio, Ph.D., Cognitive Scientist,
author of The State of Perfection

*The problem is never how to get new innovative thoughts into your mind, but how to get the old ones out.*

—Dee Hock
CEO Visa International.

As I was reading Sid's book, the above quote came to mind. From my experience as a teacher of adults I have found this statement to be profoundly true. Sid is offering us an alternative. Children have a natural creativity of mind waiting to learn, to be taught and sponsored. In fact, it is this childhood learning time, when the old ideas are becoming fixed, that later will be so difficult to soften.

Here is an alternative to creating these habits in the first place. The frustration with learning can be greatly alleviated if we apply the principles and processes offered in this book. If you are a parent, teacher or have ever been a young frustrated learner you will love this book.

Sid points out that the state of being is of key importance in learning, that trying to learn when frustrated, afraid etc. is not useful. Sid helps us understand the importance in the sensory channels for in-putting, representing and out-putting information.

There are many book written about NLP and the various applications to leadership, health, coaching and consulting but nothing is more relevant than education and learning.

Whether problem solving learning issues or supporting a life long learning attitude, this book points out the important application of NLP to the process of learning and leaving a legacy for teachers and learners that makes a difference.

—Judith DeLozier, Co-author of NLP II: The Next Generation

In a remarkably practical and engaging way, Sid Jacobson offers helpful and unique suggestions for how to help kids to fall in love with 'learning to learn'. It is clear that Sid is sharing a passion that he has developed for many years. I highly recommend this book!

—Stephen Gilligan, Ph.D., Psychologist, author of The Courage To Love

Also by Sid Jacobson

Meta-Cation, Vols. I, II & III

Solution States

With Dixie Elise Hickman, Ph.D.
The Power Process

# Teaching Learning

Helping Your Kids
Gain the Learning Skills
They Won't Get Taught in School

SID JACOBSON

iUniverse LLC
Bloomington

Teaching Learning
Helping Your Kids Gain the Learning Skills They Won't Get Taught in School

*This book is not intended as a substitute for the medical advice of a physician. While every effort has been made to ensure that the information here is accurate and up-to-date at the time of writing, the reader should consult a physician in matters relating to his or her health, as well as the health of their children, whenever making medical decisions.*

*iUniverse books may be ordered through booksellers or by contacting:*

*iUniverse LLC*
*1663 Liberty Drive*
*Bloomington, IN 47403*
*www.iuniverse.com*
*1-800-Authors (1-800-288-4677)*

*ISBN: 978-1-4759-9349-3 (sc)*
*ISBN: 978-1-4759-9347-9 (hc)*
*ISBN: 978-1-4759-9348-6 (e)*

*Printed in the United States of America*

*iUniverse rev. date: 07/08/2013*

# Contents

## PART 1
### *Preparing Yourself: Parent as Teacher*

## PART 2
### *Teaching skills: How to Do It*

# PART 3
*The Skills of Learning: Things Your Kids Won't Learn in School, about Learning*

# PART 4
*Troubleshooting and Getting More Help When You Need It*

# Illustrations

To my wife Cindi Lanza Jacobson, a gifted counselor and extraordinary mentor and role model to all the children in our lives. And, to all the children I've worked with over the years, as well as my nieces and nephews who I love so much.

*I must study politics and war that my sons may have liberty to study mathematics and philosophy.*
John Adams

*The reasonable man adapts himself to the world;*
*the unreasonable one persists in trying to adapt the world to himself;*
*Therefore all progress depends on the unreasonable man.*
George Bernard Shaw

# Acknowledgments

The author would like to acknowledge and thank the following people and sources for their help and guidance, as well as permission to use their material, without which this work would have been far less intelligible.

I'd like to thank Robert Dilts and Judy DeLozier for their support over the years, and regular invitations to join them as a guest trainer at NLP University in Santa Cruz, California. I appreciate their continued collaboration, support and friendship which enriches me as well as it has so many others. Robert is responsible for some of the most useful ideas in this book including the Neuro-Logical Levels.

An additional thanks to Judy, and to Joseph Riggio and Steve Gilligan, for agreeing to read advance copies of the book and for their generous comments.

I'd also like to acknowledge the contributions of the late Todd Epstein. His work in developing some of the basic principles of NLP, especially in the area of sub-modalities, and his work with Robert Dilts on Dynamic Learning contributed greatly to this the ideas in this book. Our many discussions of these ideas, and of applying NLP to all areas of living, will always be important parts of my personal growth and history.

Thanks also to Dixie Hickman, Ph.D. for her help in editing the manuscript.

I'd also like to thank my wonderful sister-in-law, Karen Jacobson, for her invaluable advice and collaboration on the illustrations in this book. She is responsible for figures 2, 4, 5, 6, 7, 8, 9, 18, 19, 20, 24, and 25. Of course the ideas in the figures belong to me and others, but her work helps bring those ideas forward much better than I am capable of.

No book on NLP is complete without acknowledgment and thanks to Richard Bandler and John Grinder, co-developers of the ever-expanding technology of Neuro-Linguistic Programming. Their genius, collective and individual, has seldom been matched in the field of human behavior and systems thinking.

A special acknowledgment goes to my many adult students and the many people who have trusted me to help them and their kids improve in learning, and in life. Much of what is here is the outgrowth of workshops I've conducted over the years, in a variety of countries and settings, especially in the UK, Singapore, Malaysia, and Romania, as well as the in United States.

All of these people helped make this book better and they deserve much of the credit for what is here that is good. The book itself, of course, is mine so any limitations or flaws are mine alone.

Finally, a special thanks goes to my wife and long-time companion Cindi Jacobson for putting up with me for all these years. The same to my parents, brothers, in-laws, nieces, nephews and other extended family, for the same reason.

# Introduction

## What this book is for

We all have dreams about how life can be, for us and those we love. We also have delusions, myths, and strange beliefs about what's possible, what's real. Some of them work for us, some don't. We develop and learn these delusions, myths and beliefs through our experiences in life. But none of us has more than a narrow range of experiences, compared to what's possible in the world. We forget that. We think our delusions, myths and beliefs are "real." We think they're "right." We think they're the only ones that "make sense." We're usually mistaken.

When we're growing up, most of us go to school. We learn. We also learn about learning. And, we make up delusions, myths and beliefs about that, too. This book is, first and foremost, about taking another look at those delusions, myths and beliefs. It's about listening to what we say to others, and ourselves, about learning, what's possible, "real," "right," or "sensible." Then we get to think about those things again and, just maybe, change our minds.

To me, the sadness in our delusions, myths and beliefs is that we spread them; in a sense we "do them" to other people, like our kids. We think things about them, their abilities, their learning and what to do for (to, about) them to get them to be successful. So we pass those beliefs along, for better or worse. Whatever you believe about your kids, you may change those as you go through the beliefs and experiments in this book.

My dream is that, sometime in the future, all learning will begin with a learning to learn. In this dream, learning to learn is taught in schools everywhere. It is systematic, inclusive, loving and fun. It prepares kids everywhere to be able to learn anything they need to, quickly, effectively, enjoyably. Then we will live in a world of people who were educated this way, so that they could live happy, healthy, productive, creative and innovative lives. It's a big dream. My part is to show you that it's possible; and that since it isn't happening in school, yet, you can begin to create it yourself. We have a lot of good technology already, and there is no need to wait.

In a real sense, we probably shouldn't have to teach kids about learning. In fact, they should probably be teaching us, but the reality is that they aren't learning, in school, the way they should be. In many cases they are unlearning some of their natural abilities and gifts. It may be that with a lot of kids we simply need to undo what happens to them in school.

This book is designed to help you develop a true *learning to learn* program for your kids. In this program, you'll be observing, helping, guiding, coaching and teaching them how to learn. That means, of course, you'll learn these skills yourself. It's never too late. What it's *not* about is "fixing" your kids. They aren't broken. It's not about making them do things they don't want to do. And it's not about taking over responsibility for everything they do or learn, in or out of school. It's also not about *what* to learn. It's about *how* to learn. Many parents only pick up a book like this to find some trick about getting their kids to do something they don't seem interested in doing. This isn't a book of tricks; it's a book about having and using a system that builds skills and supports learning that will last a lifetime.

The book is in four parts:

Part 1 is about *why* we would want to teach our own kids and *what it's about*.

Part 2 is about *how* to go about the teaching process.

Part 3 is about *which* skills to teach, specifically.

Part 4 is about *when* there are problems, how to handle them.

It is written in a sequence that builds skills, improves communication and relationships, and develops a real systematic approach to learning, in or out of school. Because it's in sequence, I recommend that you follow it in order. Sure, there may be parts you can skip, because you think you and your kids are skilled in those areas, but that doesn't mean you shouldn't look them over. Scan the whole book to see what's here, first. Then, dive in and spend the time you need to in the parts you need the most. Feel free to share it with your kids, their teachers and others you care about, when you think the time is right. And enjoy the process. Learning should be enjoyable.

## Who am I to write this?

Who am I, and why am I writing this book to you, a parent? Well, there are lots of answers to those questions, and I'll give a few. First of all, I am someone who cares a lot about people in general (sometimes too much for my own good), and most of all about kids. I have written several books for teachers prior to this one. All of them were aimed at getting the latest knowledge, techniques and skills into the hands of teachers, who could then pass it along to the people who could use it the most: the kids.

Those books came from experiences I had years ago when I was a social worker helping families and kids in a family service agency. Almost all of the people I worked with had very low incomes, came from a pretty awful school system and had many different kinds of problems. But what brought a lot of them to see me were school problems. There was one pattern that kept showing itself over and over again. Kids would be sent to me because they were getting is some kind of trouble—fights, skipping class, disrupting and the like. Also, most of them had been diagnosed with various kinds of learning disabilities. Sometimes the teachers and counselors openly recognized that the behavior problems were a direct result of the learning problems. Kids had trouble, felt stuck, stupid, embarrassed, angry or worse, and would act out in some way. But they just wanted me to "fix" the behavior. I refused.

My feeling at the time was that the aim of fixing the child (who wasn't broken in the first place) was unfair and short-sighted. I remembered how it felt when I was young and had trouble learning in school. I was frustrated too. I didn't know what to do, and I was angry because I couldn't find the help I needed a lot of the time. And I came from good schools. I imagined what it must have been like for those kids I was trying to help. Not only weren't they getting the help they needed, but then they had to go home, often to difficult family situations, in neighborhoods filled with poverty, drugs, crime and very low expectations for improvement. Not very hopeful.

My decision was to try to make a difference that would last, what we sometimes call *the difference that makes a difference*. I believed that if I could help the kids with their learning problems, the behavior would clear up on its own, and I might actually give these kids some tools that would help lift them out of some of the hopelessness and, just maybe, make a real impact on their lives.

What I found, to my surprise, was that there was nothing I *couldn't* teach these kids. *Nothing.* I found myself doing lots of experimenting to find out what made the difference in their ability to learn when they were with me, as opposed to when they were in school. At the time I was using a set of principles and skills I'd been studying from a field called Neuro-Linguistic Programming (NLP) to guide me. NLP, along with clear perception, is a combination that works. It's what most of this book is based on, so I'll share lots more of that with you as we go along. *I believe that our ability to learn is equal to our ability to solve problems and live healthy, happy and productive lives.* I wish I'd known all these things when I was a kid.

# PART 1

## Preparing Yourself:
## Parent as Teacher

# Introduction to Part 1

## You Can Do More Than You Know

Teaching your kids the learning skills in this book is like having kids to begin with. It's a choice, not a chore. Like all choices, it is something you should do consciously, on purpose, with a clear intention. You are already teaching your kids lots of things, whether you're doing it on purpose or not. Kids learn from us just by being around us, so we might as well make the learning worthwhile.

You may think that what's in this book will be over your head, too time consuming or too complicated. It isn't really. It will depend mostly on how you use it. You can make the choice to look through what is between these covers, and pick and choose the things that you think are most worth your time and effort, as well as the time and effort of the kids. Also, there is no schedule here. Quick, slow or really really slow; it's your choice. Use your good judgment and you'll find this to be a fascinating journey.

This section of the book is about clarifying these things for yourself. It doesn't involve the kids, at all. It's about you, your role in your kids' learning, your intentions and beliefs, and how much you really can do with, and for, your kids.

1

# Chapter 1

# Your Role

At some time or other most parents want, or feel compelled, to help their kids with their schoolwork. It can be a pretty scary task, too. Sometimes we don't know what we're trying to help them with much better than they do. Sometimes we don't know it at all. Sometimes we do, but we don't know how to get the idea across in a way that makes sense for our kids. We can't know all the answers. What we can know, however, are the answers to *why* we want to help in the first place. Maybe it's because they asked for the help. Maybe not. Perhaps someone else, like their teacher, asked us to help them, or motivate them, check on them, or stand over them. For lots of the parents I've worked with, it's because they are afraid. Afraid of what their kids won't know, or be able to do in a more competitive, complicated world. For some, they remember how much trouble they had, and they think, or at least hope, they can make it easier on their kids than it was for them. Sometimes they're right.

I think it really is useful to spend some time thinking about these things, here, before we get started. Preparation is valuable. Your intentions will often be your guide. If you don't have some justification that satisfies you, it sure won't satisfy them. Be able to explain yourself to your kids; it's part of the process.

Another part is that you be willing to be a *model* for what you teach them. Again, if you can't demonstrate that something is important to you, or a part of you, they won't buy it (learn it). This includes, especially, being willing to be a student for life. If you demonstrate to your kids that you really believe learning and studying are important, it will help tremendously. I've heard too many parents tell their kids: "I did my time in school. Now it's your turn." That's like blowing cigarette smoke in their faces and telling them not to smoke.

You also, certainly, want your kids to be healthy and safe, have good relationships with others, value the things you do and learn to be successful in their world. Knowing how to teach them those things is much more complicated than just saying the words to them. Most important beliefs and experiences in life are much bigger than the words we use to talk about them. How you handle the things that are really important teaches your kids how to do the same, often regardless of what you say about those things. We'll talk more about being a good role model later.

# Who are You?

So now it's your turn: "Who are you?" Before you answer, think about the question in terms of *what's most important* to you as a person. Is the first answer that comes to mind what you do for a living? A plumber, an accountant, a brick layer, a doctor, a homemaker, or whatever? Is that who you *are*, really, or is it just what you *do*. If they are the same, think about it some more. People who describe themselves as *being* what they *do* miss the richness of what it means to be a human being. What you do may be an important part of you, but you are much more.

You are more than any role you play: work, parent, spouse, friend, neighbor, whatever. There is something more central to you as a person, something that stays the same even when your role changes. More than your "personality." More than your personal preferences, likes, dislikes, things you do or don't do, your habits, or your beliefs. Do you know yourself down deep inside? Most of us probably haven't examined ourselves as completely as we could. Perhaps now would be a good time to delve a little deeper.

Good questions lead us to *more* than good answers. They lead to wisdom. For this reason, I'll be posing lots of questions throughout this book. Remember, there isn't always a right, or best, answer. Some of these questions are simply to help you think in new ways; and even lead yourself into more questions of your own. It's more about the search than the answers—a journey, not a destination.

So, in answer to the question, "Who are you?" perhaps you could start with what you believe about yourself and others, especially in relationship to your kids. Are you smart? Capable? Loving? Honest? Happy? Do you believe your kids are these things? Do you talk about it with them? Do you believe you can help them become better people? Better students? Do you know yourself well enough to answer these questions?

Just as important, maybe most important in the context of what we are doing here, is the question: "Who are you in the eyes and ears of your child—the one you want to help learn better in school and in life?" Your ability to help a child learn is directly proportional to your relationship with that child. It's crucial.

Because this is a book, I can't be with you while you read it, or while you use what's in it. I can, however, help you put it in a framework that can make it work for you in helping your kids grow and develop in ways that will be worthwhile. I'll give you steps to follow and guidelines about thinking about people, children and learning. Also, this can be a great personal growth experience for you as well as your child or children.

Parenthood is a big responsibility and a big challenge. A friend of mine often points out how great it would be if people came with an "operator's manual" that would tell us what to do when something doesn't work right. We don't have one, though, and until one comes along, those of us in the business of teaching and writing will continue to develop the parts of it that we can. Think of this book as *part* of the operator's manual you never got when your kids showed up in your life. It's the part about how people learn, or don't, and what to do to make it work better.

Many people are scared half to death of raising kids. "What if he turns out to be a criminal?" "What if she *never* learns how to behave?" "What if . . . ?" Some perspective is in order here. Think about your own life. If you remember back to when you were a kid, maybe the age of one of your own, it undoubtedly looked a lot different from how it looks now. You probably had totally different questions about your life than you do now. You would certainly describe yourself based on much different things than you did then. You may not feel the same about much of anything. Look back on some of the people you grew up with. Some probably turned out to be very successful, others not so much. Which ones turned out the way you expected? Which ones didn't? How about the ones that people said things like this about?: "He's headed for a life of crime!" or "She'll never amount to anything." or "That's the one who's going to own half this town." How many of those you expected to lead a life of crime turned out pretty normal? Be honest. How about the others, the ones everyone said were headed for stardom of some sort? How many made it? We know from many studies that what happens in school doesn't predict very well how people are going to turn out. It just doesn't.[1] The vast majority of people end up somewhere in the middle in most ways we measure, regardless of what we predicted when they were young. Sure there are exceptions, but that's what they are: exceptions.

Who you learn from is often as important as what you think you learn, because in any relationship we learn much more than surface information. That's what relationships are about. The more we know about ourselves, the more we can get out of each relationship we have. The reason for these questions about you, and my description of myself to you, is that learning in school, or in life, is a team effort. Everyone has a role—teachers, parents, professionals, and the community as a whole. To the extent you make what is in this book work for you, that is the extent to which *I* can be on the team *with* you, and help make the process more fruitful and enjoyable for you and your kids.

# Relationship and Task

*Relationship* and *Task* are different.[2] From the time we were small, we all learned to do lots of things. Tie our shoes, brush our teeth, read, count, talk, think. We learn procedures, series of tasks. Most of us are good at doing *things* (tasks), at least the ones we think are important, or ones that got drummed into us. But what about relationships? When did we learn how to do these? In class? I don't think so. In our families?

Maybe, if we were very lucky and had parents or others who knew how to teach us. Most of us just learned through trial and error and by paying attention to how others "do" relationships and using them as models. We see and hear our role models behaving in lots of different ways; and learn to copy them, whether we like it or not. And, if these role models weren't very good at relationships, well . . .

I find this whole thing odd, frankly. Half of what we need in life is to make relationships work. Otherwise, it doesn't matter what the task is. If we have to do something with other people, we need to manage the relationship with those people, or the task is going to be very tough. If the relationships are good, it makes everything easier and more effective, but we get no formal training in how to do it.

It doesn't have to be this way. We can learn to have relationships that work. It isn't hard or mysterious. In fact in NLP we know a lot about how relationships work. Any relationship. The one we have with the kids is part of the task of teaching them. It's just as important as anything else in the process.

# How Does Learning Work, and What Can You Do?

First of all, you don't have to be a teacher to teach (or a student to learn, for that matter). Sure, teachers get formal training about what to do with kids; and what to teach them. They also get some theories about why kids learn or don't learn; and a little about what to do when they don't. But they get very little training in how people *actually* learn—much less than you might think. In fact, most of them, candidly, will tell you this. Many only get a little bit of some mostly sorely outdated psychological theory about development; and a few theories that combine educational and psychological ideas about what to do in certain situations. But if you ask them how people learn—take in information, work it into their own understanding, compare and blend it with what they already know and who they are, how they store it in their minds and later retrieve it, and how this leads them to new learning—they will generally be at a loss to give you good answers. They just don't know because they haven't been taught. This isn't universal, of course, but still seems to be the norm.

7

Just as sad, they've been taught precious little about relationships. Sure they know that it's important to have good relationships with the kids in their classes, but they've never been taught how relationships work. They learned just like the rest of us. In that sense, you have an advantage over every teacher your kids will ever have. You have a relationship already. Hopefully a good one, but a relationship nonetheless. It can be the basis of helping your kids to learn. Anything.

Learning *can* be planned, organized and intentional. Most learning isn't, though. Most of what we learn, we learn on our own. The majority of that probably comes through trial and error. After a certain age; and certain life experiences, we get a lot of new learning through reading, figuring things out alone or with others, and by being in situations in which we have to experiment to get through. Trial and error, though, is a mediocre teacher. Not terrible, just mediocre. It leaves lots of gaps and disorganization. It also leaves lots of stuff that got there through luck and coincidence, rather than usefulness and good sense. Trial and error sometimes teaches *what*, sometimes *where and when*, but almost never *how*, *why* or *with whom*.

Think about how you learned to do something specific. Maybe ride a bike, drive a car, throw or kick a ball, run, swim, cook, anything. Did you have someone teach you? Probably. They probably told you or showed you some of what you needed to know. For example, in riding a bike, they probably helped you get on and showed you where to put your hands and feet. They probably helped you get your balance to begin with. They probably showed you how pushing down on the pedals moved the wheels and how pressing or squeezing the brakes, made them stop. But at some point *you* had to learn how to balance yourself in an upright position. *You* had to learn how much pressure to put on the pedals and how your feet needed to work together. *You* went from turning the handlebars to make the bike turn, to actually leaning your body gently and smoothly to make it happen. In fact, *you* learned at some point how to do all these things at the same time, in a coordinated fashion. If you didn't, you can't ride. Maybe you're good at it, though. Imagine going to a professional bike racer and having that person give you a lesson. Do you imagine this expert would tell you that you do it perfectly? With great efficiency, economy of motion, grace and power? Probably not. An expert would most likely find lots of things you do that could be changed and improved. Some of these would be things you don't even know you're doing. Maybe the positioning of your feet, the height of your seat, how far you lean, the timing of your motions, and so on. Even if they're really subtle, small changes could have a major effect on how you ride.

Now think about something much more important in your life today, probably, than riding a bike: driving a car. How many things do you actually have to do at one time? Well, there's the steering wheel, the gas and brake pedals, and perhaps a clutch pedal as well. If it isn't an automatic, that means one hand has to know what to do with the gear shift lever, coordinated along with the clutch pedal. And each one of these objects is operated in a different fashion, different pressures, in different directions, in harmony (hopefully) with one another. You have two or three mirrors to help you see behind you, as well as watching in front and to the sides. This requires some pretty sophisticated timing and coordination between what you see, and what you do with your hands and feet. And none of this includes all the rules, road conditions—even hazards—and all the other things you do while you're driving (carry on a conversation or two, maybe even on the phone, operate the radio, eat, drink and other dangerous things that people do). If you had to consciously think about any of these too much you wouldn't be able to drive at all. Unfortunately, almost everyone thinks they're really good at it, too. It's why so many keep crashing into each other. Like in bike riding, there are experts who could teach us to do it better.

Over the years we've discovered that people who are really expert at something do different things from the rest of us. Usually these are small things that never occurred to us, or that we thought were too small to make a difference. Sometimes they aren't.

Now, think for a moment about things like spelling, reading, math and other academic skills. These really are skills. Like riding a bike, driving a car or anything else, there are lots of little details that make it work and lots more that make it work *well*. None of the things that make these skills work really well are taught in school, at least as far as I can tell. Many teachers and even some people who design the curriculums don't know any better than most other people about those small details that really produce academic skills, much less excellence. Even when they do, it doesn't mean they know how to teach it to everyone in schools.

I'll give you plenty of examples later on so that you can improve your own skills while helping your kids. But here's a quick example:

9

spelling. Most people don't know that the only way to spell correctly in English is to see the word in your mind and write down (or say out loud if someone asks) what you see. Sounding out words doesn't work very well because our language isn't phonetic—meaning words aren't spelled based on how they sound. Take these words: right, write and rite. They are different words with different meanings. All three *sound* exactly the same but *look* different. There are plenty of rules about spelling that you can learn, and they will work, but that isn't what good spellers actually *do*. Well, obviously there is a skill to being able to see the words clearly in your mind when you want to spell them, and it's a skill with lots of small parts to it, like *where* you imagine seeing the word in front of you, how *big* it is, what *color*, what *kind* of writing, and more. Each of these separate parts can be taught and learned, step by step. If each one is done just right spelling is really easy. If *any* of them is done badly it can get really hard. If I've gotten you curious about the details, don't worry; we'll come back to spelling later.

Teachers are no different from the rest of us in this. They learn a lot about how to do what they do on the job. Trial and error. And lots of what works with one kid; falls flat with another. Why something works for one and not the other can become a matter of guesswork, and teachers are busy. Guessing takes time they don't have or won't spend, so they go on the best they can, like most of us. If they had someone to help them, each step of the way, it would be easier. Just as they can't help each child with each piece, there is usually no one to do it for them, either.

# Modeling

The most long lasting learning we get often comes through the process of *modeling* other people.[2] This means, literally, seeing, hearing, feeling, thinking and doing things like the other people around us. Of course the modeling process begins when we are infants and is the most intense form of learning we get when we are young. Sometimes we have learned things so well and so thoroughly; that they become a frustration to us rather than an asset. For example, you may have found yourself saying things to your kids that you swore, when you were younger, that you would never say: "Not tonight, it's a school night." "Of course you can't be hungry (cold, tired, confused, etc.); it's not the right time." "Stay away from those kids. They're a bad crowd." "Turn that racket down! You call that *music*?" When we hear those things (usually three seconds after they pour out of our mouths), we often cringe. It's like we've become our parents, teachers or the other people who raised us. We learned from them whether we liked it or not. It really doesn't help much to swear that we'll never say it again, either.

We now know a lot about how this modeling process works. We can, in fact, use it to our advantage in many ways. Wouldn't it be nice to be able to learn, or teach, the most useful things using this process? Especially since we know how well it works? We can.

## What Scares You, or Stops You?

Another really good question: "What scares you about being a parent?" At some time or another, we're all afraid of the responsibility that comes with raising kids. A lot, sometimes. And, like it or not, these fears get passed down to our kids through modeling—regardless of how much we tell ourselves we can cover them up. What do you believe your real capabilities are as a parent—a guide to a young person? Are they realistic? Do any of us even know what *realistic* is? The most important thing to remember, I think, is that you can't be a perfect parent. There is no such thing. That means you have to expect, and prepare for, things to go a little nuts from time to time. It is not a statement about your value, ability or intelligence as a parent. It's about life. The more we can accept the unexpected; and deal with it consciously, gracefully and lovingly, the better off we and our kids will be. If we are scared, frustrated, or disgusted with learning, our kids will pick it up. The sooner we handle that, the better.

## Who Is Your Child?

For years, people have come to me with all kinds of questions about what to do with their kids in some difficult situation. The questions usually begin something like: "What do you do with a kid who . . ." or "What do you do when . . ." The expectation is usually that I can give a neat three sentence answer that is like a doctor's prescription. "Take two spelling words, cut down on fat and sugar, check for allergies, have the kid do a couple of laps and everything will work out just fine." Right. The problem with asking for a specific answer to a general problem should be obvious. But we forget about that when we're frustrated, angry, confused or scared. The real answer to the question, "What do you do . . . ?" is: "First, it depends on your relationship with the child. Next, it depends on how the child works in the context of this particular problem. It might depend on other things, too."

To be able to help someone learn means that you have to relate to them in a way they can understand. You also have to know something about *how that person learns*. We're all a little different from each other when it comes to learning, though there are a lot of things we share in common. We'll go into specifics later, but for now it's vital to remember that no two people have exactly the same needs or understanding in any learning situation. Flexibility and experimentation are a must.

Also, you have to accept the interests, needs and style of your developing child, and keep that in the context of what you want to teach. Context is important. We aren't the same with every person we know. Each relationship is different and has its own context. We don't act the same in different places, like work, home, a friends' home, or our favorite restaurant. Each of these places is a different context, and requires different thinking and ways of acting. For example, there are salespeople out there who can sell millions of dollars worth of stuff to their customers, but haven't got a clue how to persuade their own kids to study. How many comedies have we all seen where the counselor or psychiatrist can't manage his or her own personal relationships?

So again, the question: "Who is your child, or each of your children?" They certainly are individuals. Any parent knows that. Here is a healthy list of other questions for you:

What are they really like? How are they like you, or different from you?
What do they really find interesting, or boring?
What is easy, or very hard for them?
What do they think is important, or worthless?
What do they find silly or funny, or sad or scary?
What are their gifts and abilities?

What would you change about them, if you could? (And what should you leave for them to develop on their own?)

What do they believe about the world, life, other people, themselves? Which of those beliefs are like yours, and which are different?

How do you get along? Do they respect you? Do you respect them?

These are important questions. I'll have more for you later. In the meantime, though, in terms of the answers to those questions, here is another: "What kind of teammate, coach or friend do you want to be with your kids, when learning is involved?"

To close this chapter, I suggest you take a few minutes to explore something in your own mind: what is it like for your kids in school, now? Imagine that you are one of your kids. What's it like to get up in the morning, as this child? What do you think about going (having to go?) to school? Pleasant? Painful? A chore you'd rather avoid?

Next, imagine you're there, in school. Sitting in one of those desks. Looking around at the classroom, the teacher, the books, the board, the rest. How do you feel? What is it like listening to the teacher, and trying to understand the new stuff? Do you feel cared for? Important? Excited? Curious? Part of something important? If not, how about confused? Ignored? Scared? Overwhelmed?

Next, imagine it's time to take a quiz or test. How does that feel? Do you feel excited and challenged? Ready to perform? Or scared? Embarrassed? Frustrated?

What about homework? Studying? Activities? Friends? How much of this—imagining you are your child—is wonderful, thrilling, encouraging and nurturing? How much isn't?

If you can really put yourself into the shoes of your kids, and go through *their experience* in your own mind, it will help you tremendously when it comes time to help them. If you can't imagine what it's like for them, you need to talk to them and find out more. Ask them these same questions. You may get a tremendous education for yourself.

# Chapter 2

# Understanding People, the Basics

What do you believe about people? About the world? Do you stop to think about this from time to time? I believe that when we take up something new, it really helps to put it into perspective: to fit it into our lives, our work, our families, our beliefs. Everyone would like to be able to instill a good set of values and beliefs in their kids. But how? It's not an easy thing to do, because it isn't just about what we tell them. It's also about how we *live* those beliefs, how we *walk the talk*. Until we know which values and beliefs we really have, we can't decide which ones we want our kids to have. Even when we've explored our own, we still have to figure out how to teach them to our kids in a way that they'll accept; a way that they'll take them, and make those values and beliefs a part of themselves.

One of the things we all know, that I mentioned earlier, is that the experience of something is bigger than the words we use to describe it. I can tell you about any experience I may have had in my life, big or small. I've traveled a great deal and seen many of the great cities of the world. My description of any of these places will always fall short of the actual experience. The same for anything else. Visiting places, meeting people, working, playing, exploring, reading, listening to music, being at a concert or movie, learning something new. Many of the most important and meaningful experiences I have ever had are difficult to share in words.

It's the same for you, if you think about the experiences you've had and how much you've learned and even changed from each one. I can tell you about any of these special things I've done, *but there just aren't enough words.* I can never really create any of those experiences for you, no matter how vividly I remember them, no matter how hard I try. You can't really give me the experiences you've had, either, no matter how special they may have been. How can we give these experiences to other people, our kids?

When you think about your values and beliefs, think about the same limitation. They aren't just words. They are much more and they're hard to share with other people, just like any special experience. Some things aren't as tangible as we would like them to be. In the beautiful, very intelligent movie *Contact*, Mathew McConaughey plays a great spiritual leader and Jodie Foster a great scientist. They are struggling, together, with the issues of what we know, what we can prove we know and how to communicate it. The spiritual leader asks the scientist: "Did you love your father?" She says: "Yes, very much." He says: "Prove it." The perplexed look on Jodie Foster's face communicates the dilemma. How? How do we convince someone of anything? That's the problem of values and beliefs, as well as for any experience that is important to us. We want to share and we need to share. How do we communicate in a way that works? How do we share value and meaning for us? Are we even fully aware of all of it?

# Basic Presuppositions

One great place to start in exploring these issues is to look at our underlying assumptions, or *presuppositions* about life. In NLP, we have a set of presuppositions that guide us. They have proven to be a very useful way of thinking about people, their problems, communication, needs and values. In fact everything we do in our field is an expression of these basic beliefs. As you look at these, and answer the questions, it will help you think about your own values and beliefs; and the ones your kids might have. These are only a start, but a good one. And by the way, you don't have to agree with all of these, but if you don't, think about *why*. There are a few questions after each explanation for you to answer for yourself. They'll help you clarify your own thinking.

Presupposition: The map is not the territory.[1]

This is a very old way of saying that our beliefs and ideas about how people, life, our kids and the world work aren't necessarily accurate. They are just a guide—a map—of how things work. You see, we don't act in the world based on how it really is. We act based on how we see, hear and think about the world, each of us, in our own way. It's how we *think* it is that we pay attention to. In that sense, we each have our own personal map, or *model*, of the world. And it's different from everyone else's. We made these maps, in our heads, largely when we were growing up. Some parts of our maps we clearly made through the eyes of a child, other parts when we were angry, lost or confused. Some parts we made up because we just didn't know what else to do at the time. Not only that, but these personal ideas about the world tend to stay the same unless we are forced to change them.

In that sense, people (even your kids) "work" just like they're supposed to. Given the maps they've developed, and the beliefs and choices they believe they have at any moment in time, they do what they think they're supposed to. It makes perfect sense to them. If we can get inside another person's model of the world—their map—and walk around a while, their behavior makes a lot more sense than it does from inside our own map. So, when things don't seem to be working the way we expect, it doesn't mean that something is wrong, or "broken." It just means there is a different map in operation.

Think about how it works for you. For most of us, just listening to the ideas other people have doesn't make us change our own ideas very often. In fact, most of the time we only listen to the ideas that appeal to us to begin with. Our maps tend to get pretty rigid. They don't always work to guide us through life anymore, and sometimes they're just wrong. Sometimes when the world doesn't seem to be working the way it should, we should change it if we can. Sometimes, though, it's time for a new map.

Questions:
1.  Do you run your relationship with your kids (or your life, for that matter) from some rigid set of rules? Where did these rules come from? Is it possible that even though they were effective back then, when you learned or made them, that they aren't anymore?
2.  When was the last time you realized something you believed was wrong? How did you handle it and change your thinking? Has it ever happened with your kids?
3.  Can you remember a time when you expected something to happen, and something very different happened instead? How did you adjust? How about the expectations you have of your kids?
4.  Have you ever had an argument with your kids (or anyone) because of some expectation that wasn't met? It happens in all relationships at some point. How do you generally handle it? Do you handle it in a way that makes the relationship stronger, a way that allows you to change your expectations in a useful way?
5.  Do you remember some things your parents, or others, told you when you were growing up that you believed at the time, but don't any longer? What happened to change your mind? How did it make you feel about the person you used to believe, but now disagree with? Different? Better? Worse?

Presupposition: All behavior has some "positive" intention, in everyone. People make the best choices they see, hear, feel or think are available to them.

No matter how weird we think other people's behavior is (kids, teachers, anyone), there is some good reason behind it (and everything they do). Sometimes you have to do a great deal of questioning and thinking to get it to make sense, but with patience and perseverance it usually will. Maybe your kids get stuck sometimes and you don't know why. Or perhaps you sometimes believe that other people are crazy, or bad, or dangerous, or stupid, or undeserving. This kind of thinking can make anything you have to do with them very difficult, painful or even impossible. However, if you assume that everyone involved is doing what makes sense to *them*, in *their map* of the world, then things will look, sound and feel different.

Questions:
1. When your kids (teachers, etc.) have acted strangely, how have you managed to step back from the situation and make sense of it?
2. Have you ever asked this question: "How is it possible that someone could think or behave this way?" Or: "Under what circumstances (or in what situation) would this kind of thinking or behavior make perfect sense?"
3. If you were to imagine that you could see the world with the innocence and naiveté of a child, how would things look different? How would you change to adjust?
4. Was there ever a time when you thought someone was doing something to hurt you, but later realized they were really trying to help? How about something that seemed crazy at first, but made perfect sense later?

Presupposition: The mind and body work together in a system.[2] A change in one part of this system will affect the other parts.

Most people realize that our thinking affects us physically, even to the point of making us sick (or well). By the same token, if we are not healthy, or even comfortable, we won't think very well. Kids are no different. Have you ever made a really brilliant, carefully worked out, rational decision when you were really angry? Most of the time we can't. In fact when most of us are angry (tired, confused, stressed, hungry), the decisions we make are just plain dumb. Our kids are no different, but sometimes we expect them to be able to come up with rational thoughts when they are all stressed out. If it doesn't work for us, it won't work for them either. However, if we learn to control our bodies and minds, and teach our kids to as well, we can do amazing things together. And let's not forget our surroundings, our environment. We should live and learn in an environment that is supportive and helpful to us in our health and our learning.

Questions:
1. How long has it been since you stopped to take stock of how you run your life and your health? Often we think a lot more about our kids' health than our own. But they learn from us! Not by what we say, but by what we do.

2. Are there any changes you would like to make in your thinking, or your environment, to give yourself and your kids a better opportunity to live and learn together?

3. When has there been a time when you realized the importance of using your mind to control your physical well-being? To exercise? Quit smoking? Lose weight? Become motivated, energetic? Have you set an example for your kids?

Presupposition: Everyone has all of the internal resources they really need to get along in life. This doesn't mean they couldn't use a little help finding and developing them.

People are resilient. They are smart. They are capable, including you and your kids. When people don't seem resilient, smart or capable, it is because they are not in touch with their own natural resources and strengths. Maybe it's a cliché we get tired of hearing, but a lot of the time, the best help we can give is to teach people to help themselves, to use their own talents and abilities. This is what we want to do with our kids, so they can take good care of themselves on their own.

Questions:
1. We've all had the experience of doing something foolish, or forgetting how to do something we know perfectly well. Later, we realize that we knew exactly what to do, but we were too flustered at the time to gather our wits. After any of those times have you ever stopped to "pre-program" yourself (in whatever way you do this)? In other words, to make sure that you would handle the situation in a planned out, rational and capable way, if it ever came up again? How did you do it?

2. Have you ever forgotten something, perhaps someone's name, or where you put something, for example, only to spontaneously remember it at a later time? Have you ever wondered what it would be like to be so in tune with your unconscious mind that you would be able to remember these things, on purpose, when you wanted to?

3. How much time do you spend actually planning how to handle difficult situations? Do you vividly imagine these things occurring, and feel the feelings you would have if you smoothly,

effectively and gracefully moved through difficulties? What would it be like to teach your kids that? What if these skills could become *automatic*?

An interesting question is: "If we all have the same resources available to us, how come we're so different?" Well, it has to do with those maps of the world that we develop in our minds. Remember, we don't experience the world as it is, but rather, we experience it through our perceptions. This means that we don't necessarily see, hear and feel the same things as the people around us, at least not in the same way. There are some things we all do in our minds when we take information in (see, hear and feel what's around us, in other words). In fact we also do these same things when we think about something, remember something or explain something to someone else. Here are three of these:[3]

Deletion

Distortion

Generalization

We call these processes *perceptual filters* because they really do act like filters, letting some things through, but not others. In fact, the filters change what gets through them on the way. These are natural processes and they affect us whether we know it or not. They're also *unavoidable,* so it's good to understand them.

Have you ever noticed, for example, that when you go someplace for the first time, you sometimes feel overwhelmed? This is especially true if it's someplace with a lot going on, like an amusement park, sporting event or tourist attraction. There is so much to see, hear and maybe feel, smell and taste that we can't take it all in. Even if we could, we'd be overloaded. Mental meltdown. So, out of self-defense, we ignore most of it. We pay attention to what we think is important and leave the rest. This is *deletion.* Hopefully, we have learned some good rules for knowing which things are really important.

You may have noticed also that the first time you go someplace, it seems to take a long time to find it. Then it seems a lot quicker to go back home. It's weird how time seems to slow down when you aren't sure where you're going. Worse still is how it slows down when you are bored, like waiting in line at the post office, bank, supermarket or movies. I've noticed how sometimes things look really big to me the first time I see them, but smaller later on. It was even truer when I was a kid. These are all examples of *distortion*. The state of mind we're in, or how we're feeling, can really affect the way things look, sound or feel to us. This may be especially true for the things people say to us. We're all a little different.

We also make *generalizations* about things. For example, we've all told people how perfect or wonderful something was, maybe a vacation, concert, sporting event, book, movie or family activity. But the *whole thing* wasn't usually perfect, just parts of it. Those parts that were the best seem biggest or most important (because we distort them), and we ignore the rest (because we delete it) so what's left seems just the way we wanted it (because we generalized it). This helps keep different times and events straight in our minds, among other things. Experiences and events are good or bad, important or not, valuable or worthless, well spent or wasted. We rarely break things down into little pieces and make measurements on each one. It isn't worth the time and effort.

The result of these three filtering mechanisms is that we all end up with our own unique experiences and ideas about everything that happens around us. This includes our opinions, beliefs and values. This makes each of our maps of the world unique, with all our own prejudices, inaccuracies and simplifications. Reality doesn't count.

# Belief Systems and Thought "Viruses"

Throughout our lives we have been gathering information and making judgments about that information, through these distortions we've been discussing. These become our generalizations about ourselves, other people and the world as a whole. We call these generalizations *beliefs*. The collection of beliefs that we have as a whole we call our *belief systems*. So, beliefs relate to each other, affect one another, and affect everything else that has to do with them. In this sense our belief system is much like any other system: all parts have to work together for the system to function properly. When the system breaks down, it's trouble.

These breakdowns are primarily what give us fits. Like any system, our belief systems can break down from outside pressure. Conflicting information would be one example. They can also break down from internal pressure, like conflicting beliefs inside us. For example, some people think all learning problems come from laziness, others from bad teaching, emotional problems, poor diet, brain damage or the alignment of the stars. At some time or another just about everything gets blamed. Knowing what to believe in this avalanche of opinions can be pretty tough.

Sometimes our belief system works just fine but still gets us into enormous trouble. Beliefs can be totally consistent, but not very useful. A good example of this is the belief that many people have that learning problems are caused by abnormalities in the brain. It makes logical sense, since learning and thinking are largely brain-based activities. Once you believe that, it makes you look for answers that are neurological and medical, rather than educational. You think of your kids as having a physical problem, with the learning difficulties being only a symptom. But learning problems are *almost never* linked to any physical problem. So the medical treatments aren't very helpful, they are expensive, and they tend to build on themselves (visits to specialists, more drugs, different dosages, dependence and more). This leads people to look in all the wrong places for solutions. Worse, this belief about neurological causes for learning difficulties is not only wrong, it's spreading. Many doctors, teachers, counselors and even the kids continue to believe it and teach it to others. It has multiplied, like a virus. These *thought viruses* are every bit as dangerous as physical ones (in fact my friend Robert Dilts has successfully demonstrated that they can cause physical problems[4]). We usually catch them in places where we come in close contact with others, like at home with our families, at work or in the doctor's office. Thought viruses are not only contagious, but they can be difficult to spot. We don't usually know we have them because they often seem so logical, and we have so much support to continue to believe them. But the symptoms can become pretty severe.

Relief, in this case, is spelled P-R-E-V-E-N-T-I-O-N. This includes repeatedly asking yourself and those around you the kinds of questions I'm asking you in this book. Who are you, and who are the people around you? What do you really believe? What are you really capable of? What limitations do you really have?

We filter information when it comes in. We talk with others about it. We decide what to believe. It helps to accept all of these filtering, communication, and belief processes as part of the cost of living. Once we do that, we can learn to recognize and work with the processes, rather than giving up, or pretending they don't exist.

# Reference Experiences[5]

No matter what we learn, it comes through some kind of experience. We see, hear and feel, and then we think about it in some way. Later, what we've learned comes out in what we say, how we communicate and act. These experiences can be things that happen in a classroom, things we notice happening around us in our daily lives, and even what we dream up. Take a look at the following diagram[6] and you'll see how these outside experiences and our internal thinking work together, and how we communicate these things to other people.

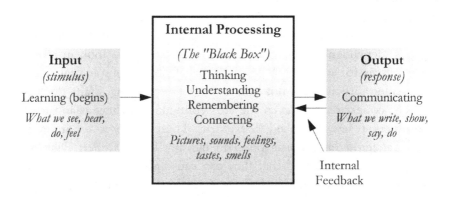

Figure 1: How We Learn, Think and Communicate

The diagram shows how we take in information and then do something with it in our brains. We call this input and processing. Then we give it to others: communicating. All this happens continually, and there is lots of feedback from outside and inside the system. It's not really complicated, but we need to know the parts to the whole process and how they're connected.

Part of what makes us human is how we *make meaning* out of these learning experiences. We judge, categorize, summarize and remember. We fit everything that happens into something we already understand and believe. My friend David Gordon has been working with these ideas for many years. He calls human beings "meaning-making machines."[7] We make everything mean something. We can't help it; it's built-in. How we each do it, though, is unique, based on our filters, beliefs and past experiences.

Once we've made something into our own unique idea, we store it away inside our minds for safekeeping. Each idea becomes part of us, like pages in a reference book. When we think about something, we go back to those memories. We remember the details we need, or gather more information, or compare one thing with another. We do this any time we are *re*-minded of them. We call these internal descriptions we make *reference experiences*. The places we've been, people we've met, the concerts and sporting events, and so on are all important reference experiences for us in our lives. For example, if someone asks me about a great concert I've been to, I might think of the Stones or the Eagles or Miles Davis or the Chicago Symphony (I know, I'm dating myself horribly . . .). Each of these comes up in my mind like movies, with images, sounds and also feelings and words I say to myself about the concert. Each one is a much fuller experience than just a title of a group or a person's name. It's the full experience of the memory that is important to me, inside. That's the real meaning, not just the words. The words are just symbols—a code really—to help us make meaning. The meaning is much bigger than the words.

All words are symbols for some meaning we make of them in our minds. For example, here is a simple word:

Chair

Think about it for a moment. When you saw it written on the page, did you hear a dictionary definition: "chair \'chear\ *n* 1: a seat with a back for one person . . . ." Probably not (I sure hope not). You probably saw an image of a chair in your mind, or felt the one you were sitting in, or looked around the room to see one. That's generally what people do. Perhaps you thought of one of the other possible meanings, for example, to "chair" a committee. Regardless, of what you did in your head, it was a collection of pictures and feelings, and maybe some words to go along. Your personal reference wasn't the same as the dictionary reference. It was more, a fuller experience. That's your reference experience: what the word means to *you*. That's how we make meaning.

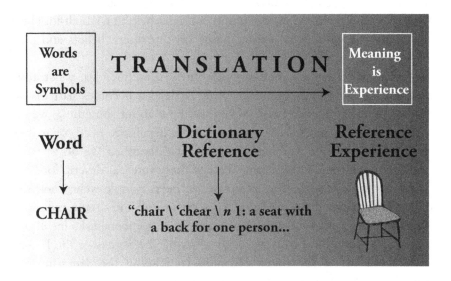

Figure 2: Words and Experience

# Changing and Learning

These reference experiences get categorized and stored in our minds as if they were reality itself, even though we made the meaning out of them through our own deletions, distortions and generalizations. They become difficult to change sometimes, as well, because they are the basis of so much of what we know and how we think. That's what makes changing our model of the world difficult, even when we need to. The truth is that we've all worked hard to develop our models, complete with opinions, rules, values, beliefs and the reference experiences to go with them. Most of us don't like to change, much less let go of, something we've worked hard at. It's natural to want to protect these things and defend ourselves, even our opinions and beliefs, when we're challenged. These processes and reference experiences are at the core of everything we learn, or teach.

The learning process is natural for kids. There are built in mechanisms that help them learn tremendous amounts of information, very quickly, very organically. When they get to school, though, the way they are usually asked to learn is very artificial. In the classroom we don't generally let them explore too much on their own. We don't give them opportunities to figure things out in their own ways, or the time they need in some cases to fit things together in a way that makes sense to them. This isn't necessarily bad, because we do have to expose them to a lot of information about the world that they just couldn't get in any other way. But it's artificial. This means they have to do things inside their minds that might not match the way they are built to learn. It's the same in every modern society I know of.

Changing is hard for some people, and learning always, on some level, involves changing. For people to change, there are at least three things they need:

Motivation
Means
Opportunity

Motivation is *why* they should change, in other words, a good reason. The means are *how* to change: the tools or processes to make the change possible. Opportunity is the *chance* to do it, maybe the time, and the proper support. People also need to feel *safe* when they're making changes, and they need to feel *ownership* of the results and even pride in what they've accomplished. Learning is the same. Kids need motivation, means, opportunity, safety and ownership of what they've learned. And motivation isn't threats; it's a good reason. Kids deserve the chance to know that what they learn might make a difference and be valuable or rewarding in some way. It's that way with all of us, and we'll come back to this topic of change soon.

# How Hard to Push?

I grew up listening to, and later playing, jazz (along with rock, blues and more). I've always admired great jazz players and been envious of great classical musicians. But, I remember when classically trained musicians would sit in with us, to play jazz, and how difficult it was for them. The disciplines, the thinking, especially the feel are so different. There are rare exceptions, however, and one of the most notable is the great trumpet player and educator, Wynton Marsalis. His first two albums won Grammy awards for album of the year, one jazz, one classical. He's the founder and director of Jazz at Lincoln Center, in New York, the largest arts organization in the world dedicated to jazz

I remember seeing him on a talk show years ago with three other great jazz legends, and they all talked about growing up, their parents, the music around them and how they were motivated to become great. When the host asked if they were pushed hard by their parents, all said the same thing: "NO!!" They stressed that too much pressure ruins the experience for kids and makes them run from practice and avoid the work it takes to become great.

Marsalis was the most direct, and funny. When asked if he was born with a trumpet, he said no, he was given his first trumpet when he was young, but didn't really connect with it. He used it to shoot off fireworks. But when he got to high school, he noticed the guys in the band got all the best girls, and the trumpet started looking pretty good . . . .

His deeper and more meaningful motivations later grew as he did. He now says: ". . . the summer I was 12, I started listening to John Coltrane, and I wanted to play. There was so much racism when we grew up, and that's part of what inspired me; I wanted to represent my humanity. The work ethic I developed at that time—I still have that." [8]

All of those great musicians said one other thing that was key. From the time they were young, they were surrounded by great music. It was in their homes, in their neighborhoods and a part of their lives. Exposure to great music gave them great taste in music, and that later inspired, even compelled them, to want to make great music of their own. Inspiration—from inside, not others—translated into art, the way it's supposed to be.

Sometimes the relationships we have can give us all we really need to change and learn: the reasons, the tools, the chance and the feeling of safety and security. For this reason, sometimes *who* does the teaching becomes very important. For example, some schools have been experimenting, more and more, with kids teaching kids. Kids often feel safer and can have more fun learning from one another. There are various names for this process, the most popular being *collaborative learning* or *peer teaching.* It's an obvious choice if you think about it. Because of the natural relationship between kids, they often understand what they need, in order to be able to learn even better than the adults around them. Many people have found that if the kids are allowed to collaborate with each other—work together—on their learning, it goes better, faster and much easier. But it depends on the quality of their relationships, which is the subject of the next chapter.

# Chapter 3

# Understanding Relationships, The Basics

Everything you do with your kids is flavored by the relationship you have with them. Teaching them is no different. Not only that, but your relationships with teachers and other school officials can have a strong influence on how your kids do in school and how they think about it. Just as kids (and all of us) need to feel safe to make changes and to learn, *they need to feel safe in their relationship with you*, for you to help them. This is about *rapport* in the relationship, that sense of safety, trust and understanding, the real connection that people develop with each other.

Familiarity is the basis of rapport. In fact, the need for familiarity is possibly the most powerful driving force in human beings, sometimes even more than the survival instinct.[1]Maybe you've known someone in your life who did very foolish or dangerous things, or even willingly went into dangerous, even life-threatening situations, because *that was what they'd always done before*. I've known criminals who were actually more afraid of trying something new than they were of being arrested or even killed. To be honest, it's one of the most difficult things to overcome when you're trying to get people to make any change. For most people, familiar = safe, even when it seems ridiculous to anyone else.

There is an old concept from social psychology called "cognitive dissonance."[2] Cognitive means thinking. Dissonance is the opposite of resonance, things working together, like in music. Musicians generally try to resonate with each other. Dissonant music sounds awful to most people because, literally, the musicians or instruments are playing off key with one another. So cognitive dissonance means our thinking isn't working, is disjointed, even with itself. We lose our sense of proportion, our ability to connect things with each other or to find the right reference experiences to help guide us. This feeling is the opposite of familiarity. Instead, it's total *confusion*. It happens in situations that are so strange (*un*familiar) that sometimes we can't figure them out at all. We feel unsteady, confused and even threatened. When this happens in a relationship, it's very uncomfortable. Maybe you've had the experience of trusting someone very deeply, and then finding out that person was extremely dishonest with you about a lot of things. It's scary. It can even make us question who we are. We might say that it shakes us to our very foundation. In our minds, that's just what it does.

Rapport, a deep relationship, between people *is* familiarity, with as little of this confusion and discomfort as possible. It's a sense of safety and understanding that comes from stability and predictability. This is what all of us want with the people we're close to, and it's vital between us and our kids. This is especially true when there are challenges or problems. The following diagram should help make this idea clear.

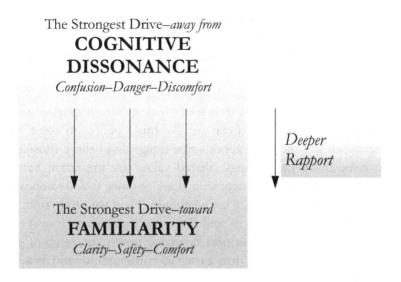

Figure 3: Rapport

Even though I've been talking about how unique each of us is, in reality people are much more alike than they are different.[3] We all have needs, and most of them are similar—at least the basics like food, clothing, shelter and basic life support. In addition to that, we're social animals. We want to belong, feel as if we are being listened to, paid attention to, considered. We want people to like us, trust us, confide in us, and treat us with respect, understanding and honesty (at least most of the time). We also want to know when someone thinks we could do better, but we want to find out in a way that doesn't hurt us or scare us.

We want rapport with the people around us who are closest, our family, friends, school mates. This sense of rapport creates three very important things:

Empathy

Trust

Understanding

*Empathy* means really feeling what another person feels. It means responding to an event or situation in the same way as someone else, complete with the thoughts and emotions that go along with it. It sends a powerful message, unconsciously—back and forth between the two people who share it—that they have a common bond. This bond is one that says they are alike in some very important and basic ways. It's special.

As empathy strengthens, so does rapport, and this leads to a feeling of *trust*. It develops from that feeling of sharing some important things, what we have in common. If we are like other people in some ways, that means we feel the same about some things and believe those same things, value those same things. Shared values are important between people, and when we find others who share ones we feel are important, it tells us a lot about who they are as people. Then we can predict how they'll feel about other things as well. This is what builds trust over time.

The third, and for our purposes extremely important, result of good rapport is that it also means it is easier to communicate and *understand* one another. And I mean understand in *every* sense of the word. Often, people who haven't communicated well, ever before, will find that they immediately see eye to eye and clearly hear the meaning behind another person's words, the moment their rapport improves. Stronger relationship, easier learning.

Another by-product of good rapport is that we can usually disagree with one another without ruining the relationship. In other words, once we have established a really strong rapport with our kids, it will be a lot easier to work out problems and disagreements. Each time we work out a problem with them, we'll not only feel better, but our relationship will get stronger. Every learning experience we create can strengthen our relationships with our kids.

# The Skills of Rapport

Over 35 years ago, the developers of my field, NLP, cracked the code on rapport.[4] For many years anthropologists, sociologists and psychologists had been trying to discover what it is that creates that special bond between people. With the addition of some insights into how the brain works and processes language, the whole puzzle came together. It turns out that the bond between people isn't so mysterious after all. Not only that, but each piece can be developed as a skill, learned, practiced and improved. More recent studies of the brain have revealed the physical structures that actually make this possible.[5]

Think about the people in your life that you have had the greatest relationships with, the most intense rapport. Isn't it true that in each case what made the relationship so strong was that you shared so much *in common*? The people we feel most comfortable with, and trust and understand the deepest, are the ones who *are most like us* in some ways. Not every way, certainly, but some very important ways. This is what creates that sense of familiarity, that we are the same in certain ways.

Here's how it works. This sense of familiarity is created between people by the signals they send back and forth to each other. These signals come in the form of spoken language and body language. The ones that work are the ones that send a message that says: "You and I share something in common." In fact, our brains are checking for this as we meet and speak with other people all the time. However, part of our brains actually do it in reverse, a lot of the time. In our minds—unconsciously—we notice what's *different* or *strange* when we're with other people. It's a defense mechanism to protect us, one that keeps us on our guard against confusion and, possibly, danger. The first question our brain wants answered when we meet someone new is: "Friend or foe?" Too much difference means, possibly foe. But when we notice (again, this is unconscious) that *we are much more the same* than different, there is a feeling of relief. We've found a friend. This is the beginning of the bond of rapport.

Many people believe that our background, race, culture, status, age and the like are the things that tie us to other people. There is some truth to that, but it is only a part of the story. Sure, when we see people our own age, who seem to be from the same background, and then hear their accent and the things they say, we feel more comfortable if they're like us. But there are many other, much more subtle signals, like body language, posture and voice tone that are at least as important in the deeper reaches of our minds.

Anyone who has traveled extensively, to different countries and cultures, has noticed that human beings all over the world are a lot more alike than they are different. However, it's the differences we *notice* first. They stand out for us. It's like walking into a room with something strange going on. Our attention is drawn to the strangeness. It should be, since that's what protects us from possible danger. It heightens our senses. It's one of the defense mechanisms we're born with. As we grow up, we learn which things are normal in our environment and which are out of the ordinary so we can make judgments about them and stay out of trouble.

When we meet someone new, our antennas go up and we pay close attention to that person and the situation. The more things we find in common with the other person, and familiar in the situation, the more we can relax. It's a normal process in the development of a new relationship. Those commonalities stay with us in our memory of that person, usually becoming the basis of the relationship. Often this first meeting becomes *our reference experience for that person*. It's why first impressions are so important. They stick.

Even in a relationship we already have, these same mechanisms apply to some extent, just less so. If we try to change something in a relationship, it triggers the antennas in the other person. So if, all of a sudden, we decide to teach our children something new, it can scare them. On the other hand, teaching them new things *on a regular basis* can be part of what is familiar. We want to make it that way so that our kids feel safe and comfortable in the learning part of our relationship with them. Then they can even enjoy it. It's important, so we need to pay attention to how we do it, each time we show them or tell them something new. With time and encouragement, the learning process itself can be a familiar part of who they are.

These skills in developing rapport, as I mentioned, can be developed like any others. Later I'll have exercises and instructions for you to practice and improve with your kids. It will all depend on your ability to communicate, the subject of the next chapter.

# Chapter 4

# Communication

There is a science to communication, and there are lots of good useful ideas and procedures to be found in the fields of communication theory, information science, linguistics and more. We don't have to get deep into these ideas. Just knowing some of the basics is plenty when we're trying to help our kids.

The basic communication model has been around for a long time, and you may already be familiar with it.[1] You may even have seen it in school. As the following diagram shows, there are four parts to any communication between two people: sender, receiver, message and context.

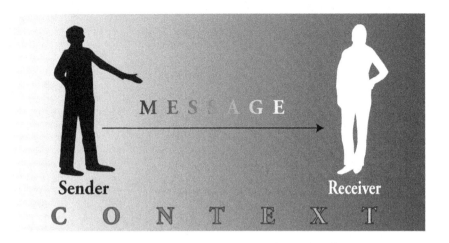

Figure 4: Basic Communication Model

It's easy to assume that when we communicate to our kids, what we think we meant has actually gotten across. We act as if the meaning is actually contained inside the message itself. Experts in communication have been studying how we get meaning from other people for a long time. Here are some estimates about how much meaning and emotion comes from each part of our communication when we're face to face with someone else:[2]

**7% Words**
**VERBAL**

**38% Tone, pitch, volume, etc.**
**VOCAL**

**55% Face & body expressions**
**VISUAL**

Everyone has to interpret what he or she sees and hears to make it mean something. As these numbers show, most of that interpretation comes from the way we communicate, not the words. For this reason, it is important to remember that the meaning is not actually contained in the message. It is in the *mind of the receiver*, your children in this case, based on how they interpret and understand the message they got from you. Clearly, this is determined in large part by how you deliver the message, where and when you give it, your tone, body language, facial expression and the other non-verbal portions of communication.

We also delete, distort and generalize when we turn our thoughts into words. Then, our kids do the same thing when they listen to us. Scary. With each idea we try to get across, we've already gone through these deletions, distortions, and generalizations *over and over*. It's like an internal version of that classroom game called telephone: one person whispers a message at one end of the class, which each other kid whispers to a neighbor, and by the time it gets to the other end it's totally transformed from the original. The following diagram shows the Basic Communication Model with these filters and interference added in.[3]

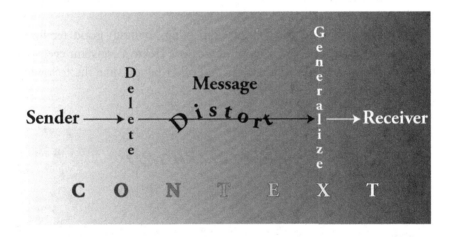

Figure 5: Basic Communication Model with Filtering and Interference

We also have some useful presuppositions about communication, specifically. These can help us keep a framework in our minds to make us as effective and clear as we can be when we're trying to get through to our kids.

Presupposition: The meaning of anything you communicate to someone, including your kids, is in the response they give you, regardless of what you actually meant.

We don't really know what we meant to someone, until they act on it in some way: the response. It is really easy to blame others for misinterpreting what we want them to do, even our kids. We know, when we think about it, that we sometimes have to be especially careful when we talk to our kids to make sure they understand. But, we also forget sometimes, especially in stressful situations. Good communicators take responsibility for getting other people to understand them. The best school teachers are gifted in this way.

People—kids—respond to what they *think* they hear, see, or understand. *Assume* that kids are responding appropriately to what you've told them or shown them. If something goes wrong, from your point of view, then figure out your part in it. How did the kids hear you, and what did they think? This will make you think and communicate differently. You'll also understand your kids much better.

All of this depends on getting (expecting, inviting) good feedback when we communicate. Good communicators create a constant cycle—a feedback loop—between themselves and other people, like the following diagram shows.

Figure 6: Basic Communication Model with the Feedback Loop

Questions:
1. Can you think of a time when you gave your kids, what you thought were careful and clear instructions, but they did something totally different? Has this ever happened, and later you figured out why? Did it ever happen in a way that convinced you that you had been confusing or unclear in your communication?
2. Can you remember an occasion when you got angry with your kids, only later to realize that you had misunderstood them? Did you promise them, or yourself, to be more careful in the future?
3. Have you ever made the conscious decision to be the best communicator you can possibly be?

Presupposition: In communication, there are no mistakes, only outcomes. There is no failure, only feedback.

I've often felt like giving up when I couldn't seem to get my point across. It's a natural reaction. I've had to train myself to remember that communication is more complicated, sometimes, than just saying the right words to someone. And because the only way we know how we're coming across is to pay attention to what we get back from others, it can become a real lesson for us.

Everything we do, successful or not, can be learned from. In communicating we need to take what other people do as feedback, to us, about how we communicate. The people around us can teach us a lot about how we communicate, behave and live. If we kick ourselves every time our kids don't understand us (or do what we ask), we might not take the time to learn from it (and correct it). That's not the example we want to set.

Questions:
1. When was the last time you found yourself consoling a friend or loved one who had made a mess of something? Did you help your friend out? Were you supportive and caring or harsh and judgmental? Did you help this person realize that the intentions were good, even if it didn't work out as planned?
2. Have you ever done the same thing for yourself? Your kids?
3. Have you ever heard, or said to someone else: "Someday you'll look back on all this and laugh?" As my old friend Richard Bandler would say: "Why wait?"

Presupposition: People show you and tell you everything you need to be able to communicate and get along with them. You just have to pay attention.

Attention. We all know that paying attention to our kids, and giving attention to our kids, is a necessity. We also know that just looking at someone isn't the same as really seeing. Just hearing isn't the same as listening. All of us could improve our skills at paying attention to the people in our lives, and the more we improve, the more we can understand those people. In fact, we can usually make the assumption that if we aren't getting along with someone, or aren't communicating well with that person, we're missing something. That goes for our kids as well.

Questions:
1. When was the last time you stopped to just look and listen, when you were having trouble with one of your kids? Did you notice new things when you did this? Things that made a real difference for you? Did you find that they were showing you or telling you something that was important, that you'd missed?
2. What would your life be like if you easily noticed all of the subtle cues and messages others around you gave out in their everyday communication?

Presupposition: An effective parent (communicator) needs to develop three things:

Flexibility
Attention
Judgment

1. *Flexibility* of behavior to find new ways to communicate with the kids and help them in any situation.
2. The *attention* skills to notice what is happening in the relationship.
3. The good *judgment* to know when good and helpful things are happening, or not, and when to make changes.

Many problems are created when we do the same things over and over, whether they work or not. The old saying, "If at first you don't succeed, try, try again." needs to be changed to: ". . . try, try again, in a *new and different way.*" People who study relationships and systems (organizations, families) will tell you that the person who is most flexible in any relationship is likely to be most in control of it.

Flexibility = options = control

Simple. Also, especially when you're trying something new, you have to pay close attention to see the results. You need to keep in mind that just because you *can* get your kids to do something new, that doesn't make it a *good idea.* I've seen many parents manipulate, or downright force, their kids to do things that they knew would be good for them, but the cost to the relationship was far worse than anything they gained.

Questions:
1. When have you realized that, though you were trying your best, you were doing something that just wasn't going to work? How did you change?
2. Have you ever had the opportunity to be tested by life in a way that demanded extreme flexibility on your part? Did it make you better able to handle difficulties creatively?
3. How do you notice when your kids aren't getting something, or doing something correctly? Are you paying attention at the right times, or finding out much later than you would like?

Presupposition: If your kids seem resistant to you, or things you suggest, it's a sign that
Either
There is a problem in the relationship between you and them, with your *rapport.*
Or
Your kids have some good reason (from their point of view) for not going along with you.

It's easy to get frustrated with our kids when they seem stubborn or unwilling. The above are the two reasons they seem that way. You have to establish rapport, a working relationship, of understanding and trust between you and your kids for them to go along with you. This is especially true when you want them to agree to new or difficult things. Also, you have to be willing to listen to, respect, and respond to them. Even if you think they're wrong or just being stubborn. The best, most persuasive, communication in the world won't overcome a poor relationship or a good reason in your kids' minds for not going along. Most important: without the relationship, you won't find out their reasons.[4]

Questions:
1. Have you ever had a great idea, but been so eager that you bowled the kids over in your excitement? What did you do to make repairs?
2. When you've had relationship problems in the past, how did you make the decision to patch things up, even if it wasn't really your responsibility? Did you decide that the relationship was more important than something silly, like the need to be "right" or "in control" in the situation?
3. When presenting ideas or plans to your kids, how much time do you give them to tell you about their concerns and objections? Do you then treat them with the respect they deserve, and take the time to answer their questions?

When someone, especially a child, doesn't understand you, or perform well while they are learning, assume the responsibility to change the way you teach them. Ask questions about what they *do understand*, and why they are doing things (procedures, tasks, other actions) the way they are. This means you have to ask yourself (or them) the following: "What images do they have in mind?" "What do they say to themselves inside?" "How do they feel?" "What do they believe about their own abilities?" "How does what I'm trying to do fit who they are, as individual people?" Remember, misunderstandings and conflicts can come in many forms.

There will always be some logic in what kids are doing, from their point of view, no matter how much it seems off base to you. If you can understand (as well as appreciate) their point of view, it will usually become obvious to you what needs to be corrected. That's the subject of the next chapter.

*When we wish to fix a new thing in either our own mind or a pupil's,*
*our conscious effort should not*
*be so much to impress and retain it as to connect it with something else*
*already there.*
William James

# Chapter 5

# Understanding the Task

## The Learning Process

I don't know how much you've thought about the learning process itself. Most of us have been taught to concentrate on *what* we should learn, rather than on *how* we should learn it. As I've said, I think this is backwards, and of course, it's one of the reasons I wrote this book. If you can make the shift from "what" to "how," my belief is that you can help your kids learn anything that is thrown at them.

Your own beliefs about learning will come through to your kids, and now is a good time to explore some of them so that you can be sure they are the ones you really want your kids to have. As in everything else, we all have basic assumptions about learning, how it works, what's worthwhile, and so on. Some of these might get in our way, and others probably help us. Here are a couple of really important ones to have and to share with your kids.

Presupposition: If something is possible for someone to do (understand, learn, create, perform), it is possible for just about anyone; it's only a question of *how*.

If you believe your abilities are very limited, you will act as if those limitations are real. They're not. If you think your kids have limitations, your expectations, and theirs, will also be limited. We've found, over many years of research, study, practice and experience, that most of these limitations are illusions.[1] We've also found that once you understand how someone does something, no matter what it is, you can learn it, as well.

One of the biggest difficulties some kids have lies in their beliefs about themselves and their abilities. Part of this is what we call self-esteem, part is simply their beliefs about what is possible for anyone. If kids believe they can't do something, they won't try. Then it becomes a self-fulfilling prophecy. We need them to understand that there is a difference between hard and impossible, between complicated and overwhelming. The best way to teach them this, of course, is to be a good role model. It also helps to tell them—in an encouraging way, rather than beating them over the head with it—that they really can do anything they put their minds to. We'll come back to ways of doing this later, but for now, here are a few more good questions.

Questions:
1. When was the last time you really impressed yourself? How about when your kids impressed you (or themselves)?
2. When you try to learn something new, now, what do you tell yourself about it at first?
   Do you believe you can do it? Do your kids have that belief?
3. Are there times when you need to remind your kids that we are *all* capable of just about anything we need to do? Do you think it might be a good idea?

Presupposition: Your kids have all the resources they need, already inside them, to be able to learn anything they need to.

The processes of learning are as natural in kids as breathing. They learn to talk, walk, get around, communicate their needs, be with other people and more, mostly without our help. Think of all the other things they learn, as well (even the ones we don't want them to). Part of being human is continually learning, whether we're aware of it or not.

Figure 7: Related Ideas Connect to Form New Learning

Let's think about the learning process itself. When we learn something new, almost always what we are really doing is incorporating it into something else we already know. For example, when you learn to drive a car, you've certainly seen it done many times before. You also know how wheels work. You've used lots of other mechanical objects before, so the relationships between the parts (turn this, and it makes that happen) make some sense to begin with. If you've ridden a bike, pulled a wagon or skated on wheels before, all of these things are in your mind already as well. So even though we think of it as totally new, it really isn't. We already have a lot of old reference experiences to draw on, as in the diagram.

Many people will tell you that *all* learning is relating what we already know to what is new. Whether it's really always that way isn't as important as the idea behind it. We automatically *look for* what we already know, the familiar, to make us feel safe and comfortable any time we are in a new situation. Sometimes we can't easily find it if the situation, or the learning, is too different from what we're used to. A good teacher will help with that. Effective teaching means guiding, or making, these connections so that the learners can stay focused on the connections without getting lost or confused too much. Some confusion is all right, but only in that it guides the kids into looking for new connections, rather than giving up. There are also times when we want to make new reference experiences for our kids. These are the times when we need to be most careful not to lose them, at least not for too long.

This, then, is what learning is about. It's about creating effective reference experiences, ideas that kids can go to quickly and easily in their minds. These become like the pieces of the puzzle they need to complete, whenever they're trying to learn something new. Just like all the pieces of the puzzle of driving a car (wheels, mechanical objects, experience, and the rest.) come together for us to be able to do it. Real learning means that the reference experiences become unconscious. This is what makes us able to do things automatically. When you drive now, you don't have to think about any of those pieces; they've all come together to form their own new set of reference experiences. So, the old pieces come together to form the new one, and it's all *unconscious and automatic*.

From this point of view, we need to be aware that all learning comes through some kind of experience, no matter what it's about. The experience can be seeing something written on a page, hearing it from someone, seeing or doing something. These are all forms of experience and some work better for some kinds of learning than others. Some also work better for some people than others, and we'll come back to that later.

For teaching to be effective, this process of connecting old references together to form new ones, through some sort of experience, needs to be *organized* and given *form*. So, there is form to teaching and learning, in addition to content. In fact many people consider setting up helpful learning experiences to be quite an art as well as a science. It's more than just telling or showing kids things—it's creating the experience that helps them learn those things themselves.

Think about how this has worked in your own life. Pick something you've learned really well, and go back in your mind to that time and place where you learned it. What did you know beforehand that made the learning possible? How did you see, hear or feel the new pieces? How did you put the whole thing together in a way that made sense to you, finally? If you had to learn it again, would you do it the same way? If not, what would you do differently? If you did it differently, how would it help you to see, hear and feel how to get the new ideas or actions into your head and body?

Questions:
1. What was it like for you in school? Were you shown and told everything you needed to see and hear, to be able to make sense out of what you were learning? How about what you needed to make the learning a part of you? Can you remember which teachers were able to do this with you really well?
2. Think back again to those special learning experiences and life lessons you've had. How were they constructed? How many were trial and error, or accidental? Are these some things that your kids could use, now or in the future, in their lives?
3. Were there any times in your life, in school or otherwise, when you had a really hard time learning to do something? What did you need back then to help you place all the pieces where you could see how they fit? Was there something you wish someone had said back then that could have helped?

# Levels of Learning

Obviously, we've been talking about learning in a very general way. Just as obviously, there are lots of different kinds of learning. For example, it isn't the same when someone is learning how to do a math problem as it is learning to drive a car, paint a picture, write a poem, or give a set of instructions. Each is a different kind of learning and requires different kinds of thinking, and teaching, to work.

A famous anthropologist named Gregory Bateson used to talk about different levels of learning. My friend Robert Dilts studied under Bateson for years and adapted Bateson's ideas to the kinds of learning

49

we've been talking about in this book.² We call these Neuro-Logical Levels of learning, and they are a very useful way of thinking about, and organizing, what we have to do when we teach our kids something. Here is one way to visualize these levels.

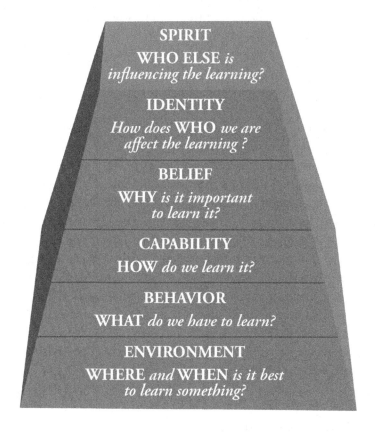

Figure 8: Neuro-Logical Levels

As you look at the diagram, imagine you are looking down on the top of a pyramid. The Spiritual, or Spirit, level is at the top, Environment at the bottom. Let's go through this arrangement from the bottom up, starting at the level of Environment, because it's easier to understand that way.

## Environment (Where? When?)

In most anything we do, a safe and properly designed environment is essential. For life itself, food, shelter, and security are essential. For learning we also need an emotionally safe environment. Think about how important it is to have a safe place just to be able to *think* clearly. This is more true for your kids. Not only that, how about the most simple and obvious environmental concerns such as seating arrangement, lighting, a comfortable work space and the like.

It is also important to consider time as well as place. Sometimes it just means avoiding interruptions. Sometimes kids just need to get certain other things done first, before school work, and you can usually figure out what that means in your case. These considerations may seem ridiculously obvious, but it's still important to be reminded of them, and to be clear about them, before you start something new or difficult with your kids. We consider environment in terms of the question: *"Where* and *when* would be the best place and time for the kids to learn something new?"* Though they may seem obvious, the following questions might help you uncover something you might have forgotten to consider.

Questions:
1. How comfortable and convenient is the physical setting your kids learn and study in? This is where you'll be working with your kids.
2. Is there some place you can set up that can serve as a somewhat permanent place for studying and learning?
3. Are there any interruptions you can anticipate that could make learning difficult for your kids? Are there chores, or activities, that you should make sure are taken care of before trying to help your kids?
4. Are there moods, or states of mind, that you know will make learning tough for your kids? Can you anticipate or prevent these? (We'll come back to this later.)

## Behavior (What?)

The next level up is the behavior level. This includes thoughts and feelings, as well as all the other activities associated with learning. For example, kids sometimes get nervous when they think about learning something new. Think of the nervousness as a behavior that can make new learning difficult.

Anything new that we learn will involve lots of small individual behaviors—making images in our minds, remembering something someone said, connecting something we see or hear with a particular memory. All these, and many more, are examples of the kinds of behaviors that are involved in learning at this level. We consider behavior in terms of the question: "*What* is it we have to do in this new learning?"

Questions:
1. How do your kids handle any feelings they may have about learning something new? What do they say to you or others about it? Does this affect the learning?
2. Have you or your kids ever stopped to think about the small individual pieces of something they (or you) were trying to learn to do?
3. Have you ever figured out exactly what you do, inside your mind, what you see hear and feel inside, when you are doing something you know well? Have you ever been able to share these small pieces with your kids?

## Capability (How?)

Next we come to the level of capability. We all know there is a difference between just doing something and really knowing how it works. For example, we can usually teach our kids how to spell certain words. "Dog." "Cat." "Mom." Even more complicated words can be done if they involve some song, rhythm or rhyme, like "Mississippi." Really knowing how to spell, however, means being able to remember or figure out how to spell many words, whenever we need to. Capability means skills, sequences, processes, procedures, strategies. It is more than just individual behaviors, and it's learned differently.

In fact, learning itself is a number of individual capabilities. We'll be going over some of them later, so that you can give them to your kids, but it's important to be aware of the processes of learning, as opposed to the content. *How* as opposed to *what*. Therefore, the central question at the capability level is: "*How* do we do anything, or learn anything we need to (as opposed to *what* do we do)?"

Questions:
1. Do you know what procedures, including the little things you do inside your head, you follow when you want to learn something new?
2. What capabilities have you shown in helping your kids learn? Do you have an idea about how you would help your kids, in general, in their learning?
3. How have your kids demonstrated their own capabilities, in general? In the learning process itself?

## Beliefs (Why?)

No matter how much you know, and how capable you are, you still may not *believe* in your abilities, or think they're worth bothering to develop. If this is the case, you won't be likely to use your abilities, even if you can. This, again, may be even more true for your kids. We all know people who act as if they are not able to do something we know they can do. Lots of us doubt ourselves, even when we've been successful at something. Beliefs and capabilities, therefore, are not built in the same ways. This difference is important to keep in mind because we have to *develop* them differently as well.

Remember those thought viruses we explored earlier? Perhaps you're one of the many people who lost confidence in yourself, or in some aspect of yourself, at some point in your life or career. Maybe some of this has been contagious, and your kids have caught it. Maybe they have difficulties in this area to begin with. This can come from school, friends or something at home.

For example, I know many parents who believe that their kids can learn what they need to in school, and ought to be left alone from there. In contrast, there are parents who think that the schools are totally incapable and that the kids need to learn everything at home. Some parents take this seriously enough to home school their kids. Some of these beliefs and attitudes toward education come from family traditions, some from the community we live in, some from personal decisions based on experiences and goals. Others may be prescribed by the schools or even come from somewhere else. I won't argue in favor of one set of beliefs over another. Different families, schools and communities would suggest different needs. I do believe, however, that these are things that families should think about consciously, talk about and even experiment with. Like a lot of other things in life, we should do this actively and choose these beliefs *on purpose*.

Questions:
1. How capable do you believe you are in teaching your kids? Do you have an idea about how you would help your kids, in general, in their learning?
2. What do you believe about your kids' capabilities? What do they believe about them?
3. What do you believe about learning? Do these beliefs serve you well? Do you want to share them with your kids, or perhaps prevent your kids from developing the same ones? Do you carry negative, limiting beliefs around with you in other areas of your life? If so, can you remember where you learned them?
4. What do you believe about the value of helping your kids in their learning?

# Identity (Who?)

The sum of your behaviors, your capabilities and your beliefs is your identity—who you are—in anything you do. We've already spent a good deal of time exploring this, but it is worthwhile to think about all of those same things again, in light of these other levels. Without a firm sense of who you are, and who your kids are, you can fall into the rut of operating on automatic pilot. This means, literally, being inconsiderate of the unique needs that you and your kids have.

We want to be clear that identity is more than the role that you play. As we said earlier, who you *are* is much different, much more, than what you do. You play many roles in your life, as do your kids. You are a member of your community, perhaps a worker in an industry, maybe a brother, sister, cousin, aunt, uncle, as well as parent. When you decide to be a teacher, guide, coach, mentor or friend to your kids in helping them to learn, this will be a distinct role, too. But none of these change who you are as a person. There is some core, central "you" that stays the same regardless of what role you may be playing at any moment in time.

The same is true for your kids. They are developing a firm identity as individuals. No matter what you may have heard or read, this continues well into adulthood. Sure, some things seem pretty much set from a very early age, maybe even infancy. But most things about people—behavior, capability, beliefs and even identity—are much more flexible than most people, even some social scientists and psychologists, are aware.

How this affects the way your kids learn is really an open question. It is very hard to make generalizations that make much sense. One thing is clear, though: sometimes, some kids have a very firm idea of what fits for them as people. They know what makes sense to them and what to make a part of themselves. It doesn't mean they can't learn math, science, art or whatever. It's just that some things won't seem to fit with who they are. If this seems vague, I apologize. My belief is that this particular area of study is so new, in the way that we're talking about it, that we don't yet have good language to describe it.[3] As with the other levels of learning, though, there is a main question here: "*Who* are you, as a person, and *who* are your kids, as individuals, and how might this affect what you try to do in helping them learn?"

Questions:
1. Again, who are you, from your own perspective? From the perspective of others?
2. Who are each of your kids? How does this affect the way they learn, or what they learn? What effect have you had, or could you have, on their ability or willingness to learn, in this sense?
3. Do you believe that your willingness or ability to help your kids learn says something about who you are as a person? Or who they are?

## Spirit (Who else?)

Finally, we have the spirit level of analysis. We mean, here, the ways in which we are connected to the world outside of ourselves and the ways your kids are connected to something outside of—bigger, more meaningful than—themselves. The word "spirit" here does not necessarily have anything to do with a religious sense of the word (but it could if you choose; that's one way of talking about it). More, it means *who else* is involved with you, your identity, your beliefs, capabilities, and behaviors. In growing up, in school especially, this is very important. None of us operates in a vacuum.

The spirit level can include relationships with other people in the learning environment. For example, I once knew a kid who would only do well in a class if he cared for, and respected, the teacher. For one year he went to a small school in which he had two teachers for his six subjects, each teaching three. His report card came back with 3 A's and 3 F's. He loved one teacher and hated the other. In talking to the teachers, I found that they each felt the same way about him as he did about them. The teacher he didn't get along with actually felt that this kid had no right to any feelings about her at all and that he needed to be forced into performing. When I suggested that he was a child with a very strong identity and that he would take this as a challenge and defeat her by continuing to fail, she got more rigid as well. She insisted that she could "break his will" and get him to do what she wanted. She failed, of course.

I've known other kids who would only do well if their family was stable. When I worked as a social worker, it became almost a foregone conclusion (through much discussion in our agency) that if the parents' marriage was failing, so would the kids' grades. Once the family would stabilize, either through reconciliation or divorce, the kids had a much better chance of stabilizing their own performance in school. The same is true for some kids depending on how things are going in their peer group. Sometimes all the kids in the crowd will perform the same, within a reasonable range. I've known many kids who didn't want to do too well, because they wouldn't fit in any longer.

Finally, there are some kids who have to be able to connect what they are learning to something important in life. These are kids who have a strong sense of societal problems and issues, the environment, religion, the greater good, as we say. They want to learn things that can help them make a difference in their community, country or even life in general. When they can make those connections, their motivation skyrockets and they do great. Perhaps you can think about famous highly accomplished people who had some firm goal from the time they were young that drove them to achieve wonderful things.

These are things you may know about your kids already. You may not. They are worth thinking and talking about.

Questions:

1. Who are the important people in your kids' lives who affect how they learn or perform in school? Teachers, relatives, friends, counselors, others?
2. Who else cares about your kids' learning? Who encourages or discourages them?
3. Is there any community organization, club, or other group that your kids can participate in, one that might help them?
4. How have you, or your kids, communicated about who is important in their learning and in their lives?

All of these levels come into play, in some way or another, when we help our kids learn. We might just need to spend a couple of minutes thinking about each level before we try to teach them something, and it will be obvious what we need to do. Some other times, however, we'll run into problems and really have to think about what level that problem exists on. If we are simply trying to do something at the wrong time, an environment level problem, we can find another more appropriate time. However, if our kids don't believe what we're trying to get across has any importance for them—a belief-level problem—we might need to do a lot more.

Our kids deserve to have what they need at every level. They deserve a good environment and respect for their time and style of learning, where and when they do it best. They deserve to be told exactly what they need to learn and do, the behavior, and how best to learn and do it, the capability. They also deserve to know why something is important, and that they do have what it takes to succeed, the beliefs that will support their learning. As much as anything, kids deserve to be considered for who they are, their individual identities, and to know that there is something outside of themselves that they are an important part of, the spirit level.

So, what is teaching? A number of things. One is understanding how the specific piece your kids need to learn is structured. What they need to do, pay attention to, see or hear in their minds, and feel is another. It means knowing what skills they need to learn and helping them make these skills a part of themselves. It also means connecting pieces of the puzzle together in a way that makes sense to them. It involves making sure that they believe they can learn what they need to and that it's worthwhile for them in their lives. This looks like an enormous task, but when you remember that children are really learning machines to begin with, you can get some perspective. Kids are built to be able to do all these things, so we just have to make sure we help them in a way that fits with the way they're built. All their learning will happen in some context, some system. Understanding the systems they learn in is the subject of the next chapter.

# Chapter 6

## Understanding Systems
## (School and Otherwise)
## And Working with Teachers

As we've said, we don't operate in a vacuum in this world. All of us are a part of something bigger than ourselves. We all need to appreciate those around us and the community, schools, organizations and other systems we're part of. You yourself are a system. Each of your kids is a system. Your family is a system. Just as your family is a kind of a system, so is the school itself. And the school operates inside the larger school system. Each school is a unique part of that larger system, as well as its own system. Systems within systems.

Most adults have learned, often the hard way, that systems seem to take on a life of their own. They seem to be much more than the individual parts, or people, inside of them. That's why, in the NLP field, we think of each person as an individual system, working within each of these other larger systems. But when we're dealing with one of these larger systems, a school for example, sometimes it tends to overwhelm us. I've found that understanding how each system works can be really helpful, especially when there are problems of some kind. The first thing to remember is that all systems follow rules. These rules are designed to make the system work, survive and flourish.

# Basic Principles of Systems

Thinking in these terms means that the system is the focus, rather than any one individual member or part of it. So sometimes when we're finding trouble, let's say between one of the teachers and one of our kids, we need to think beyond just the two of them. We need to ask ourselves what forces may be operating here, outside of that single relationship. Maybe the teacher is under some pressure from the principal or school board to perform in some way. For example, maybe test scores are being monitored or measured against some outside standard, and this is putting stress on the teacher. Possibly there is pressure on the kid from other kids or other teachers (counselors, coaches, etc.) that is affecting the relationship. Again, in terms of our Neuro-Logical Levels, the question might be: "Who else is involved in affecting what's happening in this problem?"

Finding the answers to these kinds of questions is where our communication skills come in. The currency of all our human systems is information. Without good information, we are just shooting in the dark and liable to hit anyone or anything (like our own foot). Information is "transacted" through communication, and as we said earlier, it requires clarity, clear intentions and attention to feedback. There is always more than one side to any story.

Here are some basic principles to remember about systems:

First and foremost, in any kind of system, every part has some effect on the system as a whole. Sometimes it's hard to tell immediately which parts affect which other parts, or in our case which people affect which other people. When you throw a stone into a pond, it sends ripples across the surface; the bigger the stone, the bigger the ripples. This ripple effect operates in schools and school systems too, but it isn't so obvious all of the time.

All systems tend to develop a balanced state, one that perpetuates itself. This is why they seem to have a life of their own, though it's really just an illusion. Things, systems and even people tend to stay in balance, which means they tend to continue to do whatever they're doing, regardless of what the effect is. This means that sometimes the old attitude of "we've always done it this way, so . . ." is really hard to overcome. It's especially frustrating when the system seems to be doing its thing to us or our kids, but we have to remember that this tendency to keep doing it anyway is natural. Anything that puts pressure on the system to change (us, for example) is usually resisted by this tendency toward balance. Ecology is the word we use to describe this tendency in nature. And nature is very powerful when it comes to finding a way to keep its balance.

So, understanding how to help the system change, or evolve if you like, means finding which specific kinds of changes will help the system move to *a new kind* of balance. Otherwise, the system will simply react against us to maintain its original way of being. It's normal, natural and in many ways healthy that it works this way.

You see, every organized system that people develop actually has two separate goals. The first is the obvious, usually clearly defined, goal. In a school system this is to educate the kids. But it also has another unstated goal: survival. The system itself will do what it can to keep itself going. Unfortunately, in some systems when its survival is threatened, or at least the people inside think it might be, the survival goal becomes much more important than the other one. That's why in so many places the schools seem to have stopped educating kids very well. Their survival mechanisms have taken over so completely that all their energy goes into that, and the kids and parents have to do the educational part pretty much on their own. It's a shame, but true. It's also why some teachers' organizations fight so hard against measuring the performance or academic abilities of the teachers, with tests, for example. Protecting the jobs of their members has become more important than insuring their competence. Of course if the measurements were simply taken as feedback and used to give the teachers whatever kind of help they need, instead of punishment, it could help the teachers and the system.[1]

When we're communicating to people in the school system (or any system), we need to really pay attention to the feedback we get. We need to be tuned in to all the subtle ways people communicate, reading between the lines so to speak, so that we can find out what effect we're having. Also, we need to pay attention to find out what other constraints or pressures are being placed on people in these systems that might affect us and our kids as well as them. Sometimes we need to allow enough time for the changes we introduce to move throughout the system to have the effects, or ripple effects, we're looking for. Good listening is the only way to find out.

Once you've established some rapport with the teacher (principal, school board member, whoever) you can begin to see things from their perspective. There is nothing in any relationship more valuable than being able to take someone else's viewpoint, to walk in their shoes a bit. There are lots of beliefs in education about how things should be done, and in any situation each person can have their own. From their point of view, their ideas will always make sense. Even in your own situation with one of your children, think about all the various levels and perspectives involved. Take a look at the following diagram.

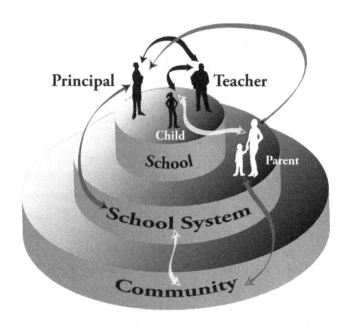

Figure 9: Various Perceptual Positions and Relationships

As you look at that diagram, it becomes obvious how many different viewpoints there can be. Even worse, how many different lines of communication are involved between each of the various parts. If any part is having trouble, or any line of communication gets snagged, it can affect the whole system. Everyone has some responsibility for making the communication work, including parents.

For nearly 20 years, I've been living and working part-time in the country of Singapore. In that country the culture dictates that the kids are pushed very hard in school *and* at home. In fact, some kids seem to be in school all day and most of the evening. Often we see them going home on trains and buses at 10 or 11 at night. It's quite common for kids to have tutoring at least several evenings a week, and this is considered a normal part of their education.

How do they do educationally? Singaporean kids (in the lower grades) usually come out as the best educated in the world, according to United Nations comparison testing. However, the level of stress on these kids is absolutely enormous. I remember riding past one of the community centers and seeing a big sign advertising upcoming stress management workshops for *pre-kindergarten children*. Imagine what it must be like to *have the need* to teach three-year-olds to handle academic stress.

The parents I work with there universally agree that they are putting way too much pressure on their kids for academic success, but they don't know what to do about it. The inherent culture of competitiveness is so powerful that they feel if they don't push their kids hard, or at least allow them to be pushed hard, that they'll have no chance of a decent future.[2] In fact, their educational system really will punish them if they don't perform well. Competition will keep them from going past certain levels of education that people in the United States would have a much easier time surpassing. The pressure is showing up in rising levels of social problems, teen drug use, rebelliousness, and so on. I've noticed the same rising academic pressures in Singapore's neighbor, Malaysia, as well as some of the other countries in Asia and Europe that I regularly visit. You may have noticed where you live, even the United States, that this increasing pressure is becoming normal in many communities. Certainly there must be a balance.

There may come a time when you feel you have to get a school or even larger system to make some changes, for whatever reason. Here are a few good principles to follow when trying to create some change within any system of people. Remember this includes a school or some part of a school, an entire school system, even a PTA or other parent organization.

1. There will be changes, anyway, over time. Change is natural in any system, especially while it is developing. School systems are always developing.
2. The system itself may have a built-in resistance to change, just to stay in balance. In other words, some people will resist change simply because it *is* change. They may have learned that change is difficult, or even dangerous, and they're simply trying to protect themselves. It doesn't mean they are bad people, or even wrong. Just like us, they need to feel safe and protected (respected, considered, important).
3. People and organizations that manage change well will thrive; those that don't will fail. But, as we said earlier, to be willing to make changes, people need at least these three things:

*Motivation*—a good reason
*Means*—a good method
*Opportunity*—a good chance for success

4. For change to go smoothly, and even succeed, people involved also need to know that they are *safe* and secure, and that this will continue to be the case. Otherwise, they'll fight to go back to the way they were.
5. Changes need to be communicated clearly to everyone involved. This may seem obvious, but anyone who has ever worked in a large organization knows that communication is one of the things that break down most often.
6. The results of changes need to be measured, reviewed and discussed at some logical interval after the change is implemented. This is to see if the changes worked to get the desired results. In fact, some changes and procedures need to be measured on a regular basis.
7. Everyone involved needs to feel that they are a part of the change, and that their ideas and opinions are at least listened to. People can usually accept changes—even those they don't want—a lot easier if they get to say their piece, express doubts and concerns, and (sometimes) moan and groan. A lot of decisions and changes are beyond the control or authority of many of the people involved. That's all right as long as they can

have some say in the matter, and feel that they can "own" the change.

8. Ownership is important because changes need to be *self-reinforcing*. That means once a change is made, it needs to perpetuate itself either by being easy and comfortable, automatic, or so effective that it's worth the extra effort. Without this, you don't have that balance in the system that's so important.

# Teachers and Systems

Some specific points about working with teachers are important here. First of all, remember that teachers modeled their own teachers. They often teach the way they were taught. It is a rare teacher who has learned to overcome this early learning. So if the teacher you're having difficulty with really seems like a bad teacher (or person), it helps to remember that they are just doing what comes naturally to them. You may want to see them as a *victim* of the teaching they got, rather than a *victimizer* of your kids. Teachers aren't withholding the good stuff, and they aren't setting your kids up to fail. They just don't always know what to do because they have become victims of that same thinking that they were exposed to as kids (or adults, or in their system). One of the most brilliant and often quoted things Albert Einstein ever said was: "You can't solve a problem with the same kind of thinking that created the problem in the first place."[3] If the teachers knew how to make the changes they needed to, in a way that worked for them within the system, they would. If you assume this, it becomes a lot easier to see the teacher as a human being like the rest of us. Then it's easy to treat him or her that way.

The idea here is to be able to create rapport with whoever is troubling you. Teachers are no different from kids when it comes to needing a good relationship to solve problems or learn new things. In talking to teachers, here are some more good guidelines to follow:

1. First and foremost, develop a relationship, good rapport, before you try anything else. Try to be as positive as possible. Show an attitude of respect and caring, along with a clear intention to be of help. Listen.

2. Try to avoid being directive or instructive, in other words telling the teacher what to do, until you have the kind of relationship that can support that. Very few people like to be told what to do (unless of course they've asked for it).

3. When you want to suggest something, set up a framework that is accepting of the teacher's needs as well as yours and your kid's. I believe the best idea for presenting things to teachers is that you are sharing something you think will help them. For example: "I've found something that seems to work *with my kids,* and it might work for you, too." In other words, you're telling the teacher that this might make his or her job (life) easier, more enjoyable and less stressful.

4. Let the teacher know that *you know* teaching is a hard job. You appreciate that it's hard and you appreciate that they really do want your kids to do well. Let the teacher know that you would like their job to be as interesting and rewarding as possible and that you want to be part of the team. Stress that you are available to help out to whatever extent the teacher wants (within reason, obviously). Always try to do this in a way that the teacher won't feel insulted, overwhelmed, invaded or challenged about their competence or their authority. No one would like that. Make sure the teacher knows that you appreciate the uniqueness of all the different kids and how difficult that makes teaching a classroom full of them. The last thing you want to do is make it harder.

5. Finally, remember, this is a *long term relationship.* You want to work with the teacher to help your kids learn. Never, if you can avoid it, do anything that will jeopardize your child's relationship with the teacher (or anyone else important in their lives). If something happens that you think might create a problem, act quickly to patch things up. This could include developing that relationship all over again, reminding the teacher of your intentions. Remember, everyone's intentions are positive, regardless of how they seem to act. The teachers. You. The kids.

Lots of parents have said to me that they really don't think they can make a difference with teachers, or in the school or school system. Sometimes it really is hard. But remember also that if anyone can make a difference, that means it's possible. If it's possible for them, it is for you, too. Good advice, always, is to avoid battles whenever you can. If you feel you really need to fight, however, choose your battles wisely. Remember that you can get yourself, the teacher, or worst of all, your child, punished if you're not careful. Make sure that you use your energy to get the most important things done. And it's always better if you *fight the problem, not the people.* Collaborate, don't compete. Get them on your side of the battle so you can tackle the problem together, and everyone can win.

# PART 2

## Teaching skills: How to Do It

*The intuitive mind is a sacred gift and the rational mind is a faithful servant.
We have created a society that honors the servant and has
forgotten the gift.*
*Albert Einstein*

*. . . those who have a higher conception of education will prize most the method of
cultivating a tree so that it fulfills to perfection its own natural conditions of growth.*
Carl Jung

# Introduction to Part 2

## Intention

I'm sure you picked up this book for a reason, or a set of reasons. If you've gotten this far, you still have that reason or reasons, maybe even more than you did when you started. This is *motivation*, one of the three things you need to make changes. Remember, you also already have a relationship with your kids. This gives you the contact, the *opportunity*, to do new things and make changes with your kids, the second piece you need. The third is the *means*—the "how"—of going about teaching your kids, and that is what this section of the book is about.

As we said earlier, there is much you can do to help your kids learn, without formal training. You just need to do some careful planning to get the results you want. First is to have a framework in mind about the learning process. You probably have a lot of that already, from the first section of this book. I believe that you can teach anything you know, once you figure out *how you know it*. You need to believe this, too. Also, we need to remember that most of what we learn doesn't come through formal lessons anyway. In fact, you've been teaching your kids all along, just not in as organized a way as you might.

In general, especially in the beginning, you'll find it really helpful to think very broadly about anything you teach. Have a bunch of questions in mind. Some of these are for yourself and some for your kids. Some are about the learning process itself; some about the specific things you want them to learn, the content. We want to always remember these two parts: the *process* and the *content*. This will help you and the kids have a framework to begin with. The following lists are a good start.

Questions to answer for you would include these:
1. *What* do I know about this topic? (Content)
2. Do I feel that this is an important thing for my kids to know? Has it been useful for me? (Content)
3. *How* do I know what I know about it? (Process. We'll talk more about this later.)
4. When I learned it, was it a good way to learn? Would I teach it the same or different now? (Process.)

Questions for the kids to ask include these:
1. Why is it important for us to learn this? How will it help? (Content)
2. What is this specific learning really about? What is natural about it? (Process and Content)
3. Where and when might this new learning be useful for us later on? (Content)
4. How does it relate to what we already know? (Process and Content)

# Messages and Meta-Messages[1]

Our intention is one of the most powerful forces we possess. We have to decide what it is and stay clear about it throughout our activities. It is what guides our actions. It is also one of the things that other people, especially those who are closest to us—our kids—will pick up quickly, even unconsciously.

Often when we communicate, we do it very clearly, but leave out what we *intend*. This can be very different from what our words *mean*. For example, has someone ever told you something that was perfectly clear, but you had no idea *why* they were telling you? Most of us have.

Usually when we ask why they're telling us, they give us an answer and it makes sense. But lots of times people don't ask when they don't know what someone else means. Kids especially. They're so used to being told what to do, sometimes they don't even know they *can* ask. Worse, sometimes they're told that they *shouldn't* ask. Worse than that, that they have *no right* to know, or are impolite to impose on an adult by *wanting* to know. Phrases like, "because I say so" are so commonplace that kids just expect to hear a lot of things that they won't understand or know the intention behind. It's too bad, and it doesn't have to be that way.

In communication theory we talk about messages and *meta*-messages. The message is the one you give directly: the words. The meta-message is the communication *about* the message that *conveys your intention*. Have you ever had someone tell you that they were really interested in what you had to say, while at the same time looking at something else, reading something on their desk, or in some way obviously not paying attention to you at all? Their stated message (they're interested) is less believable than the meta-message (they don't care). These meta-messages come in a variety of flavors from subtle body language, to certain flat voice tones, to forgetting what you said three seconds later, to complete failure to follow through on promises. These meta-messages are at least as important as the messages that go with them. Sometimes more.

To be clear to others, you must first be clear with yourself. Know the intentions and value of what you say to others, especially your kids. Then you can communicate it. The ideal is to have your meta-messages support your messages. That's what great communicators do. We call this being *congruent*.[2] If you are *in*congruent in your communication—in other words send conflicting messages and meta-messages—people won't know what to believe. It probably won't be *you*.

All of us at one time or another have complained about kids lacking incentive, self-discipline or follow-through. It's not always their fault. Sometimes the responsibility lies with the adults who gave them their instructions in the first place. Too often what kids really lack is a basic understanding about why they are doing what they've been assigned in the first place. This leads to a dilemma. They can either do whatever they've done before and hope for the best, or they can make a wild guess about what they think they are supposed to do. Lots of kids learn what most adults seem to have learned: it's safer to do nothing than to screw up. Think about some of the bureaucrats you've met.

The cure is two-fold. First, we should all try to be clear in *what* we communicate, and clear about *why*. The second is to let people know, without doubt, that they can ask us questions any time they don't understand, or need more information, no matter what that information might be. Clear on the message. Clear on the intention. We can do this with our kids, and we can teach it to our kids.

# Our Intentions in the Learning Process

So what should our intentions be when we're helping our kids learn? Well, you can probably come up with a pretty good list, if you haven't already, on your own. I, of course, have some that I think are important, so compare the following list to yours and decide if there are some more things that you should add.

## Learning can (should, at least some of the time) be fun.

Years of studies have shown that people need to involve their bodies, not just their brains, in learning.[3] One of the most effective ways is to make all learning as much fun as possible. This doesn't mean if it isn't fun, people don't learn, obviously. But who wants to do something miserable, a lot? The more fun, the more motivation, which can make the learning more effective. That should be what all of us want for all the kids.

## Learning must be safe.

When people are afraid, just as when they are unhappy, they'll avoid the situation that creates the fear and discomfort. Also, they won't learn very well. They may even attach what they learn to bad feelings, so every time that subject comes up, they'll feel bad all over again. It's really important to nurture the kids while they're learning, so that the process stays safe for them as much as possible. When problems come up, they'll be much easier to handle.

# The teaching relationship should be supportive and helpful.

So, we want the kids to feel enjoyment and safety with us. Unfortunately, lots of kids are used to being scolded, manipulated and even severely mistreated by those who teach them, in school and out. It doesn't have to be that way. Kids naturally trust adults until they learn that they shouldn't. Sure, they need to know which ones to feel safe and supported by, but it's up to us—the ones in charge of taking care of them—to make sure that they know we're on their side. We really do want to help. We really do want to be available when they need us. We really do love and care for them. Just saying so may not be enough. We may need to prove it over and over.

# Learning works.

I've met lots of kids who get overwhelmed and shut themselves off to new learning. They actually believe they aren't capable of learning new things, and they give up. It's really sad. Sometimes the only thing that works in those cases is to give them some really simple things to do, so they can experience some success. When we can pile enough successes on top of one another, in a supportive and caring relationship, it usually sinks in and they get their confidence back. It has always amazed me how hard we can make it for people to experience success, when it shouldn't be that way. We should always try to provide a learning environment in which the kids can feel successful, effective, capable and cared for.

# Learning is an active process.

I've been in a number of educational settings in which the students, kids and adults, expect to be spoon-fed new information and ideas. As an instructor, it's really frustrating because I know that learning just doesn't work like that. It's active. To learn means to do things inside our heads and bodies, not just to take information in. New information needs to be processed, thought about, connected with, connected to other things and more. Some educational settings seem to be designed to prevent this from happening. It makes the students in them become passive and lazy. I know those kids didn't start off that way. If you watch two-year-olds, you immediately notice that they seldom just sit and stare. In fact, they're usually so busy exploring that they wear out their parents. They're learning. That's how it works. We need to know that, appreciate it, use it, and expect it. The kids already know, but sometimes they need to have permission to be active in the process, or they might think they're not supposed to be (especially if they've been taught to sit still and be quiet).

## Learning is always about making connections.

We always base new learning on what we already know and can do. It always has to connect to some experience we understand. A good rule is to always begin with what the kids already know and add to it. The whole process works so much better that way, and it's so much easier and more fun. It should be automatic. But it isn't. That's why I'm reminding you now, and why we'll come back to it later.

Once you have good rapport at the beginning of a teaching session, the rest of the process gets pretty smooth. Then it's a matter of connecting ideas, information and skills together in a way that makes sense—in an environment that's safe and supportive, with clear intention. If you can do this in a way that fits for the kids, is comfortable, and even fun, it will be easy. The following chapters will take you through how the steps in the process are done.

# Chapter 7

## Rapport and Flexibility

As I've said repeatedly, if you have a clear idea about what you're doing, why and how you're doing it, it will help the kids feel more comfortable about it. If they also have a clear idea about what they're doing, and why, this will give them all the motivation they need to get started. Your rapport and motivation, for both you and your kids, will serve as a safety net for when the learning gets tough.

Remember too that each of your kids has a set of perceptual filters that distort what they're learning, sometimes in ways that make it hard for them. Since each does this differently, it means they won't learn at the same speed, or in the same way. So, flexibility is a must. It's the only way to handle all the different needs of your kids. We'll come back to how to do it later.

It's important to be flexible in maintaining good rapport during the process, or you can both lose your motivation. Rapport, the strong relationship you have with your kids, as I said earlier, is also something built out of specific skills. These are the skills of sending unconscious signals (meta-messages) to your kids that you are right there with them, sharing similar thoughts and feelings, seeing eye to eye, and hearing them clearly (see the earlier chapter: Understanding Relationships, the Basics again if you need to). Take a look at the chart below. It's a simple listing of some of the ways we can match, or pace, another person during the rapport process. It's this pacing that sends these signals, and it's a natural and continuous process between people when they are relating to each other well.

| Thinking | Background | Body language | Spoken language |
|---|---|---|---|
| ideas | race, culture | voice tone | choice of words |
| beliefs | age, status | movements, gestures | representational system |
| values | personal experiences | posture | level of difficulty |

Figure 10: Pacing Categories

Each of the things listed on the chart is something that you can communicate to your kids. You send them signals that your ideas match theirs, that your voice tone, the kinds of words you use and so on are like theirs. You have total control over this in your communication, and you should use it. The more you do, the more comfortable and open to your new ideas they'll be.

The first two of the lists above—*Thinking* and *Background*—are pretty obvious. We already think the way our kids do in some ways, and differently in others. We share the same background in most ways, though there are certainly differences in age and personal experience. The more we stress the things we share, the more we'll enhance the relationship we have with our kids. Sure, they'll want to stress the differences at times; that's part of growing up. In most ways though, they'll feel connected to us through our shared beliefs, ideas and experiences.

The next two lists—*Body language* and *Spoken language*—are the more interesting ones, in many ways. As I pointed out earlier in the book, people tend to match, or *pace*, each other when they have rapport. This is true of body language and spoken language as well as the other areas we've talked about. This means that when people are getting along really well, they tend to sit, gesture and move similarly to each other. The same is true for the choice of words and other patterns in speech. Even the tonal qualities of voice will tend to become more the same. Each person will have a unique voice, but the pitch, rhythm, speed and volume of each will be pretty close when people are in good rapport with one another. The stronger the rapport (the relationship at that moment), the more of these similarities you will find.

Also, remember, we can take some control over this natural process, and it can help us a lot in getting along with, and helping, our kids. To do this means to do the matching (pacing) process *on purpose*. To do it on purpose means we have to pay attention. We have to notice what the kids are doing with their bodies, voices and words, so that we can adjust ourselves to match them. It isn't hard; it just takes paying attention.

Practice with the experiments below, and it will help you get used to this pacing process. Pacing will become automatic—unconscious—with very little practice. Then you can trust your skills in that area and forget about it (like riding a bike).

# EXPERIMENT: OBSERVING BODY LANGUAGE

Preparation: For this experiment you'll need to be able to observe your kids during several different activities. Studying. Working on something. Playing with friends. Talking to someone else. Talking with you. Choose whatever is handy and convenient for you. You'll want to repeat this from time to time in these different situations. And, obviously, if you have several kids, you'll repeat this with each one.

Step 1:  Begin by noticing the way your child sits or stands. Basic posture: upright, slumped, balanced or leaning one way or the other.

Step 2:  Next watch for body movements. Most people don't really stand or sit still. They rock from side to side, shift their weight, and so on. Perhaps you'll notice nodding, turning or other movements of the head.

Step 3:  Try to notice hand gestures and other more subtle movements. These may look familiar to you (they may look like your own, for example).

Step 4: Pay close attention to facial expressions. Notice the mouth and eyes, especially.

Step 5: Finally, see if you can observe his or her breathing. People (kids) often don't breathe smoothly or regularly. Sometimes they hold their breath, especially when they're concentrating on something.

You may have found some parts of this more difficult than others. Hopefully you found some things you never noticed before, since almost everyone who tries this does. Also, remember that there is no right or wrong here. It's just observation. The more you see, the more you can pace, and ultimately, the more you can understand your kids. That's what it's for.

# EXPERIMENT: LISTENING TO VOICE TONE AND LANGUAGE

Preparation: For this experiment you'll need to be able to observe your kids during activities in which they're *talking*, either with others or with you.

Step 1: Begin by listening to the kinds of words and sentences your kids use. Their pronunciation, slang and so on.

Step 2: Next, begin to pay attention to what most of us call the voice or tonal qualities as they speak. Start with the volume. How loud or soft do they speak? How about the emphasis they put on certain words or phrases?

Step 3: Now, listen for the tonal quality of the voice itself. Is it resonant, nasal, breathy, scratchy, smooth?

Step 4: Next is to notice the speed (tempo) at which they speak. Sometimes it will be faster than others. Also, notice the rhythm. Some people have a very smooth rhythm, almost musical it seems. Others have a choppy or non-rhythmic voice.

Step 5: Finally, pay attention to the pitch of the voice. Is it higher or lower in pitch (high notes, low notes)? Does it stay the same, what we call a monotone? Does it go up and down a lot, like singing?

People generally seem to agree that *how* you say something is at least as important as *what* you say. This is what conveys those meta-messages we spoke of earlier. And they come in the form of body language and voice tone. This is what makes us unique, as well. We each have a personal communication style. We learned it growing up, watching and listening to other people, our family members especially. And, like a lot of what we've been talking about, we didn't pay much attention while we were learning it. We can now. We can also observe our kids while they go through this learning process. We don't want to cramp their style, but we do want to observe it. We also want to be able to respond to it, by pacing, when we're trying to strengthen our relationship with them. The more we can appreciate their style, the more we can understand them, as unique individuals.

You'll also find that, as the kids' states of mind change, so will all these things you were observing. The whole package of our body language and voice tone is an indicator of what kind of state of mind we're in. This can be a big help when you're trying to work with them, since some states of mind are great for learning and others are awful. It's the same for all of us.

So the question here becomes, if you need to, can you notice, and then duplicate, the body language and speaking style of your kids, at least enough to enhance the rapport you have with them? This is actually a pretty good question to ask yourself about all of your important relationships. It's also a good way to gain much greater flexibility as a person. Your kids can learn from that, too, since the better you are at dealing with them, the more they can learn about dealing with everyone. When you feel ready, try the following experiment.

# EXPERIMENT: BASIC PACING

Preparation: For this experiment you'll need to get together with one of your kids. It doesn't matter too much what you're doing; it can be a simple project or even just a conversation.

Step 1: Decide what aspect of body language or voice tone you'd like to experiment with. Choose something specific that you noticed in your child when you were observing. Make it one you feel comfortable in changing, in yourself, something you can do smoothly and easily. Here is the list:

| BODY | VOICE |
|---|---|
| posture | words, pronunciation |
| movement | volume |
| gestures | tonal quality |
| facial expression | speed (tempo), rhythm |
| breathing | pitch (high, low) |

Step 2: Get together with your child, and begin to observe, as you're talking and listening, what he or she is doing in the area you've chosen. For example, if it's the volume of the voice, just notice, first, how loud or soft it is. Try not to stare or focus in a way that becomes obvious or strange. This won't help with the rapport you're trying to improve.

Step 3: Next, gradually and smoothly change what you're doing so that it matches the child. Again, if it's the volume of your voice, simply begin to speak at exactly the same one as the child.

Step 4: Notice if there is any obvious change in your child. There may or may not be right away.

Step 5: Choose another aspect of body language or voice tone, and repeat the above until you can match that as well.

The goal here is to be able to match on all of the things we've listed. All of the body language, gestures, expressions, voice tone patterns and so on. This is what people really do when they're in great rapport with each other anyway; you're just doing the same thing on purpose instead of by accident.

Avoid being hard on yourself if any part of this is difficult. Some of it takes some practice, for example noticing and duplicating someone else's breathing patterns, or the rhythm of their voice. You really will get good at it if you practice, though. Also, it's probably a good idea to try to be fairly subtle until you can do it gracefully. Otherwise you'll look and sound awkward, and that certainly isn't the goal. In fact, some of this will feel strange and awkward at first anyway, like lots of things that are new to you. You may find that you are somewhat rigid in the way that you move or speak, either literally or figuratively. Practice can be a great help in loosening up, if you want it to be.

All of us would like to have great relationships with the people in our lives who are important to us. Learning to smoothly blend in with them, even in communication style, is a big help. It is also, again, at the heart of really understanding anyone else. Once we do that, they can understand us.

# Chapter 8

# Kinds of learning: Six Categories

We all know there are lots of different kinds of things we have to learn. Riding a bike isn't the same as spelling, doing math or operating a computer. Each takes different kinds of skills and different thinking. In this chapter I want to take a big picture look at the learning process, just to make sure we have a good framework in mind. Later we'll get down to the smaller pieces. It's easier that way.

## Skill Categories

Learning is natural, but it is also a natural set of skills. Friends of mine named Robert Dilts and the late Todd Epstein developed some categories[1] of different kinds of skills we've found very useful in our field. It doesn't take much expertise to figure out which categories fit for anything you're trying to teach, and it makes the process a lot more logical and easy.

Here are the categories:

Conceptual
Analytical
Observational
Procedural
Interactive
Relational

*Conceptual* skill is the ability to put a whole idea—the big picture—together, out of a bunch of smaller pieces, like those puzzles we talked about earlier. Figuring out how small parts of something relate to each other and fit together is a skill that can be learned and practiced. Understanding how it all fits together inside of something that is bigger, and how that in turn fits into something bigger, and so forth, is what we're talking about here. We sometimes call this "chunking up," in other words going to larger and larger chunks of the whole piece. For example, if we were talking about a math problem, this would mean understanding how and why the numbers work the way they do and how this math problem relates to other ones like it. It could also include how the problem relates to our everyday life.

*Analytical* skills are the opposite of conceptual skills, sort of. When we *analyze* something we don't put it together; we take it apart. So, figuring out how some big piece naturally breaks down into its components is a separate skill from figuring out how they get built up. This also includes categorizing, or cataloging, the basic elements that make up the whole. Big chunks get broken down into smaller ones, so we sometimes call this "chunking down." So, again in our math problem, this would be how we look at and talk about each of the individual pieces of the problem, numbers, formula, and so on.

*Observational* skills, obviously, require using our eyes and our ears to see and hear what is happening around us. It also includes the ability to gather relevant information in the moment it's happening, what we call "real time." In other words, see and hear what's around you, notice what's important, and use the information. Better than math, as an example, would be sports. How we notice other players, positions, where the ball is, the sights and sounds that let us react appropriately. The experiments in the last chapter on observing your kids also fall into this category.

*Procedural* skills involve the abilities we have to remember, and then follow, a set of steps properly. This means getting from some beginning point to some ending point, in the right order. It also means knowing which step leads to the next (and hopefully why) so we can get to the objective. We need to know how to start and finish things. This is a very difficult skill for many people. In our math problem, it's knowing how to begin, follow the steps and finish the problem. Even in sports it's important to know what order to do things in. Think about hitting a tennis ball, baseball or a golf ball, and all the little things we have to do in the right sequence to get the ball to go in the direction we want.

*Interactive* skills involve dealing effectively with other people. It includes knowing how to get them to respond to us as well as appropriately responding to them. We mean here, especially, noticing the way other people are reacting to us—and what to do about it if it isn't working out. Certainly this includes our observational skills and to some extent our procedural skills to be truly effective. If you think about our discussions on rapport, this will become clear. In teaching kids, it's important that we know how to deal with them, and that they know how to deal with us. We need to pay attention to each other while we're doing things together.

*Relational* skills also involve communicating well with other people, but these include a broader category of skills: understanding our various roles, differences in culture, ages, understandings, and how to handle different situations. Relational skills also include how to create the relationship in the first place, keep it going strong and, especially, what to do when there are problems. To me, the ability to manage our relationships includes all the other skills in this list.

Any time we're trying to help, or teach, our kids, is a good time to think about these six different skills. Obviously, depending on what we're trying to accomplish, some will be more important than others. This will shape what we do from that point forward. We'll come back to some specifics later on.

# Neuro-Logical Levels

Another good point is to remember our Neuro-Logical Levels. I simply want to mention them, to keep them in mind, as we go through the teaching process, and the skills involved. Much of what you'll be teaching your kids will be *behavior* and *capability* level skills: *what* to do and *how* to do it. Sometimes you'll run into a belief or identity level issue, and it will usually be obvious. If you've established good rapport and answered the questions about why the material is important, it will usually take care of itself. Every once in a while, though, some kind of problem will turn up that makes thinking about this important. We'll talk more at length about this in the section on trouble-shooting.

# The Bandura "Learning Curve"

Another natural process shows up in learning a lot of the time, and it's good to be aware of this one, before you get started. Like many things in life, learning isn't always a neat and tidy process that moves ahead at a steady pace. In fact, real learning seldom works this way. Instead, it goes in fits and starts, moves quickly, moves slowly, stops, reaches plateaus. Psychologists have been plotting graphs and curves of these processes for many years, and it *can* get very complicated, but it doesn't have to.

This messy process has some predictable patterns that we should keep in mind. There are four main phases of learning something from scratch and progressing all the way up to knowing it thoroughly. These were described many years ago by a psychologist named Albert Bandura.[2] The stages of learning are these:

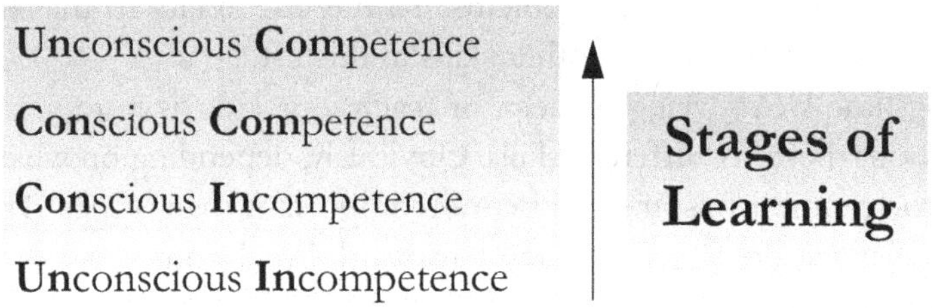

Unconscious **Competence**

Conscious **Competence**

Conscious **Incompetence**

Unconscious **Incompetence**

**Stages of Learning**

Figure 11: Stages of Learning

Learning progresses through these stages, as I mentioned, in some predictable ways. If you understand some of the pitfalls in the process, it can make it easier to guard against problems. In fact, just understanding this can eliminate some of the problems altogether. Here is a summary of one of Bandura's graphs that shows these natural stages, including a couple of the problem areas.

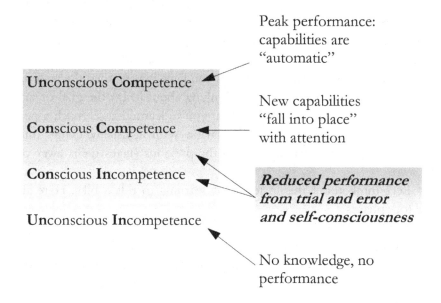

Peak performance: capabilities are "automatic"

**Un**conscious **Comp**etence

New capabilities "fall into place" with attention

**Con**scious **Comp**etence

**Con**scious **In**competence

*Reduced performance from trial and error and self-consciousness*

**Un**conscious **In**competence

No knowledge, no performance

Figure 12: Problem Areas in the Learning Curve

Here's what this means and how these stages work.

**Un**conscious **In**competence means that you don't know the new thing you need to learn, and you don't even know you don't know. This is the very beginning, before you've discovered the new learning even exists. Ignorance is bliss.

**Con**scious **In**competence is the next step. Here you find out that you don't know it. At this point you *know about* the new knowledge, but you also know you don't *know* it yet, or how to do it. It can be a bit uncomfortable if you think this new thing is important to know. It might also be a really good motivator to learn.

**Con**scious **Comp**etence is the stage in which you've now learned the knowledge or skills to the extent that you can use it. However, at this stage you can only do it if you concentrate on it and stay focused. In this stage you have to pay attention to avoid mistakes, but you're capable as long as you concentrate. This is usually an encouraging point in the learning, but can cause difficulties when you try to get everything to work smoothly with what you already knew before. In other words, during the learning process, in the **Con**scious **In**competence and **Con**scious **Com**petence stages, as you devote more of your concentration on the new learning you tend to make more mistakes in other areas. Overall performance often suffers. This can be surprising, and even discouraging, when it happens, but it's a natural part of the process.

**Un**conscious **Com**petence means you have now learned the material *so well* that you can use it without thinking about it. It's the goal of any thorough learning. It means that what you've learned is so much a part of you that it's *automatic* in your behavior. With it, usually, comes total confidence. The performance lag in the previous stages melts away on its own.

Let's think about this in terms of learning to ride a bike. Here are the four phases.

**Un**conscious **In**competence
> There is a point, when you're young, when you don't even know this is something that you can learn. You don't know about bikes yet.

**Con**scious **In**competence
> Later, you'll see someone riding, then ask about it. Someone will explain it to you and probably tell you that it will be your turn to have a bike soon. That's when you'll want to learn and even begin to try.

**Con**scious **Com**petence
> Next, with some help and practice, you'll get to the stage where you can ride a little, but you have to work at it, paying attention to holding yourself up, peddling, steering and the rest. At this stage you can ride, but you can't do much else because all your attention is taken up with doing it safely and going in the right direction.

**Un**conscious **Com**petence
> Finally, with practice, you can just get on and ride, paying attention to the countryside, the people you're talking to, the soft

drink you're drinking, or whatever. At this point in your learning, you don't have to think about riding the bike at all. It's automatic. This learning stays with you, needing very little refreshing in the future.

What this means, for us, is several things. The first one is that the first and last stages are the easy ones. The old saying, "Ignorance is bliss," describes **Unconscious Inc**ompetence perfectly. It doesn't bother you about what you don't know, if you don't know about it. Of course once the new knowledge becomes automatic, or built in for you—**Unconscious Comp**etence—you again don't have to think about it. Unconscious is easy.

The middle two stages are where the real work is. When you're first learning something it can be hard, and this can make staying motivated difficult. When we don't improve at things as smoothly or quickly as we like, we can get discouraged. So attention to both those things, the learning and the motivation, are important. Even when you've learned something to the level of conscious competence, it can be difficult to integrate into yourself and your other learnings. A strange thing happens sometimes during this integration process. With some people, and some learnings, we seem to go through a process of sliding backwards at this point—actually getting worse—at what we're learning *and the things we thought we already knew.*

I once ran into a common example of this in a group of adults I was working with. This group runs the computer systems for a major corporation, and they were in the middle of a big change in the way they did things. Almost everyone involved had to learn lots of new things, really fast. Not only were they overwhelmed with the new learning, but a number of them also told me they were *having trouble with things they already knew how to do.* Things that were fairly straightforward, everyday tasks were now becoming confusing and inefficient for these folks. These tasks were mostly the ones they had conscious competence about, ones they could do, but that still required attention and clear thinking to do well. They found that they just didn't have enough "brain power" to learn the new systems and still do these other normal everyday things. It made them feel dumb, and really shook their personal confidence, in some cases. *This is a normal stage in the learning process and it doesn't last.* When I explained all of this to them, especially that it was normal, they were quite relieved. You, too, have probably never noticed these stages happening in your learning (at least not this clearly), but they happen nevertheless.

This same kind of getting stuck happens in kids all the time. Even little ones. A good example is when a child is just learning to walk. They've finished the crawling stage pretty well, but they aren't too steady on their feet yet. This is often the same time they're learning to talk. Sometimes they will actually go back to crawling for a while, because it's too much effort to walk and talk at the same time (for some grownups I know, as well). This apparent slide backwards can really scare parents when they see it. They, quite naturally, think that the child was walking better before, and they wonder what's wrong. Again, when parents learn that this is normal, it's a nice relief.

This natural process is nothing to worry about, just to notice and pay attention to. Usually, when you understand that this is natural and *will pass all by itself* as you progress, you can just relax. People deserve to know this. Most of us have realized that any time we're having any sort of difficulty in our lives, it's a lot easier if we know two things: first, it's normal; and second, there is an end in sight. Our kids need to know about this, too.

# Chapter 9

# Paying Attention to Paying Attention

Probably since the dawn of mankind, people have been complaining that others just don't pay attention. What they really mean is: "They just don't pay attention to what I want them to." It really is different. I used to have parents complain to me on a regular basis that the kids don't listen. Of course what they really meant was that they don't do what their parents told them to. I'm being picky on purpose. If you listen to the words, without understanding the meaning, it's easy to get caught in the same kind of thinking that created the problem in the first place.

If there is any such thing as a secret to getting kids (or anyone) to pay attention to what we want them to, it's probably this: Find out *how* they pay attention in the first place. If you can do that, and create strong rapport, you can guide their attention much more easily. Remember, we delete, distort and generalize all the time, and so do our kids. It's not that we're *not* paying attention; it's just a question of *what* we're paying attention *to*.

This all may seem more technical than it needs to be. It might be, but some time thinking about these things can be really helpful. I'll try to make it as logical as possible, in this chapter, so you can take what you need and apply it in your own situation with your kids.

There are some principles we came up with in our field a number of years ago that include a number of different ways people pay attention, as well as how they chunk information. We call these *Sorting Principles*.[1] This means, literally, how people sort things out from their experience, all that they see, hear and feel, in any moment, in any situation. What things do we choose to notice out of all that we see? How do we know which thing that someone said was most important? What guides our decisions about what is important? Good questions.

The idea here is that we are *programmed* to sort things out, including what we pay attention to, in any situation. How the programming is done isn't important, since it's very fluid and we can change it. What *is* important is noticing that the programming is active and working in our kids and us. It affects every aspect of teaching and learning. We call these sorting principles *Meta-programs* (programs that run other programs) for that reason. It means there is programming in us that tells us which programs to run inside ourselves—for paying attention to things—in each kind of situation. These programs are closely related to our attitudes and beliefs, so paying attention to them, especially if there is some kind of problem, can be really helpful.

There are long lists of these Meta-programs, and they aren't all relevant here, so I'll go over only the ones that I believe are the most useful for us. Also, as you look at these, you'll notice that in most cases they are listed as "either-or" combinations, but that isn't really how they work. There is no right or wrong, better or worse in any of these, just different ways of looking at the world. They also may seem extreme and disconnected from each other. They aren't. There is a range, or balance, that occurs in each one of these programs, like most things in life.

| Relationships and communication | Convincers |
|---|---|
| Task & Relationship<br>Primary Representational System | Time frame<br>Number of examples<br>Input source |
| **Working, learning & thinking styles** | **Motivators** |
| Independent, Collaboration, Proximity<br>Matching, Mis-matching<br>Chunk sizes | Toward & Away From<br>Proactive & Reactive<br>Possibility & Necessity<br>Internal & External |

Figure 13: Meta-Program Sorting Principles

## Relationships and Communication

Task and Relationship
Primary Representational System

We've already talked about task and relationship a bit. As I said earlier, the most important thing in teaching your kids is to make sure the relationship is solid before you try to begin the task. There is, of course, a balance you want to achieve here. There will be plenty of times that your kids need your attention and caring a lot more than they need to concentrate fully on a math problem or other task. Be willing to shift your attention to the relationship whenever you get the signal from your kids. When you go back to the task, it will be a lot easier. It will also help maintain the motivation to keep going when the learning gets tough.

You may be familiar with the concept of learning styles. These come in lots of forms,[2] but one of the most important has to do with which *senses* your kids pay most attention to: what they see, what they hear or what they feel. Obviously this changes from time to time, in fact in some cases moment to moment. However, some kids (people) have a tendency to favor one kind of input most of the time. Maybe your kids prefer visual information (what they see) to auditory (what they hear) much more often than the reverse. Or maybe they prefer kinesthetic (what they

95

feel) over anything almost all the time. We have to be really careful about generalizations here, but in some kids strong preferences do exist.

We can also think about all the different ways input comes in, in terms of schoolwork and learning. Let's say you've noticed that your kids believe what others tell them more than what they see, or read. Or maybe the reverse is true, meaning they believe what they read or see more than what anyone says. Some kids seem to need to have a full experience—to actively do something—to give them the feeling that they understand it, or can appreciate it. You can even think through your own experiences of learning in this respect. You might notice one of these patterns is generally true for you as well.

These ways of taking in knowledge can affect the way kids are convinced of things, how they make decisions about them, even whether they notice them or not. Certainly giving your kids what they need to learn in the way that has the most impact on them will help, and we'll explore this in the next chapter, in some detail. But you can be thinking about it, for now, in terms of what your kids believe, understand and appreciate. Sometimes it's how they get the message, not the message itself. Ultimately, from my point of view, kids need to be able to take in any kind of information that's useful and relevant, in or out of school. We'll talk more about that later, too.

## Convincers

Time Frame
Number of Examples
Input Source

How are you convinced that you know something—that you've really learned it? This can be an important thing to know. It could be with your kids, too. For example, do you know that you've learned something well because you can *do it well consistently*, pretty much all the time? Or, in contrast, do you just have to do something well for a couple of weeks to know that you have it down? These are examples of using time itself to convince you of something. Some people seem to have favorite time periods that they use, either because they seem to work for them or because they learned them from someone else. Think about how this creeps into the workplace: "Six month trial period" or "Two week probation" or "Annual bonus" or "Quarterly report" or "Seven day waiting period." Time is important to us, and we use it for things that don't always make sense (but sometimes do). Maybe your kids need a set period of time to do something successfully before they believe they know it. For example, if they can do something for three weeks, they feel comfortable with it. If this is the case, you can use that time frame along with them. Or, you can change it if it seems like it's causing more trouble than it's worth.

Maybe you don't think of time in that way at all, though. Some people need a number of things to happen to convince them that they know something. For example: "I know if I can do this just three times, I'll have it down cold." Or: "If my kids can pass the next three spelling tests with 80% correct, then I'll know they're on the right track." Sound familiar? These kinds of "number of examples" decisions creep into our lives pretty often, and as with time periods, they might make sense and they might not. We all know people who are convinced they can do something because they did it once, even though they seem to have failed consistently ever since that first time. Not a good convincer. On the other hand, and just as troublesome, there are plenty of people who seem to do very well at something on a regular basis, but still aren't satisfied. Your kids may be stuck in some way like this. You can help them.

We should also remember that sometimes the kids are only paying attention to what they see, or what they hear or how they feel about what they've learned. They might only pay attention depending on who the information is coming from. For example, the convincer for your child might be that the *teacher* praised them one time, and that's enough. It can be confusing if this is the case after *you've* been praising them for weeks and it didn't seem to have any effect. The *source* of the praise matters. Not just that they *hear* it, but *who* they hear it *from*. The same could be true of a voice tone, more than the words. It might be a facial expression, a pat on the back or a hug, or any other kind of signal they get from someone. Sometimes it's the *signal*; sometimes it's the *source*.

Talking with your kids about these issues can be one of the most valuable lessons they, and you, can ever have. The more we mature, the more we get to decide what success means to us. This means choosing what *criteria* we use, at least in our own minds and experience. Talking about, and agreeing on, what constitutes success in learning can enhance your relationship with your kids, increase their motivation and help them develop a clear idea about their own abilities in learning and every other area of their lives. The sooner they are able to learn what works for them, in measurable ways, the sooner they can shoot for those specific targets. In the long run it will save a lot of time, too.

## Motivators

Toward and Away From
Proactive and Reactive
Possibility and Necessity
Internal and External

Just as we are convinced of certain things in certain ways, we're motivated by certain kinds of input, from some sources more than others. What kicks me into high gear when I'm trying to learn something might be totally different from what works for you or your kids. Any adult who works at any job knows from experience that everyone is motivated by slightly different things and from different people.

For example, some people don't get working until they are under some kind of threat of pain or discomfort. They respond well to scolding from the boss, or a deadline beyond which disaster will happen. But, as a psychiatrist I worked with once pointed out to me, for some people a deadline is simply *an instruction for how to be LATE!* For them, the pain, or threat of it, doesn't seem to work. But maybe a reward will. So, some people respond to pain, others to rewards—sticks or carrots. We call this contrast: Toward pleasure vs. Away From pain. Certainly none of us only responds to one or the other, but some people seem to pay attention to one much more than the other in certain circumstances. In school, some kids work hard for those good grades and praises from the teachers. Others only work hard when they're under the threat of poor grades, lack of privileges, extra work and so forth.

This is closely related to another pair of programs called Possibility vs. Necessity and Proactive vs. Reactive. In other words, some of us will see what's possible and take the bull by the horns to make it happen (Possibility, Proactive). We seem to have vision and initiative. Others will wait until they have no choice (Reactive) and just have to do something (Necessity). I know this seems like one is good and the other bad, and I don't really mean it that way. There are lots of times in life when we should just step aside and let things happen on their own and "let sleeping dogs lie." The secret, like in most things in life, is knowing which one will work better for us and under what circumstances.

For our kids, we generally want them to move toward the good things they can get in learning (Toward), to notice what they might get out of it (Possibility) and act independently, with initiative (Proactive). Getting them there is another story. Think about when you were a kid in school. Were you the kind who wasn't really motivated to write your paper until the night before? If so, by that time you felt like you had no choice; it was do or die. Then you could work furiously until late into the night (or all night) and get the job done (most of the time). That was me. There are plenty of people who really did take the teacher's constant advice to get started as soon as the assignment was given, working smoothly and steadily all the way through, maybe even handing in their work early. I never understood those people back then. Now I do. They were motivated in a different way than I was. I didn't get to change this in myself until I was in graduate school and I felt like I had no choice but to change it.

A lot of this has to do with maturity in general. When we're growing up, we learn about what's expected of us and how we work best. What most of us generally consider mature is to look forward at what's possible, how good life can be if we invest time and effort into making it that way, and then we show initiative. We often respect self-starters. They seem to get the job done without having to be told. A lot of this has to do with whether we get our motivation from others (External) or build it in ourselves (Internal). As we get older, we have more internal motivations to get things done, because we have fewer people standing over us. The exception is work. Many people, unfortunately, act at work as if they were still in school, waiting to be told (or threatened about) what to do. Sometimes in every other area of their lives they are proactive, energized and moving forward—but not on the job. People who are self-employed don't usually act that way, or they can't stay in business. I think if we learned to get some control over this internal motivation when we were kids, it would easily carry over. The successful people I know seem to have this pretty well worked out.

So for our kids, we want them to move generally in the following direction:

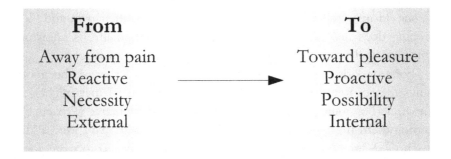

| From | To |
|---|---|
| Away from pain | Toward pleasure |
| Reactive | Proactive |
| Necessity | Possibility |
| External | Internal |

Figure 14: Directionalization

## Working, Learning and Thinking Styles

Independent, Collaboration, Proximity
Matching, Mis-matching
Chunk Sizes

Everything we've been talking about affects motivation, decision making (convincing us and our kids that they are learning effectively), and the relationship we have with them. It also affects the way they feel about themselves. A lot of it is a matter of style. For every kid who seems to match some image of the perfect combination of attitudes, there is another who doesn't but still does just fine. It's finding the combination that works best for each that's the trick. And, unfortunately, it's no trick. It would be easier if it were. It takes talking, asking questions, observing and checking to find out what works best and is most comfortable.

Think about how you work and learn best, in various situations. Some people do just great all by themselves. We just wait, and they show up with the job done fine. They really seem to do better alone, and *Independent* from other people. In contrast, there are those who have to work in teams to be most effective. They work best in *Collaboration* with others. Maybe it helps them generate ideas or motivation, perhaps it allows them to get needed input throughout the process of their work, or maybe they just like the relationships and feel more comfortable that way. Most adults have had plenty of opportunity to be in both kinds of situations, and sometimes they like one better than the other, and sometimes the combination is helpful. One kind of combination is a setup that allows you to work by yourself, but to have lots of people available that you can call on for help whenever you need to. These other people are in close *Proximity* and can act as consultants, mentors, collaborators, or whatever else seems appropriate.

Kids get the opportunity to explore these different kinds of relationships as well. The one they have with you when you are helping to teach them is the most important for our purposes here. Often the kids will just tell us to leave them alone so they can work out something on their own. Sometimes this really is a good idea, and sometimes it isn't. But it is worth giving the benefit of the doubt if you aren't sure. If they can do this, and come to you only when they need help, you may be developing that kind of Proximity relationship that really works. And, of course, sometimes you'll want to do things with them, in a Collaborative way, as a team. I believe this is one of the smartest things to ask your kids about each time you want to give them something new. Decide, between you, what will work the best. Check it. Find out. Change it if you need to. Remember:

Independent    Leave the kids alone, as long as they're all right
Collaboration  Work together as a team, until you get the idea not to
Proximity      Let them work alone, but stay close by for consultation

Another kind of thinking involves comparisons with what we already know, or have already experienced, when we're learning. For example, we talked earlier about how driving a car is like riding a bike, and how it isn't. This can be a great way to start when you want to share something new with the kids. If they can relate the new idea, in some way, to what they already know (*Match*) then they might find it easier to learn. It's also important to remember that if it's really something new, it will also be different in some ways (*Mis-match*).

There is another interesting aspect to this Match vs. Mis-match concept that affects much more than the new information. Sometimes, when kids are learning something new, they remember the last time they learned something new. Not the information, the learning experience itself. If this was a great experience, they want it to be the same—a Match—in terms of the experience. But it might not be and this can lead to disappointment or worse. Maybe the opposite is true, in that the previous learning experience was an unpleasant one, and they want it to be different this time: a Mis-match. That can happen as well. The point is that these Matches and Mis-matches happen on the level of the experience—the feelings about learning—as well as the content of the learning. This is another one of those things that the kids will sometimes let us know right at the start.

| Mis-match | "Not another new idea, Mom, don't you remember the last time? |
| Match | "Come on Dad, do it like you did when we worked on those math problems. Make it fun like it was then!" |

Certainly the kids deserve the best learning experiences we can give them. One of the best ways is to be able to point out the good parts that Match and separate out the bad ones that Mis-match. We can do this together with them. It will be what helps them learn the difference between a cup that is half-empty and one that is half-full.

There is a wonderful book about writing, and life, that tells a story about an experience the author had when she was a child.

> . . . thirty years ago my older brother, who was ten years old at the time, was trying to get a report on birds written that he'd had three months to write, which was due the next day. We were out at our family cabin in Bolinas, and he was at the kitchen table close to tears, surrounded by binder paper and pencils and unopened books on birds, immobilized by the hugeness of the task ahead. Then my father sat down beside him, put his arm around my brother's shoulder, and said, "Bird by bird, buddy. Just take it bird by bird."[3]

The book this is from is called *Bird by Bird: Some Instructions on Writing and Life* and it's filled with stories about how to think about these things. Highly recommended.

We often talk about taking things in bite-size chunks, but the two-part question is: "What does that really mean, and by the way, whose bites?" We have probably all had the problem of being overwhelmed by a big project of some sort and at some point realizing that we need to break it down into pieces that we can handle without scaring ourselves. A classic Chinese saying says: "A journey of a thousand miles begins with a single step."[4] So, picking the right size piece to learn (teach, study, whatever) is important for our motivation as well. It's also important for making sense out of certain kinds of material. We call this choosing the right Chunk size.

Some people find it easier to think in big picture terms, chunking up as we discussed earlier. They like to have broad outlines or ideas about what they are doing. Literally, for those of us who prefer this kind of thinking, we feel comfortable if we can step back, so to speak, from the picture we have in mind, and see all of it at once. In fact, some kinds of thinking and learning require this. On the other hand, other people are more comfortable with small details than with the whole concept, idea or system: chunking down. They want a thin slice, not the whole pie. Often their question would be, "What's the first step, so I can get started? I'll come back and ask for more when I get that done."

Maybe you had this classic test in school when you were a kid (it was very popular in schools when I was young). The teacher passes out the test. It's actually a set of instructions to be followed. The first instruction is to read through the whole thing, before you begin. But, it's long and there are lots of complicated instructions, so I, like most of the kids in my class, started doing them. It included things like "circle all the 3's on the page" or "underline the first 5 capital letters you find" or "put a box in the left hand corner." Many of the instructions made no sense at all, and I vividly remember being one of the students that asked the teacher to explain what was meant. She just kept saying: "Read the instructions." By the time we got to the bottom of the page it was a mess. The last instruction—remember, the one we were supposed to read before beginning—said something like: "Now that you've read all of the instructions, ignore them, write your name in the upper right hand corner, and put your pencil down." There was no escape, either you made a complete mess and wasted a lot of time, or you handed in a nice neat piece of paper with just your name at the top.

The question of what size pieces to help your kids learn is not one you can always answer beforehand. If you know that your kids do better with big pieces first—and then break them down into smaller ones—fine. Or if you know that they generally do better with the smaller ones first—before building up the whole puzzle—also fine. Most of us have some natural preferences. But sometimes the *nature of the learning* will make one style work better than the other. All of us are overwhelmed by some things, no matter how much we prefer the big picture and, by the same token, sometimes details will drive us crazy, no matter how much we generally prefer those.

Best is to find out by asking the question at the beginning. Your kids will often tell you or show you what you need to do. I believe, in general, that an overview of what, why and how is good to start with, but if it seems like too much, stop. Go to details, or steps, or the first step, depending on what you're teaching.

I'll come back to more examples of how to do this in the specific pieces in Part III. For now, it's valuable to keep the idea of "chunk size" in mind, even for yourself as you read this.

In terms of all these ideas about attention, the one overriding factor is to notice it. Observation is one of your strongest tools. Kids will show you and tell you what they are paying attention to. Then you can ask yourself if the things they are paying attention to are the ones that will help them to learn what they need to learn. I think it's vital to be able to ask your kids about what they notice. And just as importantly, about what they don't, or didn't, notice while they were working on something. My hope is that this brief discussion on the different ways we can pay attention, and focus ourselves, will help you to help your kids.

# Chapter 10

# Common Sense(s): Using the Five Senses You Were Born with

In our field, and indeed in much of the educational community, we've known for a long time that there is a *sensory basis* to the way we learn.[1] As we've said, we see, hear and feel and some of us do much better with some sensory information than with others.

So teaching (communicating) means getting what we see, hear and feel across to someone else. We need them to be able to see the picture, hear the sounds and words and feel the feelings that are built into the new things they're learning. It isn't magical, or even difficult, but it is important. A lot of what people call learning disabilities are just symptoms of doing something with the sensory information that simply doesn't work very well.

I also know that many people seem to have a difficult time seeing clear images in their minds in the first place. Some have trouble hearing or remembering voices or words well, or even paying attention to what (or how) they feel. Perhaps you're one of them. Relax. Most of the time, it's just a matter of practice in paying attention. We'll do some exercises that should help. The idea is to make our internal thoughts clear to us, and then we can make them clear for the kids.

In my view there are two main parts to doing this well. First, we need to be able to give them the pictures, sounds and feelings they need that constitute the new information. But second, and in the long run much more important, we need to help them develop the skills to be able to use all the senses well, so that they can understand different kinds of information easily, and be able to learn from anyone, regardless of what sensory information that person generally gives. You see, one of the main difficulties between teachers and students comes in the form of a mis-match between the way the teacher puts out the information and the way the student takes it in. If the teacher only puts it out in words, and the student needs a picture connected to a feeling, it can be difficult to make the translation. And, that's what it is: a translation from one sense to another. It's not that it can't be done; it's just more difficult for some kinds of information than others. It can be much more difficult if the relationship between the teacher and student isn't very good. On the other hand, if the relationship is very, very good, this kind of problem usually goes away altogether. That's why we've spent so much time on relationships.[2]

Again, the secret in teaching is to be able to transfer what you actually know, the pictures, sounds and feelings, so that your kids can get the same ones in their minds that you have in yours. To be able to do this, sometimes you have to figure out what really is in your mind first. How do you know what you know?

Here's a simple example. Let's say you want to teach your kids how to call someone on the phone. What are the actual things you have to be able to do, in making a phone call? Well, first, before you can do it you have to pick up the receiver, something physical, and put it up to your ear. Then you have to make sure you get a dial tone. So this is something you have to listen for. Then you have to know the number (we'll come back to that in a moment). Once you know the number, you have to physically push each of the buttons, one at a time. Then you have to wait for it to ring, or give a busy signal, again something to listen for. Then you wait and talk to the person, or hang up, whichever is appropriate.

What about knowing the number? You can do this by remembering it, looking it up in the phone book, or having someone tell you; each of these requires something different in the way of understanding. If you are remembering it, how are you doing that?

> Do you see the person's face, and then hear the number in your mind?
>
> Do you imagine you can hear their voice, and see the number in your mind?
>
> Either way, do you see or hear the whole number at one time, or do you have it in two chunks, one three numbers, followed by another that is four (in the United States, anyway)?

Looking for it in a telephone directory requires a whole other set of skills, including reading, understanding alphabetical order, knowing the proper sections of the book and so on. And if someone tells you the number, you have to hear it correctly, then punch the numbers in, in the same order they gave them to you (How many times have you forgotten the number somewhere between their words, your brain and your fingers?).

This can be a lot more complicated than you thought, huh? Well, what we've just done here is called *task analysis*.[3] This means figuring out the pieces, or chunks, of any task, in this case looking up a number. Though it sounds complicated and even overwhelming at first, it isn't really. With a little bit of practice it can be kind of fun. You can even make this into a game with your kids.

One of the things that make this easier is learning to listen carefully to the language your kids use when they talk (or anyone, for that matter). We communicate in words, but also in patterns of words and ideas. We tell people the way we think about things by some of the words that we use, specifically sensory-based words. Our language actually includes sensory information. It happens in the verbs, adjectives and adverbs, what we call the predicates. These words tell people how we *represent*—think about—what we say to one another. Our language breaks down into what linguists call *representational systems*. Take a look at the list that follows and notice how the words are organized into visual words, auditory words, kinesthetic words, and words that are unspecific as far as sensory processing.

| VISUAL | AUDITORY | KINESTHETIC | UNSPECIFIED |
|---|---|---|---|
| see | listen | bite | seem |
| view | hear | burst | be |
| observe | overhear | bend | aware |
| witness | sound | bind | have |
| sight | order | break | think |
| spot | ask | fall | believe |
| look | beg | hit | allow |
| glance | ring | climb | become |
| eye | sing | feel | know |
| examine | speak | touch | understand |

Figure 15: Representational Systems in Language

Learning to listen for these different kinds of words and phrases in the way our kids talk, and carefully using them ourselves, can really help in getting our ideas across. It turns out that, most of the time when we talk, we primarily will use one of the systems more than the others. Sometimes we'll use two, but rarely will we use visual, auditory and kinesthetic all at the same time. From one moment, or one topic, to the next, we'll have a favorite way of thinking about what we're talking about. This will get us to use a favorite kind of word to go along with that thinking. In other words, when we're thinking in pictures, we'll use visual words. Remembering sounds or words people said, we'd tend to use auditory words. Feelings: kinesthetic words.

For example, let's say you're describing a trip you took to an exciting new place. You might come back and tell your friends "all about" your wonderful trip, but I doubt it. Most likely, you'll concentrate on one sensory aspect or the other. For example:

| | |
|---|---|
| Visual | the beautiful scenery, the landscape |
| | what you saw people wearing, the local styles |
| | the architecture or the artwork |
| Auditory | all those wonderful stories, the unique language |
| | the special music, the unique local sounds |
| | sounds of nature, or even how quiet it was |
| Kinesthetic | how exciting the trip was or how relaxed you felt |
| | the hiking, climbing and other physical activities |

the cold weather and how you had to bundle up to stay warm

You can probably easily tell from the above lists, which is more likely for you. Sometimes it's just about you and your personal preferences. Sometimes there is something special about the place that gets your attention in some way. People who come to where I live in the summertime usually talk about how hot and humid it is, and they wonder how the locals survive. They even swear never to come back. Then they remember the food, and it all changes . . . .

As I said, only rarely will we use visual, auditory and kinesthetic all at the same time. The same is true for our kids. It also turns out, that when any two people have established good rapport, their language changes so that they both use, primarily, the same representational system (or systems) as each other. In other words, they speak the "same language." This is part of what creates that sharing of common experience we talked about earlier. It's very natural. You do it most of the time.

This means we can purposely use the same words, or kind of words, as our kids to help enhance the rapport between us. Also, we can carefully use the appropriate words to describe any task we want to help them learn. So if we remember our idea of task analysis, we can really use this. It makes sense that as we figure out what the *sensory steps* are in any task, we can describe those steps using the sensory words that go along with those steps. It's natural with a little practice.

For example, let's look at our telephone-dialing task. Here are the steps:

| | |
|---|---|
| 1. Pick up the receiver and put it up to your ear | physical movement, kinesthetic |
| 2. Listen for a dial tone | hear, auditory |
| 3. Get the number | see or hear it in your mind or hear it from someone or look it up |
| 4. Physically push each button in the right order | see, act, visual and kinesthetic |
| 5. Listen for ring or busy signal | auditory |
| 6. Talk or hang up | act |

Figure 16: The Tasks in Making a Phone Call

So, in describing this to your kids, you want to clearly use the appropriate visual, auditory or kinesthetic words to get these steps across, in the right order. When we think about it this way, it seems kind of obvious, but it's easy to miss out on some of the description if we aren't careful. We might accidentally skip some of the steps, or be vague in describing them. Here's an example of being too vague, for some kids:

"All right, son, here's what you have to do. You have to pick up the receiver, and punch the numbers in, one at a time, then wait for grandma to say hello." This might be what people normally do, but it also might not be enough for some kids. Now, let's try it this way (the representational—sensory—words and phrases are in *italics*):

"All right son, we have to do several things to *talk* to Grandma on the phone. First you have to *pick up* the receiver part of the phone, the part you've *seen* us *hold*. Now *hold* it up to your ear like you've *seen* us do. Do you *hear* a sound? It's a *buzzing* sound, right? That's *called* a dial tone.

Now, I'm going to *tell* you some numbers, one at a time. Here's the first number: eight. Now, do you *see* the button on the phone that has an eight on it? *Press* that button and *listen* for the *sound the phone makes* when you do. Do you *hear* it? It's a different kind of a beep than the sound it made before when it was just *buzzing*, the dial tone. Now here's the next number: four. *Press* the button with the four on it. It *made a beep* again, didn't it? And this beep *sounded different* than the last one, huh? OK, there are seven numbers in all that we have to dial. These seven numbers work to make Grandma's phone number. Everyone has a special set of numbers for each phone, and they're all different. Here's the next . . . .

Now that you've *dialed* all seven numbers, by *pressing* the buttons, you have to *wait* a few seconds, but *listen*. Do you *hear* another sound? It's kind of a *ringing sound that goes on and off*, right? It's not a *buzzing sound that goes on and off*, like the dial tone, is it? If that happens, it means we have to *call back later*, because Grandma is *talking* on the phone with someone else already. If you *get that ringing sound*, going on and off, it means she's *not using* her phone, so we have to *give her some time* to *come to the phone* and *pick it up*. Can you *imagine* grandma *getting up* out of that chair she likes so much, and *walking across the room* to *pick up* the phone? If she *doesn't pick it up* after about eight or nine rings, it probably means she isn't home, and we have to *call back later* . . ."

Notice how all the senses are used, and in the order that matches what the little boy has to do. It may seem like overkill, and for most kids it would be. But sometimes it's worth it. If they don't get what you tried to give them the first time, do it again with more detail.

As I've repeatedly said, one of the most useful ways to help your kids learn something is to teach them how *you* understand it. *How*, not what. What pictures, sounds, words, and feelings do you have that make up your understanding and appreciation for what you are doing? How can you convey this to your kids in a way that makes it easy and natural for them to duplicate? This is even more important when you're trying to share something more difficult, complicated, or conceptual in nature than dialing the phone. It doesn't matter what it is; inside your brain it's made out of pictures, sounds and feelings: reference experiences.

111

To get the idea a little clearer, let's start with single words, rather than whole procedures (like dialing the phone). As you look at each of the words on the following list, pay attention to what comes up in your mind. You may want to jot down a note or two in each case. What happens when you think of:

chair
electricity
experience
communication
relationship
politics
teaching
parenting

What did you discover as you thought about each one of these words? Did you notice that the ones near the end of the list were a little more complicated than the ones at the beginning? If you think about a chair, for example, it's a solid object we're all familiar with, and we talked earlier about what most people do when they see or hear the word.

Each of the other words on the list is harder to see, hear or feel, but we do something specific in our minds anyway. When you thought of electricity, you might have seen sparks in your mind, or wires, or noticed something electrical in the room, such as the lights. You may have remembered getting a shock when you touched something. Possible you imagined wiring diagrams, or power stations. Maybe it conjured up other words in your mind, like "power" or "light." You have to have some kind of idea in mind, that's built out of pictures, sounds, feelings, or a combination. Otherwise, it won't have any real meaning for you. The other words on the list work the same way. Maybe with the words teaching, or parenting, you even remembered specific personal experiences you've had. They might even have had some special feeling or emotion attached to them. You may even have gone off somewhere in your mind for a few moments as the memories became clearer or more complete. Some words will do that to us, won't they?

In terms of teaching our kids, it's the same thing. First we figure out what something means to us, in our minds. Then we figure out how to translate it into words, and share it with them so they can do the same thing inside their own minds. The best teachers are the ones that leave their students with a complete set of images, sounds and feelings. The central question, in this entire book, is to figure out how to do that really well. Once you can do that, then the kids can build on what you (or others) give them to make their own meanings.

For practice let's think about some other simple things you might want to help your kids learn about. Here are three short lists:

| Math | Language | Social Studies |
|---|---|---|
| addition | sentence structure | country |
| multiplication | paragraph | cultural belief |
| area | metaphor | war |
| space | symbolism | politics |
| mathematics | writing | history |

Notice again how the words near the bottom of each of the three lists are a bit more broad, or conceptual, than the ones near the top. Choose the first one on any of the three lists and stop, now, and think about it for a moment. What pictures come to mind? What words or other sounds? What feelings, or even memories and experiences come up for you?

Now, using that word, figure out what you would have to do in explaining *your understanding* of that word to your kids. How would you describe the images you have in mind in a way that would make sense? How would you set up the explanation in some order, or steps to follow, that would break it down so they could think about it the same way? What questions do you think might come up for them as you do?

As you go down to the words lower on the list, the more conceptual ones, you may find that your images get more complicated, or maybe less clear. The more complicated the concept, usually, the more involved the explanation.

For example, if I think of something historical, it's not a thing; it's more of a process, a series of events. So I end up describing something in the form of a story: the people, the actions and more. In fact, for me, I often remember movies I've seen about those events. That's how my memory sometimes works. How is it for you?

Sometimes, though, it's possible to explain something more easily through another kind of experience and a discussion. I remember an old

Bruce Springsteen song *My Home Town*. It's about his father taking him out in the car, and showing him their town, explaining the true meaning of a hometown. Later in the song he puts his own son on his knee and teaches him what it means to have a home. It's a beautiful song, and it conveys much more than a dictionary could ever do. Great teaching. Think back on how you learned about these things and about how you'd like to give them to your kids.

So, here are some steps that you'll follow when you're ready:
1. Make sure you understand what it is you'd like to help the kids with.
2. Figure out *how* you know what you know about it.
   Do you have some visual *image*, or a movie in *mind*?
   What do you *say to yourself* about this, or what else do you *hear*? Other people's *voices* describing it, or explaining it to you? Your own voice?
   How do you *feel* about this idea or concept? Does it trigger some emotion, sensation or movement in your body? Does it make you want to *do something*?
3. Think about how your kids would naturally think about something like this, in a way that would make sense to them.
4. Come up with a plan to give them what you have in your mind, in a way that would naturally fit for them.
5. Practice your delivery, at least in your mind a few times, so that you can do it smoothly.
6. Try it out.
7. Get feedback.

Here are some more guidelines for making sure you can give sensory-based descriptions, and use them the way your kids can best learn.

# Choose your words carefully.

Use all of the representational systems in your speech. In other words, be able to tell your kids what you see, hear and feel when you think about something.

# Listen to the words your kids use.

Ask your kids how they understand what it is you're trying to teach. What do they think about, with what they know so far? Listen for what kinds of words they use: visual (seeing), auditory (hearing) or kinesthetic (feeling). Be willing to switch your words to the ones they are using most. Later, when they understand in that sense, include the others.

# Use aids that address the different senses.

Find or develop teaching aids and materials that use all the senses, and especially the ones your kids seem most comfortable with. This means some pictures, charts, flash cards and other visuals. Also, find some tapes or CD's, rhymes, word games or other kinds of aids that use sounds. Finally, something they can physically do, touch or play with to add in the feelings. The kids will let you know, usually pretty quickly, which ones are most interesting and important for them. Get them involved in choosing, as well.

# Analyze the task for its sensory basis.

Some things require you to have a clear picture in mind to understand them. Others require sounds or feelings. For example, to spell properly, at some point you have to be able to see the letters in the word, and write them down. To repeat back some words, precisely, such as in memorizing a famous saying, quote or speech, it helps to hear the words in your head. To be able to operate different types of apparatus, musical instruments, paintbrushes, keyboards and the like, touch and feel are crucial.

# Use all the senses when you speak to more than one person.

Use all of the senses when you speak to groups of people, at least long enough to establish good rapport and mutual understanding between you and your audience. Great communicators do this naturally.

# Break things down.

Break down tasks that need to be learned into the smallest possible chunks; even down to the level of the senses. Literally, what pictures to have in mind, what to say to yourself, what to feel or whatever else is appropriate and necessary.

# Let the kids teach you what they've learned.

Once you've helped your kids learn something, remember to make sure they've learned it. This means getting them to show and tell you what they know, teaching it back to you. Teaching, in order to learn, has become an accepted method over the years. The classic medical school learning procedure for a new medical treatment is "see one, do one, teach one." Get the kids to do it with each other, if appropriate.

I know this way of thinking about learning can seem strange. It's different from what people usually think about, but that's what makes it special. Once you get past the strangeness, you'll be glad you did.

There are some wonderful scenes in a movie called *Nobody's Fool*, with a man named Sully (played brilliantly by Paul Newman) and his grandson, Will. In an early scene Sully takes Will to explore an old home he had as a child. As Sully goes inside, he has a memory that takes him away in his mind for a few moments, forgetting that he has left Will standing on the walk outside. When he realizes it, he goes out and finds that Will has become very frightened and upset. Sully has forgotten how easily young kids can get scared and realizes he's made a serious mistake. He knows he should do something to make amends. His decision is to teach the boy about courage:

Sully:  You know what I used to do when I was your age? I'd try to be brave for exactly a minute. And the next time I'd try to be brave for two minutes.

Will:  What were you scared of?

Sully:  I don't remember. But hey, when you get to be my age you won't remember, either. Here. (He hands Will a stopwatch.) You can time yourself with it. When the big hand goes around once, that'll be a minute. When it goes around again, it'll be two minutes. And you can tell how long you've been brave.

Then we see Will go to sleep holding the stopwatch. Later in the movie, something happens that frightens Will. He sees that a man has left his artificial leg by the door of a restaurant they've gone into, while the man goes to sit down and have a drink. Will is clearly scared of the leg. The man asks Will to bring him the leg.

Sully: You want to take it to him?

Will shakes his head, and backs up, clearly afraid.

Sully: It's not alive. It ain't gonna bite ya.

Will stiffens up, even more scared.

Sully: You still got that stopwatch?

Will nods yes, still speechless.

Sully: Want to see if it works?

Will takes out the watch and hands it to Sully. Sully gives him the leg. Will walks slowly across the room and hands it to the man, who has been watching the whole scene. The man takes the leg and bows to Will, then kisses him on the head. Will turns to Sully and smiles, proudly. Sully raises his fist and whispers: "Yeah."

*The only source of knowledge is experience.*
Albert Einstein

# Chapter 11

# Creating and Setting Up Learning Experiences

Several years ago my wife and I took a course in stand-up comedy at one of the local universities. Both of us had lots of experience on stages doing training and public speaking, and usually being funny, but it's not the same. The final exam was held in a hotel ballroom, open to the public (and advertised on the radio). We had to do our routines in front of several hundred people. For some people the hardest part seemed to be writing the material. For some it was delivering it well. There were several who were just plain terrified, of course. There is both an art and a craft to delivering an act, and both need to be mastered. To do it well, and get genuine laughter from a real live audience, is worth every bit of the effort and struggle.

Perhaps you are one of those people who can't tell a joke. Be honest, now. Some of us can, and some of us can't. Some people just can't seem to make even the best jokes work. Like everything else, though, there are principles and skills to be learned that can make it work. First of all, there are three basic parts to a joke:

Set-up
Delivery
Punch line

There is also some idea or principle behind the joke that makes it funny, often something weird and unexpected. Some people just don't get that part, and for them the joke won't work no matter how hard, or long, you try to explain it (don't bother; life is too short). Some can't do the set-up, and once they've blown that, it's really hard to recover. For others, it's something else in the delivery, others the punch. Like a lot of things in life, there is an underlying principle, a beginning, middle and end. Sometimes there is also a segue: a connection of some sort to what comes next. Sometimes we also have a tie-up to bring it to a close. Teaching can be a lot like this.

# The Underlying Principle

## Skill Categories

Asking a lot of questions beforehand can make all the difference. You can start with the categories and ask yourself *what kind of learning* this is. What are the *essential elements* you want the kids to learn. Sometimes some of these categories won't make any sense, or be important in what you're teaching, but it's good to think it through first so you can concentrate on the ones that are important. Here they are again, with some questions to help you:

Conceptual: The ability to conceptualize, or see, the whole picture and relate or fit it into a larger framework.
1.   What does the whole picture look like to me, when I think about what I'm about to help my kids learn?
2.   Do I have a way of giving them this big picture that will make sense to them?

Analytical: The ability to break the whole idea down into its component pieces, to categorize its elements.

1.  How does this big picture break down into smaller pieces that make sense?
2.  Is there some way I can show, or tell, the kids about this in a way that will help them see the relationship between those pieces and the whole thing?

Observational: The ability to see and hear the relevant information in whatever you're doing as it happens.

1.  Is this the kind of skill that requires the kids to watch and listen for something while they are doing it?
2.  If so, how can I help them focus their attention on those things?

Procedural: The ability to remember and follow a set of steps in the right order to accomplish whatever the task is.

1.  Does this learning require the kids to go through a series of actions, or questions, or steps of some kind to get to the end?
2.  If so, how can I help them remember each one and keep them in order?

Interactive: The ability to notice how we're getting along with someone moment to moment and react accordingly.

1.  Is this new piece I want to teach them a "people skill?"
2.  If so, is it one I'm good at? Can I help them understand what to watch and listen for? Can I help them learn to pick up on the messages and ideas other people send, and communicate with them effectively?

Relational: The ability to recognize and respond appropriately to the roles, culture or context involved in a relationship.

1.  Does this require the kids to appreciate the kinds of relationships between other people they're involved with?
2.  Is there some way I can model, or demonstrate, this for them to help them appreciate what's important here?

# Neuro-Logical Levels

Neuro-Logical Levels can also be a big help. The questions we looked at earlier were about the general conditions you and your kids need to have for learning. In other words, how things need to look, sound and feel between you for the best results. But these levels of understanding can be applied directly to each specific new thing your kids need to learn. In fact, that's where the whole idea came from in the first place. So, each time you're about to teach your kids something new, you can ask yourself the following set of questions.

Environment: Where and when?
1. Is now the best time to try something new with the kids? Are the kids in a good state for learning (or can we all get into one)?
2. Do you have the physical setting arranged in a sensible and comfortable way?
3. If not, what do you need to do?

Behavior: What?
1. Do you know what you will do to help the kids learn this new idea or skill?
2. What are the tasks involved? How can you figure them out?

Capability: How?
1. What skills and abilities do you actually need to help the kids learn this particular new piece?
2. What actual skills and abilities do the kids need? (Remember, the skills are different from just *what* to do; they are, rather, *how* to do it.)
3. Do you need to help the kids develop some set of skills before going on?

Belief: Why?
1. Do you believe that the kids are capable of learning this new thing and that you can help them?
2. Do both you and the kids believe that the learning is worthwhile?
3. If not, what can you do about it?

Identity: Who?
1. Does teaching this fit with who you are as a person?
2. Is the new learning something that will fit into *who* the kids are, as individuals?
3. Do you need to help your kids see themselves differently somehow?

Spirit: Who else?
1. Is there anyone else who can help, or should be involved in this specific learning?
2. Would your kids find it best to learn this with someone else helping?
3. Can you, or they, ask for help if it's needed?

As in any learning, both you and the kids have specific responsibilities in each learning experience you set up. Sometimes clarifying these responsibilities is helpful. It's almost always easier and a lot more fun as a team, anyway, and you can use that to take some of the pressure off. Part of your responsibility in helping the kids learn is to figure out the answers to the questions above.

# The Delivery

Once you've figured out the nature of the learning itself, the underlying principle, the next step you need is to figure out how to deliver it to the kids *in a way that they can take it* and make it a part of themselves.

First, remember that you want to create as full an experience as possible. This is the difference between *experiential* learning and simple rote memorizing. Experience gets it into the entire body so that it becomes a part of the kids instead of just some information that seems somehow disconnected. How do you do that? Well, it depends on each thing you teach.

Let's take a math problem; any one will do. Here are the different ways you can help your kids learn how to do it:

Tell the kids what to do

Show them how to do it                 **Less Experiential**

Do it with them, side by side

Get them to do it on their own

Make it into a puzzle, game, song or poem

                                        **More Experiential**
Have them make some pieces (paper, tile,
blocks, anything) each of which represents
some part of the problem, and arrange them
according to the steps

Figure 17: Levels of Experiential Learning

None of the things on that list are good or bad, or necessarily better than any of the others. As you go down the list, though, each one gets more fully experiential and involves more of the senses, deeper understanding and more participation. This is what makes learning work. You don't need to do this with everything, of course. That would be ridiculous. Often, just telling the kids what to do will be plenty. This is especially true if they already understand the underlying principle and can relate the new piece to something they already know. There will be times, though, when using a more experiential and elaborate approach will really help. As a general rule, this is true if the concept is very new and you think the kids may have trouble connecting it with what they already know. Fortunately, you don't have to reinvent the wheel here, because there are plenty of books and guides available in book stores and libraries to give you specific activities you can do for many kinds of learning.[1]

I was once on a call-in radio program, answering questions about how parents can help their kids learn, when I got a fairly typical call from a mother of a five-year-old. She said that when they read together, she had to do all the work. The little boy had his favorites and would sit there listening to his mom read them over and over and ask for more. When she told him to read, though, he still wanted *her* to do it for him.

As she spoke, I remember getting several interesting impressions. First, they seemed to be in good shape in terms of their relationship, his interest in the material or stories, and their enjoyment of the time they were spending together. But, also, any of us might wonder if five years old isn't a bit young to be expecting a lot of initiative. This is especially the case since it's something challenging at that age: reading. My point to this mother was two-fold. First, as long as she was willing to do it, why should he? Second, if she wanted to break this pattern, she should do it in a way that: 1. Maintained the good *relationship* and 2. Kept him *interested and enthusiastic.* The best way, I thought, was to make it into a game of some sort, in which they would *take turns* reading. I'm sure you could think of lots of ways to do this, and, in fact, it's fairly common advice. You could include rewards, use a tape recorder to play with later, and so on. The most important thing: don't turn it into a chore, or he won't want to do it anymore.

I remember an old friend telling me about how he taught his son the importance of fairness, after a note from the teacher suggesting a lesson would be useful (you can imagine what might have led up to that note). My friend bought a candy bar and told his son they would share it. Then he cut it, but one "half" was a lot bigger than the other, and my friend took that one. His son screamed at him and said he couldn't do that. The father asked why not, since he was a lot bigger. You can guess the rest. Not new, but a good example. You can make the point without a lecture or any kind of punishment. It creates a memory: sights, sounds, feelings.

In an earlier book of mine, I repeated the following story, which makes the same point and a whole lot more. It was told by the great actress Liv Ullman, who at the time of that book was UNICEF's official Ambassador of Goodwill—the first woman to hold such a position. In an interview she described an example of brilliant teaching.[2]

> My daughter told me when she was ten or so that her teacher had done something marvelous: she said they were going to have a lesson about awareness of the world. This was in a school in Norway. Everybody was to bring some wonderful cakes and things from home, and in the intermission all the goodies were collected by the teacher. And she said, "The biggest part of the group, you are the Third World." Then to the smaller

group, "You are the Iron Curtain countries." Then to the smallest group, "You are Europe and the United States."

Then the smallest group—to which my daughter did not belong—got most of the cakes. Then to the Iron Curtain countries, somewhat less was given, a lot less. Then to this big group where Linn was sitting, two or three cakes were given—or not even that. And they were furious! They said, "But we are the biggest group—how come we get so much less than them?" And the teacher just said, "If you belong, remember where you belong. This is how it is." Linn that day didn't really understand. The children bad-mouthed the teacher, thought she was crazy. It only dawned on them weeks later what had happened. And it's with Linn still as a part of her conscience.

Even if you don't consider yourself to be creative in these ways, all is not lost. There are scores of books, filled with activities you can do with your kids around learning things, and some of my favorites are listed in the back of this book. Of course that's not what this book you have in your hands is about; this one is about learning to learn, itself. You can, however, get lots of ideas about helping your kids in creative ways, just by browsing through your local book store's sections on parenting and education.

## Delivery Guidelines

I guess no matter what you do with your kids to help them learn, sometimes it won't go as planned. But that doesn't mean you've done something wrong, or even that it won't be useful in the long run. It might mean you need to do something different, though. In the last section of the book I'll go over some typical problems that happen in helping kids learn, but for now here are some guidelines:

1. Maintain a good strong *relationship*, a working rapport, at all times. As long as you have that, you can keep working at the learning as long as you need to.

2.  Make the *psychogeography* work for you, like the stage in a comedy show or play. The physical setting—the layout—is important. Set it up so that it helps rather than getting in the way. If you find you need to change it, go ahead.

3.  The more *doing*, the better. We all learn better by actually engaging our brains and bodies all at once in whatever the learning is. Show, tell, touch and do as much as possible.

4.  Let the kids be *involved* in, and have *ownership* of, what they learn. If you do it, it's yours; if they do it, it's theirs.

5.  Let the kids *ask* all the *questions* they need to. This doesn't necessarily mean you have to answer them; sometimes just asking helps make the pictures and words clearer in their minds. It also lets you know a lot about what they understand.

6.  Give them the *whole picture*, and break it down into all the *pieces* they need, conceptual and analytical. Let them show and tell it back to you.

7.  Get as much *feedback* as you can on what they understand and on how you're doing in helping them. Let them be honest, and don't take criticism personally. Sometimes if they're critical, it's because they're embarrassed, frustrated or scared. Sometimes it's because they're just trying to get out of the work, or get you out of it for a while. Sometimes, you really do need to change something. Being able to talk frankly is important. Be willing.

8.  Make it *fun* for yourself as well as the kids. An awful lot of research has shown that the more fun people are having, the better they learn.[3]

9.  The more you can do *together*, the easier and more fun it will be for both of you. Later you can give it to them to do on their own.

10. It's OK if it's a *challenge*, as long as it's within reach—and they know it. If they think it's impossible, they'll probably give up.

11. Be *patient* with yourself as well as the kids. If anyone (you or them) gets stuck, it's OK to stop, take a break, ask for help, or go back to the drawing board. Learning is *not a race*, no matter what you may have heard to the contrary.

12. There is *no right or wrong way* to teach something or help someone learn. Some things we do will create the right experiences and some won't. Use your creativity. Borrow creativity from others.

# The Set-Up

Once you know what you're going to do, it's time to figure out how to introduce it to the kids. How something *starts* often sets the tone for what follows. A learning experience is really no different. Unfortunately, there is no perfect set-up to any single learning experience. It's a matter of relationship, context, mood, timing and intention. Like a good joke. Use your foresight, patience and practice.

In general, the kids need and deserve to know something about each of the following:

What this new learning is about
What it's a part of (the bigger picture)
Why it's important
When they might need it in the future
How it relates to what they already know
How you're going to help them

The question in each case, of course, is how best to do it. One of the principles that always seems to help is to remember that we learn by modeling others. Our kids learn a lot of what they learn, by modeling us. They see and hear what we do. They listen to our stories. If the stories make sense, they can be a great way to start.

## Metaphors

The concept we're talking about here is *metaphor*.[4] A metaphor, in case you've forgotten studying them as a kid, is a *story* that is really about something else besides what it actually tells. So when we see a good movie or read a good book, the story we see and hear is really about more, in some way. In fact, if it makes a real impact, it's usually because it's about *us*. We see ourselves in the characters; we find similarities, ways to relate the story to our own lives. This is how we begin to learn from the time we are little children. All those fairy tales, religious tales, family stories and more are meant to teach us things about our own lives. It works, though usually on an unconscious level.

You can adapt this principle to teaching your kids. You can give them metaphors (stories, examples, comparisons, analogies) that will help them learn to connect new information with themselves in a way that makes sense. It can actually take a lot of the burden off of you and make the whole process more interesting and fun, as well. Of course you also want to be cautious not to get long winded, irrelevant, boring or too moralistic or your kids won't want to hang around with you anymore . . . .

## Experiences, Universal and Personal

So, how do we do this? Well, I like to recommend that we start by finding some experiences that are related to what we want to teach the kids. Let's go back to our example of learning to drive a car. If you remember the parts you already know from *similar* experiences like riding a bike, skating and so on, it makes it easier. If you present it that way to the kids, they can relate each one of the earlier experiences to driving in some way. Any comparison makes learning easier. This is a basic part of learning, and you can use it.

When there is stress in the learning, the tendency is to get overwhelmed and forget that there are pieces of it that are already familiar. Take math. When we first learn about numbers, most of us count whatever is around. Food, toys, our fingers and toes. Later when we already know how to add numbers, and we're trying to learn to multiply them, we're taught that multiplication is just a more sophisticated kind of addition. Even something pretty complex, like calculus, has its basis in the real world of physics, laws of motion, and so on. If you can learn it that way, it's a lot easier.

Once the kids are old enough, meaning they've had a broad enough series of experiences, you can begin to use more *universal* (or relatively universal) experiences as metaphors. What do I mean by universal? Well, there seem to be things that we all know, or at least have experienced at some time. The sun comes up and goes down. It gets hot and cold, sunny and rainy. We've all tripped and fallen before. We've all looked at something we found beautiful. We've heard music we love and music we can't stand. We go someplace new, meet new people, and taste new foods. Surprise, joy, laughter, pain and fear. Learning. These are *universals*.

Everyone knows them. They are things we can all share and relate to. It is always possible to fall back on a universal experience to relate to a new one, since you know that the kids can relate to it.

As an interesting exercise, each time you are about to give your kids something new, try to find out what the most basic and universal part of the new idea is, the part that you absolutely know they can relate to.

# The Punch Line

A big finish always leaves them asking for more. It's a good principle in teaching your kids.

There is a wonderful movie called *Renaissance Man*, with Danny DeVito that's worth a look if you've never seen it. In the movie he finds himself, pretty much against his will, teaching a group of young US Army recruits who have lots of academic problems. He ends up teaching them what *he* loves: Shakespeare. At first it makes no sense to them at all, because of the language and the complexity of the relationships. But he's able to teach them that Shakespeare's plays are really metaphors. He helps them see that many of the stories are universal and that each of them can relate their own personal experiences to things the Bard talked about 500 years ago. These are wonderful lessons about learning and life, and they change the lives of those students in dramatic, and funny, ways.

# The Tie-Up

One extremely valuable thing you can do, once your kids have the idea about what you're teaching them, is to help them take what they've learned right into the future, to see and hear what it will be like later, when they really need to know it. We call this process *future-pacing*, which simply means making sure that they remember later what they're learning now. Ideally, they need to remember it *at the specific time* when they need it. That means the moment they need the new learning, the pictures, sounds, words and feelings will pop back into their minds, automatically.

*Needing* the new learning comes in three flavors. First, when they are asked to use the new knowledge directly, for example on a test. Second, when they need it to relate to some other new, but similar, idea it's connected with. Third, when they need it later in their lives. For example, imagine going to a party. You get introduced to someone, and hear his or her name for the first time, when you walk in. Later, someone asks you: "Who is that person over there?" This is like the test. You hope the name pops back up. Sometime later you might try to remember all the people you met at the party. Still later you may get together with friends and talk about all the people you'd like to invite to a meeting, and while you make up the list, you might want that person's name to come up again. The face and name need to come back into your mind, even though this meeting is only slightly related to the party where you originally met the person.

So, how do we get this learning and memory process to happen? Well, that's the primary subject of a later chapter, but here are a few tips:

1. Ask the kids plenty of questions about how they'll use what you're giving them when it's time.
2. Ask them to imagine all the other kinds of times, not directly related, that they think might be helpful to know the new material.
3. Have the kids actually spend a few minutes imagining they are going through a testing situation in class, or other related situation, and repeating what they've just learned as if it's actually happening. In other words: rehearse.
4. Tell the kids, that you know they'll remember what they've learned whenever they need to. Encourage them to remember.

Some people who write jokes actually start with a good underlying principle and a punch line, and then work backwards to develop the delivery and the set-up. We can do the same. Ask yourself what you want the kids to come away with after you've given them something new. What kind of experience do you want them to take with them? If you know where and when they'll need to know the new material, you can imagine how they'll use it in the future. Then imagine what steps they would need to go through so they can do that.

One great way to finish is to compliment your kids for doing a good job, or at least giving it their best. Then it's a nice touch to thank them for working so hard. This will make it a lot easier the next time you want to teach them something. It will also help your relationship with them.

It's respectful. Just as valuable, this is a really nice way to model good manners and ways of maintaining good relationships with other people. A generally good idea.

# After the Act

After anything you do that's important in life, it's a good idea to go back over it in your mind, in retrospect, to decide how well you did and what you would change. Here are some questions to help you focus on how you've done:

1.  What worked really well in helping the kids understand, in each area of the lesson?
    > The underlying principle
    > The set-up
    > The delivery
    > The punch line
    > The tie-up
2.  Can you use the same approach again in other kinds of lessons?
3.  What didn't work in each area?
    > The underlying principle
    > The set-up
    > The delivery
    > The punch line
    > The tie-up
4.  What changes would you make, based on what worked and what didn't, if you had it to do over again?
    > The underlying principle
    > The set-up
    > The delivery
    > The punch line
    > The tie-up
5.  Were you able to make the whole process interesting and fun?
6.  Do you know how you will relate back to this lesson, in future lessons?

# PART 3

## The Skills of Learning: Things Your Kids Won't Learn in School, about Learning

*In teaching, you must simply work your pupil into such a state of interest in what you are going to teach him that every other object of attention is banished from his mind; then reveal it to him so impressively that he will remember the occasion to his dying day; and finally fill him with devouring curiosity to know what the next steps in connection with the subject are.*

William James

# Introduction to Part 3

## Teaching Your Kids What They Really Need to Learn

This section of the book is about the things your kids aren't going to learn in school. These are the "how to learn" skills: what your kids need to do when they're supposed to learn something. If you can help them see and hear what to do, and feel comfortable and even motivated and excited, when they are learning something new, it will take them through the rest of their lives as real learners. What follows are the skills that professionals in the education community know are necessary in learning—they just never seem to teach them in school. In each chapter I'll give you as much as you need to be able to get the skills into your kids. You'll find stories, examples, experiments and other guides.

In addition, each chapter describes skills you'll recognize as things that you need, and use, in many areas of your life. You probably don't think about it when you're using them, though. The same will be true of your kids, of course, but they haven't learned to do them nearly as well as they could. You'll probably also find that you could use improvement in some or all of these areas yourself. Most of us could.

One special note: As I mentioned, there are experiments in these chapters. Some are for you to do on your own, either to learn about the concept or process, or to prepare to teach it to the kids. Some people look at these and say to themselves something like: "Oh no, more work to do, just like the school work I could never handle." Rather than thinking of the exercises as a chore, though, how about seeing each one as a step on the path to more personal development? You could say: "Oh wow, I get to learn something that will help me in many areas of my life!" Isn't that what we want our kids to do when it's time for them to do assignments? Personally, I think these kinds of exercises are fun, and I have a great time doing them. Maybe you will, too.

Remember also, this isn't a race. Take your time with the reading, the exercises and your kids. Take all the time you need, in fact. Remember, this is life-long learning and these skills will help in just about everything you and your kids do. Look at this path as one you can walk at your own pace. Enjoy it as a stroll, or jog along when you feel the energy, but make sure you take in the scenery. Respect yourself and your kids' time and energy. Do what is comfortable for all of you. The exercises are meant to start you down this path, and it's one without end. Happy trails.

# Chapter 12

# How to Control Your State of Mind

My nephew Charlie is a great kid. His mother Jaye is also a great schoolteacher, and she often knows just what to do when kids are having trouble. Charlie came home one day after baseball practice in tears, angry and yelling. He'd had some trouble at practice, and he was embarrassed and inconsolable. Jaye asked him what had happened, and he told her. He didn't want to play any more, and he wanted to quit. She was really stuck for a few moments. Then she remembered that he'd had a great game just a few weeks before. So she asked him: "Charlie, didn't you have a great hit a few weeks ago, when your team won the game right at the end?" He said, "Yeah." She then asked him to remind her about that game, because she couldn't remember exactly what happened. As he described the game to her, especially how he hit that great game winning base hit, he began to light up. She kept him talking, giving her more details. He began to feel better the more he talked, and within a few minutes he was back on top of the world, just like he had been when he made the game-winning hit. The anger and tears had disappeared.

All of us know one thing for sure. Sometimes we do things really well, and we know it's because we are in a great state of mind. Then, maybe the next day, we try to do the same thing and we're terrible at it. Not the same state of mind. This experience is so common that we take it for granted but what we know is this: *our state of mind often controls our abilities.* What most people don't know is that *we have* a tremendous amount of *control over our states of mind.* There are lots of ways to do it, and most of them are really pretty simple. That's what we'll explore in this chapter.

## The Underlying Principle

The first and easiest way, most of the time, to learn to control our states is to use our memories (our dreams, fantasies and just plain imagination work just as well). It turns out that, for some neurological reasons,[1] when we remember an experience we've had, really vividly in our minds, it brings back the state of mind we were in at the time of the experience. In other words, if we remember a time when we were really feeling great, and remember it really clearly in our minds, we feel great again. By the same token, if we remember some time when we were embarrassed or felt foolish, we get those feelings back too.

Here's why. There is a phenomenon called *state dependent learning* that says:

> *When you are in a particular state of mind, and you learn something, to remember it later you have to go back into the same state of mind.*

In other words, remembering what you've *learned depends* on your *state* of mind. You have to go back to the same one you were in when you learned it the first time.[2] So when Charlie was describing how well he'd done for his mom, he had to go back into the state he was in when he'd done really well, just to remember it. This changed his state to the one he was in then, and he felt great. A quick change. The diagram below shows the relationship between our memory and imagination and state of mind, and how that controls our abilities.

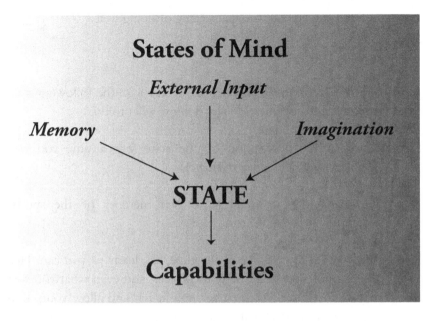

Figure 18: State of Mind and Capability

We've all experienced changes like this before in ourselves as well as in other people, like our kids. Let's think about some common examples of this. For each of these, do the following experiment:

## EXPERIMENT: CHANGING FEELINGS

Preparation: To begin with, take a look at the following list of unpleasant and more pleasant experiences. I'm going to ask you to remember examples of each after you do.

A time you were embarrassed
   then
A recent party or celebration that was fun

A time you did something really badly or clumsily
   then
A time you did something really well

Something you've had trouble learning or doing well
   then
Something you learned really easily

Now, for each of those experiences, go through the following steps. Read through these steps first, so you'll know what to do.

Step 1: Look at the description of the state (e.g. a time you were embarrassed) and close your eyes.

Step 2: Go back in your mind to a clear memory of the specific example.

Step 3: See what it looked like at the time, as clearly as you can. Hear the sounds that were there, the voices, and even what you were saying to yourself. Remember how it felt and allow yourself to have those feelings again.

Do this for each of the experiences in the list, and pay close attention to how it makes you feel inside. Compare the first feeling with the second in each of the pairs of memories listed above.

In each pair of examples, you should have had a very different experience going from the first to the second, provided that you actually vividly remembered the original experiences. For some people, clearly seeing or hearing all the sounds is more difficult than for others, but if you remembered the experience, it should have changed the way you felt when you started, to something like what the original memory felt like. So first you felt the unpleasant feelings that went with the first memory, followed by the much better feelings that went with the second. That's the way we work.

Think about memory itself for a moment. I just asked you to use your memory in specific ways to get back states of mind you've had before. Do you know exactly how you did it? When you recall some event or experience, how do you actually remember it? What causes the images and sounds in your head to come flooding back to you? What is the mechanism that causes you to react to something with a response, whether the response is an act, thought, or feeling? How do you know that when you've got a visual image, or some sounds in your mind, the feelings that come up are really the ones that went with that particular memory? We generally take these psychological processes for granted. It's a lot better if we can use them on purpose.

We have all had the experience of walking down the street, minding our own (or someone else's) business, and suddenly being struck with a memory. Often, if we pay attention to our surroundings, we can identify some object, sound, or smell that seems to be the cause of our sudden recall. It could be almost anything. A stranger's facial expression, or even posture, can remind us of someone we know. This leads to a memory that involved that person we know, and suddenly the images, sounds, and feelings that go with it come up in our minds. It is as if we are not in our present surroundings any longer, but rather hurled back in time to that former, perhaps forgotten, place, with that person again.

Familiar? Of course. The process that makes it work is something we understand pretty well, now. This basic sort of relationship between what we see hear and feel, and the state we get from these things, is something that psychologists have been studying for many years. And because we know, pretty much, how it works, we can use it to help ourselves.

The first to explore it, in the laboratory, most thoroughly was Pavlov,[3] in his experiments with dogs, well over a hundred years ago. Everyone who has a dog knows that a dog will begin to drool when you bring out the supper dish (I do the same when I see a pizza). It's normal, and it's actually the first step in the digestion of food. Pavlov wanted to know if he could exert some *influence* on this naturally occurring process and bring it under some control. So, each time he showed the food to the dog, he rang a bell. He did this a number of times, so that the dog would "associate" the food and the bell with each other. After a while he would *only* ring the bell for the dog, without showing it the food. Sure enough, the dog would begin to drool. The experiments get more complicated, but the idea is that under the right "conditions" just ringing a bell would get the dog to drool, just as if there was food in sight. We call making this new connection *conditioning*. It's a basic form of learning,[4] and it's shown in this diagram.

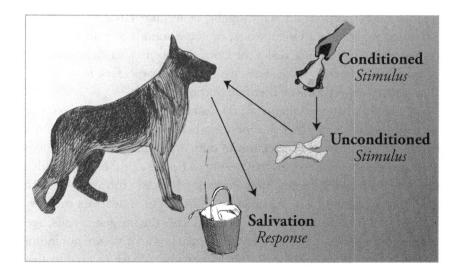

Figure 19: Pavlovian (Classical) Conditioning

This also explains the triggering mechanism we have been talking about in *us*. That facial expression that brings back our powerful memory is like Pavlov's bell. It is like a *conditioned stimulus:* a signal that causes a *response* in us. In the NLP field we call these *anchors.* Many people believe that a lot of our responses to the things around us have been conditioned (in this and in similar ways). We have a big advantage, though: we can just use our memory and our imagination to make it work for all kinds of things. This includes the states of mind we need for learning, studying, taking tests or performing in any way that's important to us. The same is true for our kids.

For example, when I asked you to think back to something you'd done very well, how did you do it? Certainly you did some sort of search through the files in your memory for that kind of experience. But, more specifically, *how?* Did you sort through a series of pictures in your mind until you had a feeling of doing well? Did these pictures look like a series of snapshots? Did they look more like a movie? Or perhaps, did you simply say some words like "good job" or "well done" to yourself, and then feel it? Which senses, sights, sounds, smells or tastes did you use, and how did you use them?

Just to test yourself, do it again with a different example. Remember another time that you did something really well, but this time pay close attention to what you do in your mind to bring back the memory. What pictures, movies, sounds, words or other process do you use to find and then re-create that memory? Find out how you do it, in your mind, and you'll have a really valuable tool.

This is a basic awareness experiment to determine what stimulates you to this memory. In other words, if just before you got into the state you made the visual image of the scene in your mind, *that's* the trigger, or *stimulus*, for that memory, which is the *response* (stimulus—response). If it was something you said, then that's it. Each of these is a part of the experience. Perhaps just calling up one part brings on the whole memory, the feelings and the complete state of mind.

We call that stimulus a *naturally occurring anchor* because it was already there. You didn't have to make it like Pavlov did with the bell. These natural anchors can be almost anything, as long as they work. For some people there will usually be a visual image, for others a sound, or another feeling. Some people even get a particular taste in their mouths or a smell just before the memory or state comes back, maybe several things at once. When you find out exactly what happens in your mind, you can do it on purpose. Practice can make it easier and even stronger.

Think about how many naturally occurring anchors we have. They are everywhere in our lives, and they really do affect us. Here are some common experiences, just to help get you thinking about it:

The smell when you walk into a bakery, reminding you of being a kid
A certain person's voice that makes you feel good the moment you hear it
The special look someone gives you that has special meaning for you
A favorite song from when you were a teenager that takes you back in time
An old movie that was special to you that comes on late at night
A photograph (yearbook or album) of a special time years ago
The feeling you get when you walk into your favorite restaurant

Anchors are extremely powerful tools. They are only tools, however, when *you are controlling them* rather than the other way around. Keep in mind that the list above includes some *nice* ones, but we have plenty we'd rather not think about at all. Until now, you probably wouldn't have

143

thought of using the process on purpose. You *could* have if you'd known how. The following diagram shows the anchoring process.

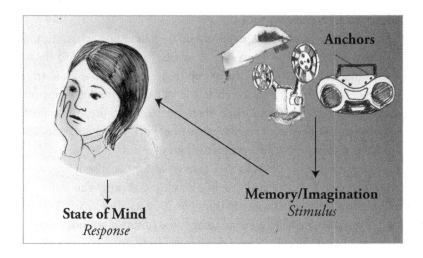

Figure 20: Anchoring

You can also create, artificially like Pavlov did, other anchors to get you into the useful states you want. It is much simpler for us to do it ourselves than it is to do it with a dog. The first step is to practice creating anchors in yourself, at will. Remember, an anchor can be almost anything. Here are a few experiments for you to play with to explore the process. They're kind of fun, and you can do them now or later depending on what's most convenient for you.

## EXPERIMENT: WRITTEN ANCHORS

Preparation: For this experiment you'll need some paper and something to write with, (or a computer if you prefer), and it will be easiest to do in a quiet place, without too many distractions.

Step 1: Choose any of the following experiences you'd like to have again right now:

A really fun time
A feeling of confidence
A great personal accomplishment
The knowledge that you are capable at something
An experience of learning, or remembering, something easily
A feeling of safety and security inside
A memory of organizing yourself, or something, really well
Creativity
Enthusiasm and excitement

Step 2: When you've chosen one (or something else if you'd like), remember a time when you had that experience. Make the memory as vivid as possible, complete with pictures, sounds, feelings and even tastes and smells if you can.

Step 3: When the memory is really as clear as you can get it, and you have as much of that original feeling as you can, begin to write down a description of what you see and hear in your mind. It doesn't have to be too detailed, a short paragraph on what you see and another on the words and sounds you hear should be plenty. If you enjoy being more thorough, it can be even more fun.

Step 4: Now set it aside and go do something else for a few minutes.

Step 5: When you come back, simply read your description of what you saw and heard and pay attention to what happens inside your mind. Notice how the memory comes back just from reading what you wrote. Pay attention to how the feelings—your actual state of mind—change back again to the way they were during the memory, just from reading your own description.

# EXPERIMENT: YOUR MIND'S OWN VIDEO

Preparation: This time you won't need to write anything, just a quiet place, without too many distractions. Read through the instructions a couple of times just to be clear.

Step 1: For variety, choose another of those great experiences from the list:

A really fun time
A feeling of confidence
A great personal accomplishment
The knowledge that you are capable at something
An experience of learning, or remembering, something easily
A feeling of safety and security inside
A memory of organizing yourself, or something, really well
Creativity
Enthusiasm and excitement

Step 2: When you've chosen one (or something else if you'd like), again remember a time when you had that experience. Remember to make the memory as clear as possible: pictures, sounds, feelings, tastes and smells. It helps many people to close their eyes when doing this.

Step 3: When you have it nice and clear and the feelings are as strong as you can get them, imagine that you have a video recorder in your mind, a special camera that can record all that you see, hear, feel, taste and smell. Imagine making a videotape that you can play back whenever you want to from now on. It doesn't have to be too long, 15 seconds is enough, but of course if you are enjoying the experience all over again, make your imaginary tape as long as you'd like.

Step 4: Now, imagine stopping the taping and putting the tape in a safe place in your mind where you can get it back easily. Again take a break and go do something else for a few minutes.

Step 5: When you come back, close your eyes again, and imagine getting the tape back from wherever you put it in your mind. Play it back so that you can watch and listen to it again. Pay attention to what happens inside your mind. Notice how the feelings—your actual state of mind—change back again to the way they were during the memory.

There is a reason human beings created writing, photography, film, video and all the other ways we have of reproducing words, sounds and images. These are all different forms of *external memory sources*. They are ways of preserving memories in a way that doesn't rely on us to do it in our minds. The reason they work is partly because they are reliable ways of storing words, pictures and ideas but also partly because when we get a small part of them, we fill in the rest ourselves, in our own minds. Think about looking at a photograph you've taken of some vacation or special event, for example. One photo doesn't really show all that much, but the memory of the event comes back, and we get much more of the original experience than just the picture. Well, we can certainly do the same inside our minds if we think about it and plan for it. We can create the same feelings just by thinking about the events, with or without the paper or pictures. And it doesn't matter what the event is. It can be anything that produces a feeling or state of mind we might want to have again some time. Now, try the following experiment.

## EXPERIMENT: TOUCH ANCHORS

Preparation: Just like in the last experiment with your mental videotape, to do this experiment you only need a quiet place to concentrate for a few minutes. Again, it will help to read through the instructions a couple of times first.

Step 1: For this experiment, choose either of the states you just used, either the one you wrote about or the one you made an imaginary tape of.

Step 2: Re-create the state again by either reading what you wrote or playing back your imaginary videotape. Make it as strong and vivid as you can in your mind and feel the feelings as fully as possible.

Step 3: When it's nice and strong, press the tips of your thumb and forefinger together, on your left hand. Do this with gentle but firm pressure and hold it for 15 to 30 seconds while you imagine being back in this memory.

Step 4: Next, get up and go do something else for about five minutes.

Step 5: When you come back, immediately press your thumb and forefinger together exactly as you did before and hold it. Make sure to use the same touch, the same pressure. Pay attention to your feelings and the images and sounds in your mind. Does the memory—the feelings and state of mind—come back, fully and realistically?

If not, repeat the whole procedure another time or two and it should.

This touching of the thumb and forefinger is another kind of anchor. It can be just as effective as reading your description or playing back that mental video. We've done these anchoring experiments with many thousands of people in a wide variety of settings (and countries). It seems that the location and pressure used in a physical touch anchor can be very crucial in some people. Even a slight variation can be enough to reduce the effectiveness of the anchor considerably, so make sure you get the touch just right. Another point I want to make is that any touch you choose as an anchor *should be one you don't normally use*. If you happen to spend a lot of time touching your thumb and forefinger together, choose some other kind of touch, perhaps another finger and your thumb, as your anchor. This makes sense if you think about it. If Pavlov tried to use his conditioning methods on a dog that lived in a bell factory, how would the dog make the connection? Bells would be associated with *everything*, and therefore, nothing specific.

If this process sounds a bit too mechanical, I apologize. Often when people first learn these concepts they remark that they don't much appreciate being compared with dogs (or other animals). I don't like it either, but the techniques work, plain and simple. Conditioning—anchoring—is a fact of life. As you practice anchoring, it will seem much more natural to you, and it will make perfect sense to your kids.

# The Set-Up

I've found a number of ways to introduce this idea to kids over the years. Especially with boys (in the past, now I do this with all kids), I usually start by talking about sports. Many people and almost all kids are unaware of a profession called "sports psychology." It is a profession in which specialists, psychologists or others trained in the techniques, help athletes perform their best. They help them out of slumps, help them stay focused, help them communicate better with teammates and coaches and even more. The anchoring process I just described is one of the main things they do. All athletes who are any good know that the mental game is just as important as the physical one, and if they can get into the state of mind that they perform best in, they'll be able to master it. So sports psychologists help athletes of all kinds learn to remember the times they played or performed best, clearly seeing the images and hearing the sounds to create the feelings. Then they help them to anchor it in some way so that they can take it onto the field or the place they have to be at their best. Almost every professional baseball, football, basketball and tennis player has had exposure to sports psychology. It's a major part of the martial arts. Virtually all Olympic athletes work with sports psychologists, and most golfers have as well, so this isn't something strange or unusual. Athletes want to get "in the zone," the state in which they do their best. When I talk with kids about this, they usually get really interested, really fast.

Some kids who aren't interested in sports are interested in things like theater or music. The training that actors get includes much of this same kind of technique and even more than athletes use. They create states that help them be "in character." And every musician who's any good at all knows what it's like to be "in the groove." Athletes, actors and musicians all work at helping each other get into their best states. I usually tell kids that I'm ready to give them what the professionals use, rather than making them wait. That also usually gets their attention.

The other "secret" is that this will help them in studying, taking tests, understanding their teachers and what they read, and even in staying (or getting) out of trouble. This is, of course, what we're most concerned with here, but sometimes teaching them with something more interesting, at first, keeps them motivated while they learn. Most kids, also, relate very easily to the idea of states of mind. They've had experiences just like Charlie did with Jaye when he changed from feeling miserable to feeling great in just a few minutes. Think about specific examples of times this has happened with your own kids, and remind them of those (over and over and over). And by the way, they'll almost always learn to use this process more easily than adults (yes, even you).

# The Delivery

Remember, as we said earlier, while you're helping your kids learn this, the following principles apply:

Maintain a good strong *relationship*.
Make the *psychogeography* work for all of you.
The more *doing*, the better.
Let the kids be *involved* and have *ownership*.
Let the kids *ask* all the *questions* they need to.
Give them the *whole picture*, and break it down into all the *pieces* they need.
Get as much *feedback* as you can.
Make it *fun* for yourself as well as the kids.
The more you can do *together*, the easier and more fun it will be.
It's OK if it's a *challenge*.
Be *patient*.
There is *no right or wrong way* to teach something or help someone learn.

Here are the four basic things you want them to learn about states of mind:

1. They can get into the states they need by using their memories;
2. They can stay in the state as long as they need to by holding the images in mind;
3. They can save the state for the future (studying, learning, tests) by anchoring;
4. They can get back in it quickly and easily by using the anchor.

# EXPERIMENT: TEACHING ABOUT STATES

Preparation: For this experiment with your kids, as in all of the following ones, choose a time when you can be relaxed and free from too many distractions. Do this in a comfortable place. You won't need any special materials for writing or anything else. Again, read through the steps so that you can plan it out in a way that makes sense for you and the kids. Go over it in your mind a couple of times, and if you want, you can do it in stages, rather than all at once. Feel free to take breaks and keep it light, especially with this exercise. You'll notice the steps are in a more generalized form than the earlier experiments. That's so you can be flexible and do them in a way that makes sense in the context of your kids and the relationship you have with them.

Step 1: Begin by talking with the kids about great experiences they've had. You can remind them with photos or stories or things you bought on trips, or other naturally occurring anchors. Get them to talk with you about how much fun the experiences were. For example, if it's a vacation you took to some place, have them tell you about their favorite things. Ask them to tell you how it looked, sounded and felt. Have them talk about the food and the smells to make it more complete. As you do this, pay attention to how their state changes. The more they get into it (the state, see how it's built into our language?), the more obvious it should be. When they are really back into the experience, ask them a loaded question: "Wouldn't it be great if we could feel like that whenever we wanted to?" (If the answer isn't yes, something is wrong.)

Step 2: Now you get to show them how to do it with their memories. Have them choose three or four really good ones and talk about each one. Help them notice how their feelings change each time. Then do the same for some *other* experiences, ones that will help them in their learning. Have them tell you about some of the following (choose one or two, and go on from there if they are interested, but don't overwhelm them):

A time they did something really well
Something they learned really easily
Their favorite subject
Their favorite sport, hobby or other activity
A time when they feel safe and secure
A time when they're organized
Something that makes them feel enthusiastic and excited
A feeling of self-confidence

Step 3: With the ones they really get into, ask them about when they think each one might help them in life or in school. For example, when they learned something easily, you might ask: "What other things would you like to have be that easy?" Or, for a time when they feel safe and secure: "Are there ever times, say in school, that you feel bad and you wish you felt safe like this instead?" Or, when they can be organized: "Where else do you wish you could be organized like that?" Usually they will have answers for each question like this, but you can always suggest some that you know would be helpful.

Step 4: Talk with them about how each of these creates a special kind of state of mind. And each state of mind is really good for some things, but not so good for others. Part of learning to run our own lives is figuring out which states are good for which things, and learning to control them.

This exercise is usually more than enough to get the idea across. They should be able to understand about states of mind and how we can change them ourselves from this. If you do just this with your kids, you'll probably notice a difference without doing anything else. Kids are clever when it comes to using these ideas. The more you let them know it's for them, it's natural, it's valuable and that they can do it on their own, the more they'll use it (which doesn't mean you can't ask about it to remind them from time to time).

There is more you can do, however, because they still haven't learned about anchors, only about states. Remember, anchors come in many different flavors. They can be something you write down, a video you take in your mind, a touch, something else you see while you are thinking of something, a photo, a gift someone gave you and lots more. So it can really help to give your kids some of the experiences you've had, if you did the experiments I gave you, so that they can have even more control over their states.

# EXPERIMENT: TEACHING ABOUT ANCHORS

Preparation: For this experiment, the same ideas apply as in the last one. You need a comfortable place and time, few distractions, etc. You can do it right after the one you just finished, or at some other time. Use your judgment.

Step 1: Choose the memory, and state of mind, your kids went into that was most fun for them in the last exercise. Tell them you want to do it again, since they liked it, and make it even better by adding something to it.

Step 2: Ask them to describe it for you again, so they get back into it, see what they saw, hear the sounds and have the feelings.

Step 3: Now, ask them to close their eyes and go back in time, in their mind, to that actual time when the event they remember was happening. (For instance, if it was the time they were learning something well, go back and actually be in that place, perhaps a classroom, again. See the person teaching them, hear their voice, feel what it was like.) Ask them to spend a little time enjoying the experience again and make sure they are really into it.

Step 4: Next, ask them to imagine that they have a *magic video camera* inside their mind. They are to make a video of all the sights, sounds, feelings and even tastes and smells from this memory, so they can play it back again whenever they want. Have them "record" for about two minutes, then imagine putting the camera and the video away someplace safe. Then have them come back to here and now, open their eyes and take a short break (cookies are an excellent idea at this moment).

Step 5:   After the break, ask them to try something out. Have them close
          their eyes again, imagine pulling out the imaginary video and the
          magic video camera from wherever they put it, and play back the
          video of the memory all over again. Ask them to pay attention
          to how it makes them feel.

          Note: The vast majority of the time, this will take them
          right back into the state they were in before. If for some
          reason it doesn't, ask them if they were able to play back
          the video, seeing, hearing and feeling everything as they
          did earlier. If not, practice it with them a couple of
          times until they can. It is rare that you would have to do
          this, but in case you do, it's worth the extra effort. Some
          kids need a little more practice.

Step 6:   Explain to them that the imaginary video they made is one kind
          of anchor that can help them get back the good feelings—the
          state of mind—that they had back then in the memory. Any
          time they want to get that state back again, they only have to
          play back the video. And it will work from now on. Encourage
          them to practice on their own. Bedtime works great.[5]

Obviously, you can do this over and over with as many different
experiences and memories as you and your kids would like. It can be as
fun as you make it and, in fact, you can ask them to tell you about their
favorite imaginary tapes any time you want. This is like mental pushups
for state of mind training. The more practice, the better.

The other part of practice that makes this work really well, is
practicing when they will use these great states of mind in the future.
For example, with the state in which they learned something really easily,
when might they want to be able to learn something else just as easily?
Have them imagine going into a difficult class, or with some material
they find tough to handle, and playing their tape back just when it's
time to learn the new stuff. Have them practice it until it seems like it's
automatic, so that as soon as they go into that class, the tape seems to
play back all by itself. It really will make it easier for them. You might
remind them just before they have that tough class, and ask them about
it right afterwards to make sure they remembered. Have them tell you

if it made the learning easier. This will help put the whole idea together for them. The more you practice it with them, the more automatic it will become. In NLP this rehearsal process is called: *future-pacing*. It helps with what traditional psychologists and educators call *transfer of learning*. We want to make sure that whatever our kids learn, they can take with them (transfer it) to the place they need it. Just as teachers want the kids to take what they learn into the real world, we want them to take their learning skills into the real classroom. The process is shown in the diagram below.

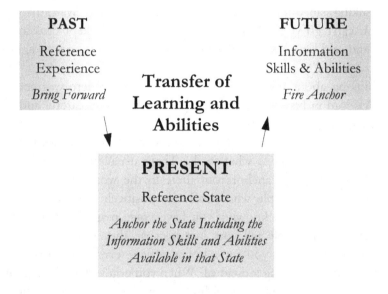

Figure 21: Future Pacing: Transfer of Learning

I use the imaginary video method in this exercise with kids because they usually like it the best. But you can repeat the same thing and have them squeeze their thumb and finger together like you did. They have four fingers to choose from and two hands, so they can make eight different anchors this way if they want. They just have to remember which ones are which.

My wife has been doing this with her clients for years, in counseling. She keeps some polished stones in her pocket and when she helps get someone into the state they really want, she takes one out, puts it into their hand, and tells them a story about it. She tells them to keep it with them and squeeze it whenever they need that state. It's their anchor. More than one person has called her from across the country to ask for a new stone because theirs got lost!

# The Punch Line

I remember years ago when I was in college, walking down the street with a friend of mine. We came to an intersection and the light was red. Naturally, as I'd always done, I stopped and waited for the light. He just kept walking, since there were no cars coming. I said, "Wait, the light's red, you can't go yet." He just turned slightly, as he kept crossing the street, and said over his shoulder to me, "Are you going to let a light tell you what to do?"

Thinking about this years later, I thought that there was certainly some wisdom in his statement to me. Sure, I'm pretty careful and I try to follow the rules most of the time, but there are some times when acting like a robot just isn't that smart. A stoplight is an anchor that we understand. It tells us what to do. That's usually a good thing. But think of all the other anchors out there in the world that aren't. Are you one of those people who absolutely positively has to answer the phone if it rings, even knowing you have voice mail? Do you have to do what certain people tell you, just because they yell it at you? Do you feel nervous when you see a police officer, even though you are a well-behaved law-abiding individual? When you notice that it's lunchtime, do you automatically start to feel hungry and have to get something to eat? Do you have to feel afraid or stupid if someone says it's time to take a test? Think about all of the anchors (triggers, signals) there are out there in our lives that make us feel, think and do things we don't want. Remember, your kids have them, too, and lots of those anchors are in school.

Talk with them about this. Ask them: "What would you like to *de*-anchor? What would you like to anchor for yourself in its place? You can, you know. It's just a matter of deciding what you'd like to feel and be able to do."

For example, if your kids get nervous taking tests, they need anchors to be calm and focused instead. That's what the kids who do really well are feeling, and yours can too. All they have to do is remember a time when they did feel that way (taking a test, or some other time—it doesn't really matter) and make another little videotape in their mind. Or have a good luck charm of some sort that can serve as the anchor. Or squeeze their thumb and finger together. Or sing their favorite song in their head, one that always makes them feel safe, calm and in control. Or have some image, or symbol, in their mind that they can easily recall. They don't need you for this once they've learned the process, but you can help them if they want. Eventually they'll do it better themselves anyway.

Also, again in the long run, what makes us most successful is to have access to lots of useful states of mind when we need them. Here is a list of generally useful states of mind from a book I wrote for business people on problem solving:[6]

Openness to Change
Learning
Taking Other Viewpoints: Perspective
Creativity
Focus
Planning, Setting Goals and Outcomes
Handling Constraints or Adversity
Breaking Habits
Taking Action, Motivation
Willingness to Take Risks
Feeling Safe and Secure
Decision Making
Clarity and Understanding
Developing Effective Relationships
Gaining and Maintaining Rapport
Being Healthy
Finishing

It should be pretty obvious why we would need to be able to do each of those things from time to time in our lives and how having a particular state of mind would be helpful in each case. Knowing your kids (and yourself, for that matter) can point out areas where some special work could be helpful. The idea, of course, is that at some time or other we're all able to do these things. If we can simply remember those times, we can go back into those states and anchor them for the future. Each anchor then becomes a tool just for us, or for the kids. My advice: fill the toolbox.

# The Tie-Up

People have been asking me for years what I think about kids studying with music playing, or the television on. "Isn't that going to ruin their concentration?" "Won't it prevent them from learning anything?" "Couldn't they get their material confused with what they see and hear from the TV or stereo?" Here is the absolute, totally tested and verified answer to that: maybe, maybe not. Like anything else, some people work better in certain kinds of environments than others. The secret is to create one that works for you, or your kids. I've known plenty of adults and kids who do just fine, even better sometimes, with lots of stuff going on around them. Test it with your own kids. Also, be aware that if they have gotten used to the music, it could be a really *good* anchor for them to get into a comfortable focused state of mind. One of my nieces once told me that, while taking a test, she remembers which songs she listened to while she was studying. This helps her remember the material and makes the tests more fun (imagine that, and I didn't even teach her this). And she's smart as a whip (currently working on her Ph.D. in computer science). Taking the music away could be trouble. You have to check these things out to know for sure.

In my experience, the one thing that seems to hold most true is that kids, like all of us, should have a study space that works for them, that is consistent and in their control. If that means music, so be it (as long as it doesn't drive everyone else nuts . . .).

# Chapter 13

# How to Come to Your Senses
# (And Remember What
# You Learned Later)

When I was finishing up college, I had two friends, fellow students, who were both chess masters. Each had grown up competing up and down the East Coast of the United States from the time they were young. One talked me into playing once, despite my protests of a total lack of skill. Checkmate in four moves. He actually had the gall to ask me, afterwards, if I was kidding, or if I was really that bad. The most interesting thing they told me, though, was that they could play without the board! I thought *they* were kidding, until they showed me. They were so good that they could actually visualize the board and all the pieces, and simply call out moves to each other. They told me that they each had friends in other cities who they could play with this way, over the telephone. At the time I was astonished that anyone could actually see the board and all the pieces that clearly, and remember it. They explained that it helped that there were rules and patterns, and that these same patterns occurred over and over again among good players, but that essentially you couldn't be a really good player if you couldn't do this. The whole game of chess was really about visualizing the board, and imagining several moves ahead to see where you and your opponent were headed. Without this skill, you'd never be any good.

# The Underlying Principle

There are obvious reasons that we've spent so much time on the senses and the different ways we can think about things, in pictures, sounds and words, and of course feelings. One is that it helps us get into great states we can use when we need to, and to help our kids do the same. Also, when we use the senses neatly and well, the teaching, and learning, can go ever so smoothly. But if we tune to the wrong channel (sense), it can be impossibly frustrating. We need to understand the essential elements that make each kind of thinking—visual, auditory and kinesthetic—make sense.

Also, I believe it's important to help the kids use all the senses and be able to learn effectively in all of them. It's fine for us, and the very best teachers, to recognize the strengths in each kid. But what about those times when the kids aren't with the very best teachers? What about when they're with people who don't really care if they learn? Remember all those teachers and classes you had when you were pretty much on your own? I do. The biggest favor we can do for the kids is to prepare them for those situations, as well as the ones with the well-trained, patient, flexible and caring teachers. By the time they get to be adults, they'll be able to handle any learning situation they're thrown into.

One piece we haven't spent time on yet, but will come up when you're working with the kids, has to do with speed. We all know some kids are quicker than others at learning some things, just like we are. Well, it's not always the kids that are quick; it can be *which sense* they're using that makes it quick.

Here's why. In the strictest terms, each kind of thinking operates at a different speed, regardless of anything else. Think about pictures for a moment. If I laid out a half dozen photographs on a table in front of you, you would be able to see them all at once. You may not notice all of the detail until you concentrate on a specific picture, but you could still see all of them. Remember what we've always heard about pictures? "A picture is worth a thousand words." In fact, if you use a computer and ever do anything with pictures or graphics, you know that scanning in a simple photograph can make a huge file on your hard disk. One picture can easily equal a couple of hundred pages of writing, in terms of disk space. That's way more than a thousand words. Pictures carry tremendous amounts of information, and you can see a number of them at once. In information science we call visualization a *simultaneous* process. We mean that you get a lot of information, all at the same time. It's really fast.

Now, think about talking. If I say a sentence to you, how many words can I say, and you hear, at one time? One. I can only give you one word at a time. Not only that, they have to be in a certain order, or they don't make any sense. In most cases, as we've said all along, when you hear each word, it brings up a reference experience, a picture, other words or sounds, and some kind of feeling. So for each word, in each sentence, you hear them one at a time, and have to translate them into something else, also one at a time. In information science we call auditory processing a *sequential* process. It's a lot slower than visual processing. Not worse, just slower.

What about feelings—kinesthetic processing? You can pay attention to how you feel, but how fast do feelings change? Well, it can seem fast, but in comparison with pictures it's really slow. And you can usually only pay attention to one feeling at a time, just like the words. What makes it even slower than words, though, is that your body has to actually physically change for your feelings to change. That physiological change takes extra time. So processing through kinesthetics is also pretty *sequential*, and it's physical. It's the slowest of the three.

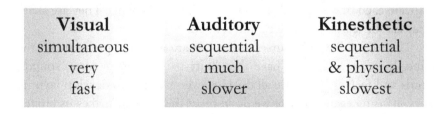

| **Visual** | **Auditory** | **Kinesthetic** |
|:---:|:---:|:---:|
| simultaneous | sequential | sequential |
| very | much | & physical |
| fast | slower | slowest |

Figure 22: Sensory Processing Speed

161

I have to emphasize something here that is very important. The speed at which kids learn is rarely the most important thing to consider. We just need to be aware of it so if things start to go too fast or too slow we can understand why and make adjustments, if it's appropriate. It might not be. It's true that people who think visually can be very quick. That is good when you have to be quick, but not always if you have to be accurate. It turns out that lots of people who are very auditory in their thinking tend also to be very precise in what they do. Lawyers, for example. When they're doing their job well they are very careful with the words they use. They work hard to get them just right. It's why contracts can be so long. This is also why some people ask so many questions that drive other people nuts. They are just trying to be really accurate. It can be frustrating to deal with if you're in a hurry, but it's often worth the wait to get the clarity and accuracy that comes with that kind of thinking.

Feelings, and thinking kinesthetically, can be really valuable as well. Sometimes many of us forget how important people's feelings are, and we end up trampling on them. The people who tend to be most oriented toward feelings often tend to be the most kind and considerate of others, and this can make them really good at relationships. They also, sometimes, tend to be extremely "values oriented" because their gut instinct tells them if something is right or wrong, or worthwhile. This is really a valuable skill. More visually oriented people sometimes tend to be more goal oriented. Sometimes they are really good at "spotting the target," "keeping their eye on the ball," "the big picture," or "the long view." Extremely auditory people often tend to be more precision oriented. These are certainly generalizations, and we need to be careful to avoid classifying individual people too much, but there is obvious value and worth in each of these perspectives. My belief is that we should all cultivate each of these skills to get their obvious benefits. They are skills. They can be learned, practiced and refined.

The nice thing, of course, is that we are all wired pretty much the same. In other words we have the ability to think in pictures, sounds, words and feelings. And, we all do. However, we tend to develop favorite ways of using each one, like we do in most things. This makes us limited in our thinking, but it's a limitation we gave ourselves, so we can get rid of it.

This may be a little late, but I have a confession to make: I was never a great student growing up. A bit of a "dim bulb" as they say, at times. Sometimes I did well, but for the most part I was just a little above average. I have two younger brothers, however, who were both way ahead of me in that department. My brother Steve used to get me downright furious, in fact. He was one of those horrible kids who *never* brought a book home and never had to do homework at night, even in high school. He always finished his work either in class or study hall. He made A's. Once we ended up in the same math course, since he was in an accelerated program. I spent hours memorizing formulas, and he didn't bother. As usual he did far better on the test. Afterwards I asked for advice.

He spent the next two hours explaining math to me, the way he thought about it in his head. He had all these big clear pictures. He understood the relationships between numbers, formulas, objects, ideas. To him it was all a big game or, more accurately, a puzzle. He just needed to have a few of the pieces, and because he knew what the whole picture was supposed to look like, he could fill in the rest. He also had lots of short cuts that sped things up a lot. More than anything, what impressed me was his ability to make really clear pictures in his mind, hold them really steady while we worked the problem and connect those internal pictures to just the right questions. He never seemed to get nervous, and in fact he had fun playing the math game.

He had learned lots of math short cuts and tricks that he showed me. Many of these he had found in books he studied, others he worked out for himself. I wasn't able to hold pictures in my mind like this, and he couldn't really teach me to do it beyond telling me to practice. Practice really is most of it, but now we do know how to teach it.

The clarity of images comes from practice *and* learning how to carefully adjust the qualities of the images. These qualities are called *sub-modalities*. The sensory modalities are, of course, the visual, auditory, kinesthetic, olfactory and gustatory parts of our experience: the five senses. The *sub*-modalities are the characteristic qualities of each of these modalities. For example, pictures each have their own characteristic size, shape and color. Sounds have volume, pitch and speed. Feelings have location, intensity and more. Here is a list of some of the main sub-modalities, to give you the idea:

| Sensory Modalities | Visual | Auditory | Kinesthetic | Olfactory-Gustatory |
|---|---|---|---|---|
| Sensory Sub-Modalities | Brightness | Sounds/Words | Intensity | Intensity |
| | Location | Volume | Location | Sweet |
| | Size | Location | Size | Sour |
| | Shape | Pitch | Temperature | Bitter |
| | Depth | Tonality/Timbre | Pressure | Salty |
| | Color | Tempo (speed) | Movement | Pungent |

Figure 23: Sensory Sub-Modalities

When you learn to adjust the sub-modalities of your internal pictures, sounds and feelings in various ways, it helps tremendously in controlling them. Your kids can also learn to make adjustments that will help hold pictures and sounds steady and clear in their minds. This will help in understanding, learning and memory. That's what the exercises we'll do are for.

# The Set-Up

Helping your kids learn about getting clear pictures, sounds and feelings inside can be a lot of fun. It will be obvious to them that it's important to be able to think clearly and remember things to do their schoolwork. But they might not know that it's just a matter of remembering to do it, and a little practice. It's what all the kids who find schoolwork really easy already do, though they don't usually know that they do it.

Asking your kids to use their memories, just like they did in the anchoring exercises, is an easy start. They can tell you what they saw, heard and felt during their favorite trip, sporting event, concert or movie. Even what their day was like. It's really pretty easy for most of them, if you don't start talking about schoolwork. You can then tell them about your experiences. Then, if you want, you can ask them about what they're working on in school and *how they think about it* (pictures, sounds and feelings). That's what you want to talk about.

This is also where having done those earlier experiments on how you think about different concepts like electricity, history, communication and so on will help. Again, if you know how you think about something, you can give those same pictures, sounds and words, and even feelings to your kids.

# The Delivery

When I was in high school, I played on the tennis team. We had a good one, with one nationally ranked player and a couple of others who were close. We practiced hard, and it was fun. But one of the other things we did after practice now and then, was switch our rackets to the other hand and continue to play. We had one left-handed player, so he would play right-handed. The rest of us played left-handed. At first we were terrible, as you'd expect. But with just a little practice, we got pretty good. We could serve, volley, hit ground strokes, pretty much everything. It was a stretch for us and it was fun.

First and foremost, when you do these exercises, make it fun. As I mentioned earlier, one of the easiest ways to do them is to make them into some sort of a game. It already is a game for a lot of the really gifted kids, so you can introduce the idea to your kids that way too. For example, on the exercises for improving visual skills, at the beginning, you can ask something like: "What's your favorite cartoon?" Then take a look at one, say in the newspaper, and ask the kids if they can remember the whole thing. Have a contest with them to see who can remember how much. You'll figure out what the winner gets . . . (remember to make sure everyone wins at some time or other).

## Visual Experiments

For years people have been coming up to me during or after workshops and saying something like this: "All this stuff is great, but I don't see pictures in my head [hear sounds clearly, notice my feelings], so I can't do any of it." I always answer their concern the same way: "Yes you do." But people aren't always clear on what I mean since they aren't always as *consciously aware* of their internal images as they think they're supposed to be. Remember we all see things in our own way, and this is just as true inside our mind's eye as it is on the outside. Some people's internal

165

pictures are faded, and some are crystal clear. Some are in full color, some muted, or black and white. Some go by really fast, so it's just a blur; others hold, steady as a rock, in space for a long time. In fact, most of us have experienced plenty of different kinds of images in our minds. Sometimes this depends on our state of mind; sometimes it's simply the skill of holding nice clear, full color, steady, detailed images. Remember, the wiring to be able to do it is there; it's knowing how to use it that counts.

I usually ask people who find this difficult to describe something for me, like their living room, or their car, or what they saw as they walked into the building we're in. Invariably people can give pretty accurate descriptions of these things. When I ask them how they're able to do that, they usually say the same thing: "I just know." When I ask how they do that, they're usually stuck. I know it's because they can recall the visual image, even if only for a moment. Remember, visualization is *fast*. They can get the information so quickly, they aren't even aware of where it came from. It's *unconscious competence*, like we discussed earlier. It's not that they can't do it. They can. They just don't know consciously *how* they're doing it. But if you can do something, you can become aware of how you do it by paying close attention.

The exercise I generally give people to do, on their own or with a little guidance, is the one that follows.

## EXPERIMENT: HOLDING PICTURES

Step 1: Choose a picture. Pick one from a magazine, a photograph or one on the wall. You choose.

Step 2: Look at the picture for about 30 seconds or so (the first time).

Step 3: Next, close your eyes and try to hold the image steady and clear, exactly as you saw it, for a minute or so.

Step 4: After that minute, open your eyes and look at the picture again. Notice how accurate the one in your mind was in comparison.

Step 5: Repeat this process a couple of times and see how much you improve.

For some people this process is, at first, impossible. For them, the image fades the moment they close their eyes. It's OK. They just need to do it some more, for a longer time. Eventually they'll be able to hold at least some part of the picture in their mind's eye. There are no rules about how long this will take, or how quickly people can improve. But in my experience, everyone who tries does improve.

For most people, though, they can do it, sort of. They find that when they open their eyes to look at the original picture, they've deleted and distorted some of it. That's pretty normal. So I suggest that they do it again a few times and see if they can get some improvement. Almost everyone can, fairly quickly, but for some it takes more practice. I've not found that I can predict very well who will quickly improve and who will take more time. What I *have* found is that just about everyone can get improvement if they take a little time each day, perhaps 10-15 minutes. In most cases, within a few months people notice they have improved. The wiring is there; it just needs a few sparks.

So for the kids, we can do the same thing, and make it fun. When you start, choose pictures you know they'll enjoy. You may want to pick some that have a lot of detail and some that don't and experiment at first. Find out how well they can do at first, then go for improvement. The easiest ones would be cartoons in the paper, in black and white. The drawings are usually pretty simple, two-dimensional, with just a few colors. This makes it easy because the kids can concentrate on just a few sizes and shapes.

If these pictures are easy, or they get easy with a little practice, you can go on to more detailed images. Work your way up to ones with plenty of variety in them, various shapes and relationships, and lots of color, eventually. Great art is good for this (and for lots of other reasons as well).

In general, as you do this, begin with "big picture" kinds of distinctions; then go for more and more detail. These features are actually handled by different parts of the brain, so you're exercising these various parts by practicing different kinds of visual distinctions. One eventual goal, of course, could be for the kids to develop total "photographic memory" which means they can see the picture in their mind with the same clarity and accuracy that they see the actual one with. This doesn't mean they (or you) will ever get that good at this. Most people don't, and it really isn't necessary for very much in our lives.

The more they practice, the better they'll get, and that's a worthwhile goal. When the kids know they can improve, it's a great help to both their skill and their belief in themselves.

Next you, and they, can repeat this same exercise, but with real things, rather than photographs. For example, choose an object in the room, and do the exercise. After that, try a part of the room, say everything along one wall. Have the kids close their eyes and describe what is there. Then they can open their eyes and see what they got right.

A fun game, one we use in our trainings to get people to pay close attention to *other people*, is to do this kind of observational exercise with a person.

# EXPERIMENT: CHANGING PICTURES

Step 1: Have your kids look at you, or someone else who wants to play, for about 30 seconds.

Step 2: Then have the kids close their eyes and hold the image of the person in their mind.

Step 3: While the kids' eyes are closed, make a small change in the person they are looking at. Perhaps move slightly to one side, or move some part of the body a bit. Change facial expression, unbutton a button, remove an earring, anything.

Step 4: Have the kids open their eyes and see if they can pick out the change.

Step 5: Repeat this as often as it's fun and make the changes smaller and more subtle as a challenge.

Step 6: When the kids get really good at this, you can expand it so that one kid is looking at three or four other people at once. Then when they close their eyes one person can make a change that they'll have to pick out. Eventually, as you play some more, each person can make a small change and the kids will have to pick all of them.

Obviously there is no limit to the variations you can make in these games and challenges. As long as it's fun, it's good training. Even better is to have the kids make up new variations they can play. They might teach you a thing or two. Some people like to add drawing into the games, so that they have to draw some aspects of what they see.

Perhaps as you were doing these things in your own mind, you found that you were talking yourself through it each time. For some people this is a help, but what we want to do here is practice using the visual sense by itself, for now, so that we exercise that. The same for your kids. Obviously some will do better with the visual part, some with the internal talking, but our goal is to get all of the kids to be able to use all of the senses really well.

One thing you can do, for now, to help the kids see the images more clearly in their minds is to have them experiment with *where* they see the picture. What I mean is, literally, which direction their eyes move when they look at the picture in their mind. Try this experiment yourself.

## EXPERIMENT: MOVING PICTURES AROUND

Step 1: Choose an image to look at, a photo, something in the room, or whatever is most interesting at this moment. It doesn't matter what it is.

Step 2: Now, cover the image or turn away from what you were looking at, and hold the image as clearly in your mind as you can.

Step 3: Next, one at a time, try moving the picture around to each of the following different locations in front of you. As you do, pay attention to whether it is easier or more difficult to hold the image clearly in mind.

  directly in front, at eye level
  directly in front, but at an angle slightly upward
  slightly up and to the left
  slightly up and to the right
  directly in front, but at an angle slightly downward
  slightly down and to the left
  slightly down and to the right

Step 4: Repeat this with a couple of different images. Try moving the image closer and farther away from you as well.

Step 5: Notice if there is one particular place where it is easiest to hold the image clearly. If so, remember exactly where that location is.

For almost everyone, some directions are easier than others. Many people find it extremely difficult, impossible even, to hold the picture in mind at all when they move it down, or down and to the right. Most people find it easier to hold the images if they are directly ahead at eye level, slightly up, or slightly up and to their left. The reason for these preferences is neurological. Without going into too much detail, the movement of the eyes literally activates different portions of the brain. In other words, when you move your eyes up and to your left, you activate different portions of your brain than if you move them down and to your right. So, moving your eyes to different locations makes a difference in what you can do because some of those parts of the brain are more involved in what you see, some in what you hear and some in what you feel. For almost everyone, this makes a real difference in their ability to clearly hold the images in their mind. There are some standard movements that work for most people, but these are just generalizations. We can really help if we can find out what works best for each kid, as well as for ourselves.

This just takes a little experimenting. Do the following simple experiment with them, and it can change their lives forever.

## EXPERIMENT: THE BEST PLACE FOR PICTURES

Step 1: Make a "movie screen" for them to hold the image on. To do this, hold up a blank plain white piece of paper, cardboard or notebook. It doesn't matter what it's made of, but it should be at least the size of a notebook so they'll have plenty of room to hold their images.

Step 2: Explain to them that you want to help them hold pictures even more clearly in their mind by finding out the best place for them to see the pictures. Give them a picture of some sort to look at, just as you did earlier. Any picture will do.

Step 3: This time, instead of having them close their eyes, have them see it on the movie screen you made and hold it directly in front of them, at eye level, about 12-18 inches away from them. This is usually very easy, but if they need to practice a bit, go ahead and give them some time.

Step 4: Tell them, again, that you want to test to find out the best place for them to see pictures in their mind. Slowly move the movie screen to the different locations you did earlier, up, down, right and left, and notice the look on the kids' faces. At each location, ask them if it is easier or more difficult to see the picture clearly. Have them notice this for themselves as well.

Step 5: When you find the best direction—and you will—test for distance as well. Find out how close the picture should be to make it easiest and most comfortable to look at.

Step 6: Talk with the kids about the value of this. Remind them that if they know where the easiest place to see the picture is, they should remember this and concentrate on using that place to look at images in their minds.

We have been exploring the relationship to people's eye movements and their ability to think and remember in different ways for over 35 years now. It is such a helpful way to go about teaching your kids that I can't emphasize it enough. We'll come back to this during the auditory and kinesthetic exercises, as well as other adjustments and refinements to help them.

## More Advanced Visual Experiments

There is a psychologist named Dr. Judy Kearins of the University of Western Australia who has devised some interesting games of this type to test the abilities of various groups of children. She would make a grid, something like a checker board, and put various small objects on it, each in its own little square. She used things like hair clips, small toys, coins, lucky charms, whatever normal every day things she could find. Then the kids would do what we just did: stare at it for 30 seconds to a minute, and then close their eyes. While their eyes were closed, Dr. Kearins would move all the objects into a pile. When they opened their eyes she would give them a few minutes to try to put all of the objects back into their original positions. In general, she found that white Australian children, who grew up with more of these objects, did much better than Aborigine kids. She thought this might have to do with their familiarity with the objects themselves, so she repeated the game in a different way. With the Aborigine kids, instead of everyday objects, she actually used small stones of different shapes. This time the Aborigine kids did much better than the white Australian kids. The reason is probably that these kids grow up out in nature, and are more used to having to identify natural shapes and objects, rather than man-made ones. She also noticed major differences in the ways that they played the games. The white Australian kids talked to themselves a lot more, coaching themselves along. The Aborigine kids seemed able to just hold the picture and work from that.[1]

Though Dr. Kearins uses this as a test of the abilities of various groups of kids, there is no reason we can't use it to *teach* rather than test. A training expert named Michelle Deck has developed training techniques that do just that. Let's say your kids have to learn a procedure, a series of steps, in a particular order. Each step of the procedure is put into a grid, much like a window with separate panes. This would look just about like the games Dr. Kearins developed. In this case though, you take each step in the procedure to be learned and draw it as a picture, or a symbol, that makes sense in some way to the kids. Then you put one in each square (window pane) in order. Then the kids would simply have to remember the pictures in each one. It works because it's easier for most of us to remember the pictures, and the overall picture, than a list of words or instructions. With practice, this could become a favorite method for your kids.[2]

We also want the kids to be able to hold more complicated things, like sequences, steps in a process or the order of things steady in their minds. Psychologists have been studying people's abilities to hold images in their minds, remember them and repeat or reproduce them for many

many years. I often believe that the tests and games that they use in their research can make great teaching tools, as well as research tools. So let's use them.

# Memory Techniques[3]

This isn't a book on memory, and I can't begin to cover the subject adequately. We can't ignore it, though, so I'm covering the aspects I think are most important. There is a vast literature, both professional and popular on the subject, and it covers a broad spectrum of information. Researchers are learning more about the brain and body mechanisms that make up how we store and recall information all the time, and it gets more and more complicated as they learn. What stays pretty much the same, though, are the principles and techniques that we can use in our everyday lives to help us, and our children, remember things that are important.

For years parents have been asking me about the many books and programs on the market designed to improve memory. Do they work? Are they really new? Which ones are best? Well, yes they work, no they aren't usually new (some are thousands of years old), and most of them are pretty much the same with slight variations. Here is a rundown of some of the major techniques.

## Stories

One way to remember some group of ideas, is to simply make up a story that includes all of the pieces. To do it really well means a complete story, with pictures, sounds and feelings. For example, let's say you send your kids to the store to pick up the following: bread, peanut butter, birdseed, light bulbs and a newspaper. You and the kids could easily make up a story about how the bird woke up in the dark, hungry and in a dirty cage. So, he needed to be fed, have his light bulb changed and clean newspaper at the bottom of the cage (I never said the story had to make sense . . .). Then the kids sit down to have their dinner along with the bird, so they have peanut butter sandwiches while they talk with their bird . . . This works, and it's fun. The longer the list, the longer the story. Also, the crazier the better.

## The "Roman Room"

Take that list of things, and imagine placing them into a familiar room, your bedroom or living room, for example. You can even do strange elaborate combinations of stories taking place in the room. Using the same list as before, you can imagine that when you walk into your living room, in your mind, you notice a light bulb is out; there is a stack of newspapers next to the door, and a peanut butter sandwich on the table. As you walk toward the sandwich, your feet slide out from under you because someone spilled birdseed all over the floor. Crazy variations work better here, too: you walk in seeing newspapers spread all over the floor, the bird yelling at you from the next room that he wants a peanut butter sandwich, and when you walk into that room he throws a light bulb at you. . . .

## Memory Links

These link together all the things you have to remember, in one strange picture. A peanut butter sandwich, flying around on a magic carpet made out of newspaper, with big light bulbs for wings, leaving a trail of birdseed across the sky.

## Memory Pegs

This one takes more preparation than the rest. First, you have to have a list of images that you permanently use for all your memory tasks. Memorize each item, in order. For example:

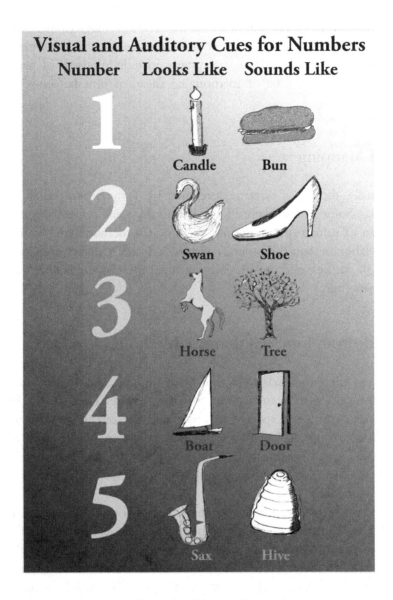

**Visual and Auditory Cues for Numbers**

| Number | Looks Like | Sounds Like |
|--------|-----------|-------------|
| 1 | Candle | Bun |
| 2 | Swan | Shoe |
| 3 | Horse | Tree |
| 4 | Boat | Door |
| 5 | Sax | Hive |

Figure 24: Memory Pegs

Associate each item you need to remember with an item on the list, in order if that matters. For our list, visualize your candle with a light bulb on it. Your swan is eating birdseed. The horse is reading the newspaper. The sailboat has a sail made out of bread and the saxophone has a jar of peanut butter sticking out of it. It's the pictures you make that help you remember what's on the list. The advantage to this method is that you can remember things in order, forwards, backwards or out of sequence just as easily. The entire systems include hundreds of pegs, so they obviously take a bit of memorizing ahead of time before you can use it effectively.

## Mind Mapping

Finally, there is a system, developed by Tony Buzan, called mind mapping. Some people like it a lot for note taking and remembering large amounts of information. I'm not going into the method here because it's more elaborate than the others, and it works very well for some people (some of my best and most highly respected friends) and is pure torture for others (me).

## The Bottom Line on Memory Methods

All of these methods work, and there are more. All of them rely on visual processes, and associations. All take practice. They are the kinds of things "memory experts" use to memorize telephone directories and other amazing feats. I do believe these methods are worth exploring, experimenting with, and playing with. You and your kids may enjoy them, or hate them. Decide for yourselves. That's why it's an exploration.

The proverbial bottom line on memory is that there are natural limits to what we can consciously remember, but we can enhance our abilities to overcome these limits. If you find a bunch of really brilliant people, or great students, and ask them how they actually remember things so well, almost none of them will tell you that they got that way from learning memory techniques (though probably a few will). Usually, they've learned their own methods and gotten used to using them regularly, which means they practiced on their own. The ones that work virtually all rely on the fact that we can visualize really well, and connect things together really well, naturally. If we connect pictures, sounds and feelings together, and relate (associate, connect) those ideas with other things we know, they'll be easier to remember. Practice (use) will make the information stick. And, if we do all of this on purpose, we'll have real control of our memory. This is what we can help the kids learn to do.

Most memory experts will tell you the trick is input, not output. In other words, how you store the information, and plan to remember it, is the really important part. If you do that well, the memories are much easier to retrieve.

## Chunk Size

We do know that there are some normal limits to what most people can remember, in terms of a sequence or series of items. Let's take, for example, a series of 16 random letters:

x r l a z b m j r e s u i w k v

If you read these, or show them, to someone and ask them to hold the list in their mind as well and long as they can, most people will be able to get a number of them right. Specifically, between five and nine (7 ± 2) right, then they'll get mixed up make mistakes. You can do the same with a set of objects, numbers, non-sense syllables (boj, lor, kel) or most other things. It seems that most people can consciously hold about 7 ± 2 pieces of information at once.[4] But if we give them those same ones with some instruction and practice, they can do better. They can learn to hold images, as we've been saying, longer and more accurately with practice. Also, they'll do way better if they group them into chunks. For example, here is the same list of 16 letters:

x r l    a z b    m j r    e s u    i w k v

With a little practice, this will be easier than the original, because we have grouped the letters. So, since we can remember each small group more easily, we can then just remember the groups. Five groups are usually a lot easier to remember than 16 individual letters. Try it yourself.

Next, as an experiment, try putting the letters in different formats, the same series, just a different view. For example:

| x | a | m | e | i |
|---|---|---|---|---|
| r | z | j | s | w |
| l | b | r | u | k |
|   |   |   |   | v |

This may have made it easier or harder for you, or perhaps produced no difference at all. But that's the point. Finding out which ways are "the difference that makes a difference" can be really helpful for you and the kids. As you play around with this, imagine how you could substitute words, numbers, objects, pictures, the steps in a process or whatever else you think might be useful. If it's really about making pictures in our minds, think of all the different things we can be making pictures of. And all the different pictures your kids have to make in their minds, in school.

A bit later, when we talk about spelling, we'll come back to some more ways to enhance the kids' abilities to see images clearly in their minds, including specific ways to adjust the sub-modalities.

## Auditory Experiments

One of the things many of us who have done various kinds of therapy with kids (of all ages) have noticed, is that many of those diagnosed (labeled) as learning disabled are remarkably talented at remembering and reproducing sounds. For example, lots of kids I've worked with who had spelling, reading and math problems are great at reciting things they've heard. This includes repeating movie dialog, making sounds of nature (some quite disgusting, but nevertheless impressive), mimicking parents and teachers, complete with voice tones and remembering exactly what people have said (or promised, and holding them to it relentlessly). This is one of the reasons that it's so surprising to be introduced to a child with a serious learning problem, and to hear them speak so articulately that it makes you do a double take.

Auditory skills are extremely valued in education in some ways but not others. In American society, visual skills are much more highly thought of—and taught to—in school. It's not necessarily like that everywhere. As I travel, I notice the differences in communication styles in different countries or even regions of a country. It's pretty obvious if you pay attention. But in the US, we are a visual culture primarily. It's the reason that so many kids diagnosed with learning problems are really just better at auditory or kinesthetic processing. It also turns out, if you pay attention, that a lot of these folks turn out to be gifted and creative in ways that aren't typical of the rest of us. As always, my personal bias is to have no bias: teach everyone the gifts of everyone else.

Think about yourself, again, for a moment. What kind of jokes do you like? What kind of music? Do you like listening to the stories people tell? What about voice tones? Do the sounds of people's voices affect you in ways that you notice, or do you notice that you don't notice them at all? Can you remember what people say, accurately, in conversation, or in speeches, jokes, sayings, etc.?

Maybe you are one of the unfortunate among us who have spent too much time watching televised court cases. The TV news stations always have expert consultants to explain what we've just witnessed. One thing that the consultants say, over and over, is to listen to the jurors after the trial has ended. The jurors usually leave the court building and face a bunch of microphones, cameras and reporters. When interviewed, they will *always* do exactly the same thing: repeat, word for word, sometimes with the same voice tone and rhythm, the words of the lawyer they voted for. Not the defendant. Not the judge, not the witnesses, experts or anyone else. The lawyer. A jury trial is all about the lawyers and their relationship to the jury. And it's about the winning lawyer's ability to get his or her words *into the minds of the jurors*. That's why they come up with little rhymes and odd phrasings (sound bytes, just like politicians use) to help people remember exactly what they said. The problem is, that's often *all* they remember. I think if I'm ever on trial, I'll hire a poet . . . .

Now the point to all this is that we want our kids to remember things they've heard that are important. That means really important, not just what someone else says is important. That means they need to *hear everything* so they can make up their own minds. Then they need to be able to hold those words, phrases, sentences and voice tones in mind, while they make up their minds about what it all means, and what it means to them.

They begin doing this when they are learning to talk. It's how they know the words. They also do it really well at some odd times. Maybe you've noticed this kind of thing before: You want your little girl to clean up her room, but she's putting it off. Finally, perhaps long after you've been able to stand it, you lose your temper and yell. "You better clean up that room right now, young lady, or else . . . ." Then you follow her, sneakily so she doesn't know, to her room. As you watch, she picks up her little girl doll and says: "You better clean up that room right now, young lady, or else . . . ."

So, we know they can remember what they hear. But how to practice? Well, there are several ways. A way to start is suggested by Tim Murphey in his great little book: *Language Hungry!* on learning foreign languages. He calls it *shadowing*[5] and it comes in two forms. First, get the kids to actually repeat back what they hear, either out loud or silently in their minds. They can do this watching TV, listening to the radio or even other people in conversation. Murphey points out that this is what kids do when they're learning to talk in the first place, but it's a good way to help them focus attention on what they hear. The second way is to have them do the same shadowing when they are talking with you. This means when you tell them something, they repeat it back immediately. Like a parrot. The difference is that you can be sure they heard you correctly, and help them if they haven't. If you think about it, this is what we do when we're teaching them to talk, as well. It's a useful process, so we might as well use it.

Another way is to do some of the same kinds of things we did with the visual information. Instead of a picture, we want our kids to be able to hear, and recognize, words, voice tones, music, sequences (sentences, lists) of things and whatever else we think is important. As with visual information, also, it often helps to have the kids move their eyes to different locations and discover if it helps them to actually hear better inside their minds. So let's start there with the following exercise.

# EXPERIMENT: THE BEST PLACE FOR SOUNDS

Step 1: Explain to the kids that you want to help them hear sounds as clearly as possible in their mind. Just like before with the pictures, by moving their eyes in different directions they will probably find that it makes a difference in how well they can hear inside.

Step 2: Begin with something fun to listen to, perhaps a CD of something that they like. This could also be a comedy recording, dialog from a movie or television show (just play the sound), radio program or something else. Start with spoken words first.

Step 3: Use your movie screen again, to help guide their eyes, and hold it directly in front of them, at eye level, as you did before. This time, though, there won't be anything to visualize, it's just to guide them to move their eyes in different directions.

Step 4: Tell them, again, that you want to test to find out the best place for them to hear sounds in their mind. Slowly move the movie screen to the different locations, up, down, right and left and notice the look on the kids' faces. At each location, ask them if it is easier or more difficult to hear the sounds clearly. Have them notice this for themselves as well. Here is the list of locations again, just so you'll remember:

directly in front, at eye level
directly in front, but at an angle slightly upward
slightly up and to the left
slightly up and to the right
directly in front, but at an angle slightly downward
slightly down and to the left
slightly down and to the right

Step 5: Find the best direction (again, you will) just as you did for pictures.

Step 6: Repeat this with the following specific sounds:

something they say to themselves, silently inside
something you read to them, from a book, newspaper or magazine
music, just instrumental, with no lyrics
songs with words and music

Note: You may find that there is some slight difference in the direction that is best to move their eyes for each of these, or not. It is definitely worth finding out.

Step 7: Talk with the kids about the value of this. Remind them that if they know where the easiest place to hear the sounds is, again, they should concentrate on using that place whenever they need to.

Just as before with the visual images, this can be the first step in learning to hear clearly on the inside. Many kids (and adults, hint, hint) discover that there is a wealth of auditory information that they never felt they had access to, but that they really do. It's just a matter of engaging the parts of our brains that help us do it best. The eye movements are one key way of doing this, and they can be just as crucial as they were with visual information.

## More advanced auditory experiments

Auditory information comes in many flavors, just like visual information does. Words, sounds, voice tones, numbers, formulas, music. We can hear sequences of these things as well. Some people use the auditory system all by itself with great skill, but most others find that it is easier to combine auditory and visual. If we can help the kids use the auditory system all by itself, when they do combine the two together it can be really impressive. This, by the way, is the basis of almost all of the super duper unbelievable fantastically successful oh-my-god-you've-got-to-be-kidding-they-can't-possibly-do-that memory enhancement programs out there on the market (and in television infomercials). They simply use some pretty basic ways of using the senses together in order to "code" things so that they get stuck together in our minds.

Anyway, we want to help the kids hear, store and recall auditory information easily and well, just as with visual information. We can use those same sequences that we used earlier; there are just fewer ways to do it.

Let's take a new series of 16 random letters:

k s j r e k l k d f l k a f v w

The same five to nine (7 ± 2) rule applies when we talk about holding them in our mind at one time. But again, we can improve on that with practice and some strategic thinking. This time, of course, instead of showing the kids the sequence, you'll read them the letters, one at a time and ask them to hold them in mind. So here are some more steps you can experiment with, to start.

## EXPERIMENT: THE BEST PLACE FOR SOUNDS—IN SEQUENCE

Step 1:  Explain to the kids, again, that you want to help them hold sounds clearly in their minds. Remind them of where their eyes should go to most clearly hold the sounds in mind, from your previous experiment with them.

Step 2:  Read the letters to them, slowly and clearly, and ask them to hold as many as they can in mind, holding their eyes in the best location for them.

Step 3:  Find out how many they can hold, for how long. Remember that most people will get between five and nine correct, but it doesn't really matter. Everyone's a little different. So let's repeat this, making a small adjustment, like before:

## EXPERIMENT: CHUNKING SEQUENCES OF SOUNDS

Step 1:  This time, tell them that you want to experiment with different ways of holding the sounds in mind.

Step 2:  Read the letters to them again, but this time in chunks, as we did earlier. Again, it may be easier if the kids can chunk the letters into smaller groups:

k s j   r e k   l k d f   l k a   f v w

Step 3: Find out how many they can hold this time, and if there is some improvement. It's perfectly all right if there isn't. Like always this is just an experiment.

Step 4: For variations, repeat this kind of exercise with numbers, words, formulas or combinations, like names and dates. Your kids probably have plenty of school examples they could use. Remember, though, this is just practice; keep it fun.

There are other adjustments we can make, using sub-modalities that will help tremendously. Try the following experiment, complete with its variations, as much as it's comfortable for both you and the kids. Again, this might be good for you to try first, since it will be just as valuable for you, and it will help you help the kids.

# EXPERIMENT: ADJUSTING THE SOUNDS

Step 1: Explain to the kids that you want to do some slightly strange experiments with sounds in their minds (as if the ones so far haven't been strange enough), and that these can be kind of fun if they play along and get creative with it. Remind them about the best place to position their eyes.

Step 2: Read them a sentence, or a saying of some sort. It should be several words long, so they have room to experiment.

Step 3: Ask them to repeat the sentence in their mind a couple of times, so they can remember it clearly.

Step 4: First, have the kids imagine that they can move the sound around; inside their mind to anyplace they want it to be. They can even imagine that it's coming from outside anyplace they'd like. Have them experiment with all different directions that the sound can come from, and find out if some are easier than others. They almost always will find some. Have them show you, so you can both remember, where the sound seems clearest and easiest to hear from. Give them plenty of time.

Step 5:  Next, ask them to imagine that they have a volume control, like on a stereo or TV, that they can use to turn the volume of the sentence up or down as much as they want. Ask them to turn the volume up louder to find out if it is easier to hear, and hold, the sentence in their mind. Have them turn it down as well. The idea, again, is to find some volume level that seems to be the easiest for them to use. Give them as much time as they need to experiment.

Step 6:  Repeat these experiments in the following ways. Have the kids experiment with:

Changing the tonality of the voice, make it more pleasant sounding, even changing it to someone's voice that they especially like

Adjusting the pitch, higher and lower ("high notes" and "low notes")

Adjusting the tempo (speed) faster and slower

Put the voice into a rhythm that is pleasant or fun to listen to

In each case, give the kids as much time as they'd like. You can experiment with them if you want; it might be fun.

All of us are strongly affected by the things people say to us, for better or worse. We put these voices inside our own heads and listen to them again and again. They change the way we think and feel, and they become an important part of our thinking. The more control we can get over this process, the more control we have over our thoughts and feelings. This also includes what we understand, learn and remember. Just doing these experiments a few times will help your kids discover the control they can have inside their own minds.

## Advanced: Connection to Kinesthetics Experiments

Just about everyone who has studied this material over the last few decades will tell you that the "kinesthetic kids" (the ones who think mostly in terms of feelings) generally have the toughest time in school. The reason is that so much of what is taught is delivered through pictures and words, and in fact is made out of pictures and words. Our educational system doesn't value feelings in the classroom very much, though it seems to have gotten better in some schools. The emphasis is on showing and telling.

When we talk about improving our kinesthetic sense, we are mostly talking about getting the kids to notice and pay attention to how they feel. What we're most interested in, here, is getting the kids to be in touch with their feelings and to gain some control over them (which doesn't mean making them into robots). In terms of schoolwork, it usually means helping them stay in a good learning state, whenever they need to.

My favorite way to help people get in touch with their feelings is to have them pay attention to what happens in different parts of their body as their state changes.

# EXPERIMENT: EXPLORING FEELINGS AND PICTURES

The idea: In this experiment we'll be exploring the sub-modalities we talked about earlier, and how changing the characteristics of the pictures inside our minds can actually change our feelings. This will serve a couple of purposes. First, we'll get to pay closer attention to feelings. Second, we'll be able to make really good states of mind even better. As always, it is a good idea to do this experiment yourself first, then with the kids. You'll definitely want to read through all the instructions, first, before getting started.

Step 1:  Remember one of those good states of mind from the last chapter. You can do this with any of those, or a different one if you want.

Step 2:  Get into the state, like you did earlier, by clearly seeing the image, hearing the sounds, and noticing the feelings that go with it. Remember that each state we go into starts with its own pictures, sounds and feelings built in. This time, pay special attention to the actual physical sensations that are part of this state of mind.

It will help to answer the following questions (you'll ask the kids these when it's their turn):

Do you feel any tension or pressure anywhere in your body? Check from the top of your head to the bottom of your feet, a little at a time.

Do you feel warm or cool anywhere? Again, check from top to bottom.

Can you pinpoint the exact location of any tension or temperature changes inside or on the surface of your skin?

How intense are the feelings that go with this state of mind?

Do you feel any movement inside, or feel as if you are moving? Or, are you feeling very still?

Do you feel in balance? Light or heavy anywhere, or all over?

Do you feel any other sensations in your body?

Once you've noticed all the feelings, we can go on to the next step.

Step 3: Now pay close attention to the visual image that goes with this state of mind. Answer the following questions as a help (again, start with yourself, but ask the kids when it's time for them to do this):

How bright is the picture, itself, in your mind?

How big is it? Is it on a screen in front of you in your mind, or are you inside of it, like it's all around you (we call this kind of image *panoramic*)?

If it's on a screen in front, how close is it to you?

Does it have depth to it, like a 3D image, or is it flat like a photograph?

Is it in full color or black and white?

Is it in motion, like a movie, or a still shot like a photo?

Is it clear and in focus?

Once you've noticed all the characteristics (the sub-modalities) of the visual image, we can go on to the next step.

Step 4:  Now we're going to make adjustments to the picture, and notice the changes in the feelings as we do each one. Do these one at a time, and take all the time you need. Remember to change the characteristic of the one you're experimenting with back to the way it was at first, before going on to the next characteristic.

As you do this, notice which changes you make in the picture cause the biggest differences in how you feel. Also, notice if any of the changes you make affect the clarity and focus of the image itself. This can come in handy later.

First, make the picture itself a little brighter in your mind (not so much that it's uncomfortable, but brighter). Notice how the feeling changes. Check all of the feelings from head to toe, like before.

Next, make it dimmer than it was (not so dim that you can't see it, but dimmer). How does the feeling change this time?

Change it back to the way it was originally.

Next, if it's on a screen in front of you in your mind, do the following. (If you are "inside" the picture—panoramic—and it's all around you, skip this one.) First make it closer and bigger (again, not so much that it is ridiculous or distorted, just closer and bigger). What happens to the way you feel this time? Check yourself all over.

Now, move it farther away from you and make it smaller. What happens to the feeling this time?

Change it back to the way it was originally.

If the picture has depth, in other words, it's a 3D image, change it so that it becomes flat like a photograph. If it's flat, make it 3D. How does that change the way you feel?

Change it back to the way it was originally.

If it's in full color, change it to black and white and shades of gray, like a black and white television. If it's in black and white to begin with, add in nice, rich, fully realistic colors. How does this change affect your feelings?

Change it back to the way it was originally.

If it's in motion, like a movie, freeze the action like a photo. If it's stopped, make it into a movie. What happens to your feelings as you do this? You can experiment with slow motion and fast motion, as well.

Change it back to the way it was originally.

Step 5: Finally, experiment with the changes you made. Adjust the visual image until it gives you the best and strongest feelings it possibly can. Leave it that way and, in general, it will stay that way from now on.

There are several really cool things about this kind of experiment. One is that we have much more control over how we feel than most people realize. Second, it's possible to fine-tune the way we feel, and therefore our state of mind, by making these adjustments. This also gives us even more practice in holding and remembering those pictures in our minds. It lets us explore how the pictures and feelings get connected, which can actually help us pay attention to our bodies better than we have before. Paying attention to how we feel is an important part of life and it's probably one of the skills that get more and more lost as our lives become more intellectual. Thinking and feeling shouldn't be two unrelated kinds of experiences, and when they are, it usually spells trouble. Let's teach the kids how these things work. It can make them healthier and happier throughout their lives, as well as helping them learn better and more easily.

# EXPERIMENT: EXPLORING FEELINGS AND SOUNDS

The idea: This time we'll be exploring the sub-modalities of sounds and how those can change our feelings. Again, I suggest you do this experiment yourself first, before doing it with the kids.

Step 1: Choose another good state of mind from the last chapter, or a different one. Once again, your choice.

Step 2: Get into the state, as you did earlier, by clearly seeing the image, hearing the sounds, and noticing the feelings that go with it. Notice what is unique and special about this state of mind. Go through the questions on feelings, just as before:

Do you feel any tension or pressure anywhere in your body? Check from the top of your head to the bottom of your feet, a little at a time.
Do you feel warm or cool anywhere? Again, check from top to bottom.
Can you pinpoint the exact location of any tension or temperature changes inside or on the surface of your skin?
How intense are the feelings that go with this state of mind?
Do you feel any movement inside, or do you feel as if you are moving, or perfectly still?
Do you feel in balance? Light or heavy anywhere, or all over?
Do you feel any other sensations in your body?
Once you've noticed all the feelings, we can go on to the next step.

Step 3: Now pay close attention to the sounds that go with this state of mind.

Answer the following questions as a help (again, start with yourself, but ask the kids when it's time for them to do this):

What sounds do you hear, in this state of mind? What do you remember hearing?

Are there voices and words? Whose voices are they? Do you hear your own voice? Are you saying something to yourself that helps create the feeling that is part of this experience? How loud or soft are these sounds and voices? Pay special attention to your own voice in your mind.

> Are these voices and sounds high or low in pitch (high notes and low notes)?
>
> How about the voice tone(s)? Is it pleasant? Strong? Smooth? What description would you give of your own voice tone in your mind?
>
> Are any or all of the voices speaking quickly or slowly? Is there a particular rhythm to them? How about any of the other sounds?
>
> Exactly where do you hear each of these sounds? Inside your head or outside? Left, right, front, back, up, down? Can you point to the exact location of each sound or voice? How about your own voice? Where exactly do you hear it?

Once you've noticed all the sub-modalities of the sounds, we can go on to the next step.

Step 4: Now we're going to make adjustments to the sounds, and notice the changes in the feelings as we do each one. As before, do these one at a time, and take all the time you need. Remember to change the characteristics all the way back to the way they started before going on to the next one.

> As you do this, notice which changes you make to the sounds cause the biggest differences in how you feel. Pay special attention to the voices, especially your own voice in your mind as you talk to yourself. Also, notice if any of the changes you make affect the clarity of the voices and sounds.

First let's experiment with the volume of various sounds and voices. Turn up the sound so that it is all louder in your mind (again, not so that it is uncomfortable, just louder). Pay attention to how it changes the feelings. Notice from head to toe.

191

Then, turn the volume down so that it is softer. Make sure that you can still hear the sounds, just that they are soft. Notice how this changes the feelings.

Change it back to the way it was originally.

Now, experiment by turning each part of the sound (assuming there are various sounds present in your mind as you do this) up or down in volume. Especially do this with your own voice, and the voices of anyone else in your mind. Make each louder and softer and pay attention to how your feelings change.

Change all of them back to the way they were originally.

Now we're going to do the same thing we did with the volume, only this time with the pitch. Experiment first by tuning the sounds so that they all seem to be higher notes than they were to start with. Notice how your feelings change as you do this.

Then, tune it down so that all the tones are deeper in pitch and pay attention to the feelings.

Change it back to the way it was originally.

Now do this with each of the individual sounds, especially the voices. Tune them up to higher pitches, then down to lower, deeper ones. Notice how each one changes the way you feel.

Change all of them back to the way they were originally.

Try changing the voice tones themselves, so that they sound different. Experiment with different tonalities and find which create more pleasant feelings inside. Do this with each voice you hear and spend careful time on your own internal voice.

Change all of them back to the way they were originally.

Now, speed up the voices and other sounds, all together. Then slow them down. How does this change the way you feel? Try adjusting the rhythm in whatever ways you can, and notice any change that makes in your feelings, as well.

Change it back to the way it was originally.

This time, do the same thing, but for each individual sound and voice. As always, concentrate on your own voice and the voices of others in your mind for this. Speed up. Slow down.

Change all of them back to the way they were originally.

Experiment with moving the various sounds around to different locations. Move them inside of and outside of your head and in different directions. Above, below, left, right. Try moving them closer to you, then farther away. Pay attention to how each one, especially the voices, changes the way you feel as they move.

Change all of them back to the way they were originally.

Step 5:  Finally, experiment with all the changes you made. Adjust all of the sounds until they give you the best and strongest feelings you can get from them. Leave it that way and, again in general, it should stay.

Different cultures are different in the ways that they pay attention. It's even possible that they process certain kinds of sounds differently, inside their brains (though research on this is unclear). In most English-speaking countries, we don't seem to pay nearly as much attention to sounds as we could. This is the reason that people often complain that other people don't listen well. It's usually true. The same thing seems to be true inside our minds. Most of us talk to ourselves just about all the time. But we don't pay much attention to it. We also hear other people talking to us in our minds, if we take the time to pay attention. Whether we pay attention or don't, these internal sounds affect us. Strongly. If we listen we can take some control over the entire process. If we don't, the process will continue to control us.

## Advanced Combination Experiments

One thing all memory experts agree on is that the more sensory information you can connect to any new idea, the easier it will be to remember.[6] So beyond the individual skills of using each of the senses, learning to connect them together can be really valuable. The last experiment showed you how the pictures and sounds in our minds can affect our feelings. Actually, all of these sensory pieces are connected together in one big system.

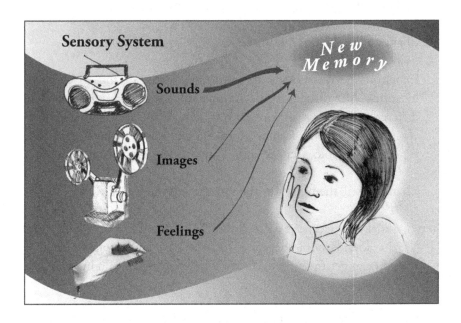

Figure 25: Our Sensory System and Memory

Each time we change a critical part of the system, the whole system changes in some way. Through exploring carefully, we can find out how each change actually affects us, but for now the important thing is to know that they do. Also, it turns out that if we carefully build a system for each experience, we can control how it looks, sounds and feels. Then it becomes a lot easier to remember. The more detail the better.

# EXPERIMENT: EXPLORING MEMORIES

The idea: This experiment is designed to help find out what makes something easier or harder to remember. It turns out that this can, partly, be based on the sub-modalities of each given memory. So we'll explore and compare a few and try to find some patterns that you and the kids can use.

Step 1: Think of three things you find easy to remember. These can be just about anything; experiences, quotations, formulas, names and dates, places you've been (or how to get there), whatever. To start with, though, you might want to choose three of the same kind of thing (three important memories, for example).

Step 2: For the first of these three, pay close attention to the visual image in your mind as you think about it. Notice the characteristics, brightness, size (or panorama), depth (3D or flat), color, motion and clarity, just as you did on the earlier images. Do the same for the sound: notice the volume, pitch, tonality, speed and location of the sounds and voices. Do this for the feelings as well, paying attention to any pressure or tension, temperature changes, where you feel these things, the intensity of the feelings, any sense of movement, your balance and anything else you notice. You may even want to make a couple of notes to yourself to help you remember.

Here again is the table to help guide you.

| Sensory Modalities | Visual | Auditory | Kinesthetic | Olfactory-Gustatory |
|---|---|---|---|---|
| Sensory Sub-Modalities | Brightness | Sounds/Words | Intensity | Intensity |
| | Location | Volume | Location | Sweet |
| | Size | Location | Size | Sour |
| | Shape | Pitch | Temperature | Bitter |
| | Depth | Tonality/Timbre | Pressure | Salty |
| | Color | Tempo (speed) | Movement | Pungent |

Figure 26: Sensory Sub-Modalities (repeat)

195

Step 3: Repeat what you just did for each of the other two you've chosen, paying close attention to all of the characteristics of the picture, sounds and feelings. Make notes if you need to.

Step 4: Now, compare these characteristics of each of these states (memories, ideas, or whatever they are). Do you notice a pattern in the characteristics? For example, are all of the visual images quite bright and clear, of the same size or similar in some other way? Do all of the sounds contain a single voice that is similar in tonality, location or volume? Is there some part of the feeling that is the same in each? Pay close attention to the similarities and, if you need to, make a note about them.

Step 5: Next, choose something that you've found difficult to remember in the past. Perhaps it is even a vague, distant, or fuzzy memory now. If you need to use something to remind you of it (a photograph, a book, etc.), do that.

Step 6: Repeat the part you did above when you carefully went through and explored the picture, sounds and feelings of this thing you've found difficult to remember. Again, if you need to, make some notes to yourself.

Note: You may find it difficult to see much of the image, hear it clearly or even have any strong feeling about it. That's the point.

Step 7: Do this again with two other things, of the same general kind as before, that you find hard to remember. Pay attention to the characteristics of the picture, sounds and feelings, and make notes about whatever you find.

Step 8: Compare the features of the memories you find difficult. Do you find patterns here as well? Perhaps all the images are in black and white, or they are small or distant, or even unclear. Maybe the sounds are indistinct or too soft to hear clearly. It might be that the feelings are dull, or even uncomfortable. Make any notes you need to about the things you find in common in these difficult to remember experiences.

For most people, these patterns become obvious right away. The things they find easy to remember give them a feeling of comfort, or confidence, or balance. Something "solid." The visual image is usually clear and bright, often looking exactly as it did originally. The same with the sounds. If you think about strong memories from your past, this is what *makes* them strong memories. Most of us find the opposite with things we don't remember well. We may have a vague sensation rather than a strong feeling. The pictures and sounds may be difficult, or even impossible, to bring back when we first try. That's why we call them "dim" "distant" or "vague" memories. We might even feel a struggle inside when we try to bring them back.

A few points are in order here. First and most important, the secret to memory is really in *preparing* to remember at the beginning, when we learn something, rather than trying to dredge it up later on (as I mentioned earlier). If we prepare properly, the memories can just pop up into our consciousness like they do when it's easy. We have to store memories, obviously, before we can recall them.

Second—what this chapter is about—if we make sure that our memories include all of the primary senses of sight, sound and feeling, they will be much stronger and easier to recall. This, literally, involves much more of our brain and body than if we just try to hold a picture by itself, or a phrase someone said, or what something felt like. If we can remember what the person looked like, the tone of their voice as well as the words, along with how we felt at the time, with all of the characteristic details, the memory is *complete* in every sense of the word. If we pay attention to all of those features when we are in the learning phase (storage, in memory terms) it will be much easier to bring them all back later (the recall phase).

Third, it's important to know that memory isn't just a function of our brain. It involves our whole body. The muscles and nerves that connect to them are as important in many memories as the connections inside our brains. This has been shown pretty conclusively in recent research.[7] This is why I'm having you spend so much time on how the pictures and sounds affect the feelings. It's a crucial part of remembering, as well as understanding in the first place. There is even strong evidence that powerful emotions, ones that really pump up our adrenaline, in some cases help make memories stronger.[8]

All of these processes have a strong sensory basis to them, inside our minds and bodies. Anything we can do to train, practice and improve our abilities to use the senses well, will improve our learning, understanding, storage and memory.

# EXPERIMENT: IMPROVING MEMORIES

In this experiment we'll be re-constructing whole experiences out of their pieces so that we control the images and feelings they give us. I strongly suggest, again, that you do this on your own first, before trying it with the kids.

Step 1: Take one of those vague, difficult-to-remember memories you were working with in the last experiment, or another if it's something you would like to retrieve.

Step 2: Explore all of the characteristics of the picture, sounds and feelings as you did earlier.

Step 3: Compare these sub-modality characteristics to the ones of the images you found easy to remember. Notice the major differences between the two memories. For example, the easier one is probably brighter, with a clearer picture and louder or more distinct sounds. It probably has a stronger feeling, as well. Make notes, if you want to, about the differences that are the most obvious.

Step 4: Now, close your eyes and relax as much as you can. Pull up the difficult memory in your mind and hold it as steady and clear as you can. Stay as relaxed as possible while you do this.

Step 5: While remaining relaxed, adjust the sub-modality characteristics, one at a time, so that they become like the easy-to-remember memory. For example, just make the picture you have in your mind brighter, without trying to do anything else. Then make the sounds louder. Next you might try adding color into the image, and slowing down the sounds, if it seems appropriate. Use the easy-to-remember characteristics as a guide. The goal is to get the difficult memory as clear as the easy one, just one small step at a time, staying relaxed and comfortable while you do it. Take all the time you need, and do your best, but don't force yourself or make yourself uncomfortable. Patience is vital with this.

Note: If this memory is too difficult, try another. You will find that you can adjust some memories much easier than others and some more quickly than others. It is very important to stay relaxed while you do this, or it probably just won't work. You may also find some very interesting patterns to which kinds of memories are easiest to adjust and get back fully. You will be able to do this completely with some memories but not others, using this method. Find out which ones you can.

Memory is dependent on lots of things, which is why it can be so fragile. It may depend on how the experience was built in the first place, where, when and with whom. You may find that the subject matter is important, or how much you were paying attention, and to which things that were happening. The emotional content, the state you were in, will certainly be a major factor, in some cases the most important. There may be other possible reasons that some memories are clearer than others as well. You will only find out if you experiment. We'll be coming back to these ideas later, in the chapter on studying.

# The Punch Line

One clear and very simple example of using these ideas—that we've been demonstrating for years—is spelling. Even though it may not be the most important thing in the world, it's a really good example of how to use the different senses, appropriately, to do things well. We found, years ago, what the differences are between the things people do inside their heads if they are good or bad at spelling. Big differences.

Maybe you remember being taught to "sound out" words to be able to spell them. I sure do. This is an excellent strategy for reading.

The problem with that auditory approach as a strategy for spelling, in a nutshell, is that words often aren't spelled the way they sound. There are exceptions to rules, silent letters, odd combinations and so on. In English we even have words that sound the same, but mean different things (right, write, rite). What good spellers do is to see the words in their mind, rather than sounding it out. The trick, obviously, is to remember exactly what the word looks like. The good news is that it's really pretty easy. I've been helping kids with this, and even doing spelling workshops for kids and their parents, for years.[9]

Here are the basic things the kids have to be able to do on a spelling test in school:

1. Hear the word
2. Remember what it looks like
3. Hold the "picture" in mind
4. Write down what they see

So here is a procedure you can follow to help your kids. The first part is to help them with their visualization skills, as we did earlier. You can make it more specific for spelling words in the following way:

1. Make your movie screen, as you did earlier
2. Show the kids the first word on their spelling list or just choose an easy one (cat, dog, etc.)
3. Have them put the word, in their mind's eye, on the screen
   Watch & listen to make sure that it's in the right place

   Note: If this is difficult, write it, or have them write it, in large letters on a piece of paper, and hold that in position, first. After they've had a little time to see it, have them hold it in their minds, then move it to the screen.

4. Adjust the *color of the word*
   Try red, black, blue, green and purple of various shades. Find out which is easiest to see clearly.
5. Adjust the *color of the background.*
   Have them imagine the screen itself changing colors. Try pale blue, pale green, pale yellow.

Find out which is easiest to see the words against, clearly.

6. Experiment with the *distance* of the viewing screen itself, until it's the clearest.
7. Try changing the *size* of letters.
8. Next adjust the *shape* & *weight* (font style) of the letters.
9. Have the kids *practice* all this, without the actual screen.
   The goal is to be able to do all this on their own "mental screen" inside their minds

We want to help the kids see the clearest possible image of the words in their minds. Again, when the kids know this, they can use it with each word they have to remember. The process will become automatic quickly, usually within a month of practice, but often much quicker.

To use the system in preparing for a spelling test, do the following steps:

1. *Show* the kids the first word on the list.
2. Have the kids take a mental *"snapshot"* of the word.
3. Ask them to *visualize*, and hold, the word on the mental screen in their mind.
4. Ask them to spell the word *backwards* first. That is, call out the letters in reverse order, from right to left—then forwards.
   This is to make sure they can clearly see the word. It's just as easy to spell backwards as forwards if you can, and they can't sound it out backwards.
5. Remind them how they did it, and practice.
6. Repeat this with each word they see on the list.
7. *Say* the first word on the list to them and make sure that they can get the image back clearly in mind (practice saying the word and having them see it at the same time if it's necessary, though it usually isn't).
8. *Practice* taking the spelling test, like it will be in class.

Good spellers clearly hear the words that are spoken during a test. They make clear images, and can hold the word in mind while they write it down. Maybe you're one of those people who have to write down words, to see them, to know if you have them right. Really good spellers do the same thing, only they do it in their mind's eye. They also feel funny if they don't have it quite right. You might do the same if you've written it down wrong. The only time they sound it out is if they aren't sure they've got the picture in mind. Sounding out the word, to spell it, is a backup strategy. So the entire process can involve pictures, sounds and feelings.

Spelling is just an example of this process. It can work for lots of other things as well, really anything that needs to be memorized in this way: formulas, multiplication tables, dates and places and more. Spend time with the kids going over the different kinds of things they have to know, and ask them to come up with ways to see, hear and remember them. They'll surprise you.

# The Tie-Up

Think about all the games you played as a kid, and the ones your kids play now. I'll bet you can come up with some that you did pretty well, too. It may not be chess, like those guys I mentioned at the beginning of this chapter. What about Monopoly? Remember what's next to what? Or cards: who picked up what, and what you had in the last hand you played. Maybe you're one of those people who collected baseball cards, or dolls, or coins, or stamps, or marbles, or butterflies, or whatever. I'll bet you could remember which ones you had. If you did baseball cards, you might even have been one of those kids who could quote statistics like an announcer on TV. This is part of growing up, and the things we choose to remember, the ones that are important to us, we seem to find a way to hold on to. My brother and I can still recite parts of comedy albums we listened to when we were kids. Your kids are no different. They are already playing games, singing songs, telling jokes and other activities that use these same skills. In fact, a lot of them are more complicated than anything we ever had, like computer games, video games and more. Maybe you can think of ways to enhance them so that they learn the variety that they need to, and can use them in the classroom and the rest of their lives. Better yet, maybe they can come up with some.

We've been doing these experiments with many thousands of adults, as well as children, in workshops all over the world for over 30 years now. The results are always that people discover things about their own thinking that they never knew. And they gain skill in thinking in ways that they didn't even know were possible. Maybe you can even get your kids to impress themselves.

*Children are wired for sound, but print is an optional accessory that must be painstakingly bolted on. This basic fact about human nature should be the starting point for any discussion of how to teach our children to read and write. We need to understand how the contraption called writing works, how the mind of the child works, how to get the two to mesh.*
Steven Pinker

# Chapter 14

# How to Learn From Reading

One of my two greatest lessons about reading came from a case study by a very famous psychiatrist named Milton H. Erickson, M.D. Erickson is generally considered to be the father of modern hypnosis and possibly the greatest psychiatrist that ever lived. In this particular case, Erickson worked with a 70-year-old woman who had been illiterate all of her life. He, however, believed she had all she needed, since she had tried to learn many times over the years. Erickson felt she simply needed to put the pieces together in a new way. He insisted to her, repeatedly, that he was not going to teach her ". . . anything that she did not already know and had known for a long time." Under hypnosis he had her "draw" shapes that were actually pieces of letters. Then he repeated this in her normal waking state. Over a series of a few sessions, he had her put these together, and then showed her a book, newspaper and magazine to verify that their letters matched hers. He taught her "letter building," "word building" and "naming." Then, the dictionary. Each piece was taught first under hypnosis, then fully awake. She learned to write (and read) in three weeks. Erickson believed that our unconscious minds know much more than our conscious minds ever could, and that "both minds" could learn to work together. He also believed that it is crucial to use exactly what people present to you to help them. He used her thinking, her abilities and her beliefs to help her. The result: she wrote and read voraciously for the rest of her life.[1]

This case shaped many of my ideas about reading problems in children and adults. Applying this idea to people with "dyslexia" I've been impressed that all of these people can read perfectly normally, as far as I can tell, once I help them discover what parts of the process are causing them difficulty. I've helped dozens (perhaps hundreds) of people individually and in workshops get rid of their reading disorders, usually in a matter of a few minutes. It hasn't seemed to matter what kind of problem they were having (reversing letters or words, seeing words jumble on the page, getting constantly confused trying to make sense out of the material, whatever). The things I've done with them have worked all of the time, in my experience. And they're all simple tools that I'll share with you here. Remember, though, I'm not talking about the *mechanics* of learning how to read. I'm talking about *understanding and learning* from reading in this chapter. I'll give some tips on mechanics later.

# The Underlying Principle

The fact that you are reading this means that you know reading can be valuable. Otherwise you wouldn't be doing it. In many cases the kids just don't know that. It's part of the learning process because if they can attach a value to it, they'll do it more and learn it faster and better. If it's hard at first, or even painful, it can stop the process dead in its tracks. With virtually every child or adult with a reading problem that I ever helped, the problem developed in the early stages. And it wasn't their fault. The teachers of these poor people just didn't do, often because they didn't know how to do, what was needed at the time. The good news, I discovered, is that you can find the point where the problem was, fix it, and the learning will take over naturally as it should have in the first place. It's usually easy as well, if you know how reading works.

Learning to read is different from learning from reading, so I want to be clear at the start about that. The two are different, and learned at different times, in different ways, and involve somewhat different skills.

The first part—actually learning how to read—means looking at the words on a page and knowing what they are (correctly). I'm not going to spend time on this here, mainly because it would take an entire book. Also, that book was written already by Diane McGuinness and is called *Why Our Children Can't Read and What We Can Do About It.*[2] Since that one, there have been several others, as well. If your child is having problems with these mechanics of reading, get one of these books, and whatever other help you need. Reading specialists are now generally quite well-trained in helping to resolve these basic reading problems.

Once the mechanics are taken care of, the second part of reading is the understanding and learning that comes from it. The person who taught me most about understanding what we read was a seven-year-old boy. This was the second major lesson I had about reading, so I'll tell you about it. His dad called me for an appointment a couple of days before my lesson was to begin, and told me that he had a second-grader with absolutely zero comprehension. When I asked him what he meant by zero, he said that his little boy could read really well, out loud, in fact better than anyone else in his class, according to his teacher. But, when you asked him what he'd just read, he had no idea. In fact, he had never gotten even one question right on any reading test. Well, I thought this was just way too cool.

So I asked Dad to bring him in to my office, and to bring his reading books with him so we'd have something to work with (and because I still didn't believe it). They came in a couple of days later, and I liked them both immediately. The boy was nice, obviously bright and well spoken for a seven-year-old, friendly and eager. So we sat down, and I asked him to show me his books. He had two. The first was one of those picture books, with about nine pictures on a page, with a sentence under each one that described what was in the picture. The other had no illustrations. I decided to start with the illustrated one and see what happened.

We opened to the first page, and the first picture, up in the upper left hand corner of the page. It was a picture of a cow in a field, jumping over a fence. I asked him to read the sentence underneath the picture to me:

Boy: The cow jumped over the fence.
Me: Good. What's that mean?
Boy: I have no idea.

Me:   Huh? But . . . you just read it to me fine.

Boy:  Uh, huh.

Me:   Well . . . read it again.

Boy:  The cow jumped over the fence.

Me:   (With enthusiasm) *Great!* Now, what's that mean?

Boy:  I don't know.

Me:   (Finding it difficult to breathe) OK, let's look at the words. What's that word (pointing to "cow")?

Boy:  Cow.

Me:   Good. Do you know what a cow is?

Boy:  Sure. An animal, where we get our milk from. I've seen them before, everybody knows what a cow is.

Me:   OK. How about this word (fence).

Boy:  Fence.

Me:   And do you know what a fence is?

Boy:  (Being wonderfully patient with me, like his dad) Of course. We have a fence around our yard. You see them all the time.

Me:   (Still confused, looking over at Dad) Is this what it's like all the time?

Dad:  Yep.

Me:   Wow. (Turning back to the boy) OK. Here's what we're going to do. You know what a cow is, right?

Boy:  Yeah.

Me:   And you know what a fence is.

Boy:  (Nods)

Me:   So what would it look like if a cow was jumping over a fence? Can you tell me?

Boy:  Sure. First you'd have a cow, like in a field. Then there'd be this fence going across and the cow would be jumping, in the air, over the fence. So he'd be up over the fence in the air (showing me with his hands, communicating beautifully).

Me:   (More enthusiastic than ever) *GREAT!* Now, read that sentence again, one more time!

Boy:  The cow jumped over the fence.

Me:   Right! What's that mean?!

Boy:  I don't know.

Me:   (Just about losing it . . .) Well . . . Uh . . . *look at the picture!*

Boy: (Looks at the picture for about 3 seconds, gets wide-eyed, slaps himself on the forehead, *hard*) That's the picture we just made, of the cow jumping over a fence!

Me: (Whining) I know.

Boy: (Almost screaming) *That's what it means??!!*

Me: Yeah!

Boy: (Still real loud and very upset) So all the pictures are the same as the words?

Me: (Apologetic) Uh, huh.

Boy: Are they all like that?

Me: (More apologetic) Uh, huh.

Boy: Why didn't they tell me that?!

Me: (Almost pleading) I don't know.

Boy: (Still upset) Why didn't they?

Me: (Trying bravely . . .) Maybe you were absent that day?

Boy: I don't think so . . . .

We talked for a while and looked at the book. He looked over the rest of the pictures, read the words, and connected them together in his mind just fine, with no trouble. After a few minutes, when we all calmed down from the ordeal of discovery, and his disappointment with his teachers, I asked him to pick up the other book.

This one, remember, had no pictures. So I told him the object here was to make your own, in your mind, just like we did with the first picture of the cow jumping over the fence. So we looked at a paragraph. I had him read the first sentence, and construct the picture in his mind, step by step using each word in the sentence. When he had a nice clear image, I asked him to imagine holding that image up in the left hand corner in his mind's eye. Then we did the same thing with the next sentence. This time, though, I asked him to put that picture right next to the other one, just to the right. We repeated this until the end of the paragraph. At the end he had five or six pictures (one for each sentence) arranged in a row, left to right. I had him read the paragraph to me one more time. Then I asked him to describe each of the pictures to me, in order, one at a time. He could do this easily.

At this point, Dad jumped in and said: "You know, I don't read so good either. I wonder if this is the same problem I have." All three of us talked about the whole process for a few minutes. I told them that the task of reading is to make your own pictures out of the words. Then you can also add in sounds and feelings, if that's what the words tell you to do. Comprehension is being able to do this part. Remembering later is being able to get back the pictures, sounds and feelings—the whole movie you've made in your head. Obviously some reading will be easier than others, depending on how much the author gives you. The more the author tells you about the movie in his or her head, the easier it is to make the same one in yours.

Since both of them needed a little practice, I told them to do it together for a couple of weeks, and give me a call and let me know how they were doing. It just so happened that the day after our session together, the boy had had a comprehension test in class. Dad told me he got an 85%, a really good grade.

Many of us have had the feeling, at some point in our lives, that there was some secret that everyone else knew but we didn't. And that secret was the one thing keeping us from success and happiness in our lives. Sometimes, at least in this case, it's true, only it isn't really a secret. It's just some crucial piece of information that pulls everything else together and makes it work. In the case of reading, the secret is to be able to get the *reference experience*, the pictures, sounds and feelings, out of the words we read, and put them together in our mind the way the person who wrote it did in theirs. Being able to remember it, usually, means to get back the reference experiences we made. There may be certain cases in which we have to get back the actual words themselves, like in memorizing a poem or the lines in a play, but those are relatively rare.

Simply stated, the steps in successful reading are clear. It's being able to do each one, and remembering to do each one, until it becomes automatic, that makes reading a smooth, natural and productive (and enjoyable) process. The steps in understanding and learning from reading would include:

Seeing the words
Understanding what each word is and what it means
Translating each word, or at least the whole idea, into its reference experience (picture, sound, feeling)
Gathering the reference experiences together into a coherent sensible package
Remembering the package later on when it's important

# The Set-Up

My friend Claudia has two wonderful kids. Her oldest is Camille. A friend of theirs brought some children's books over for Camille when she was about three. Camille walked over and started to go through the books, looking at the covers. Then she started to read the titles to Claudia and her friend. They were stunned. Claudia asked: "When did you learn how to read?" Camille just laughed.

Kids want to be able to read. It's that simple. If you sit and read a book or the paper in front of a young child they become immediately curious. They'll often come over and look over your shoulder or get between you and the paper (so will your cat, but that's different . . .). The kids want to do it with you. When they are old enough to be read to, say at bedtime, this curiosity expands. Just like little Camille, they'll pick up a lot naturally, if you show them what it's all about. Simply pointing out the words in their favorite stories, as you say each one, will help those connections to get made. Doing it over and over (and over, as you beg your kids: "Please, not *that* story again!") is actually what makes it easier and more fun for them.

It doesn't matter what age your kids are, you can read things that are interesting to them, and share those things. If your kids have trouble, you'll usually know, and you can help them by reading along with them or even just talking about what things mean to you. Like anything else, you have those reference experiences in your mind each time you read something, so ask the kids what their internal experiences are. We'll cover this in more detail next.

# The Delivery

I don't know if you are one of those people who are, in a sense, addicted to reading. What I mean by that is, whenever and wherever you land (sit, lie down, find yourself stuck to a spot) you look around immediately for what there is to read. The doctor's office. The supermarket checkout line. Bus. Plane. Stuck in traffic. Anyplace. If there is something there, you pick it up, look at it, read it. No matter if it would normally hold any interest at all, it's just there, so it has to be read. Are you like that? I am. Reading material jumps into my hands and eyes wherever I am, whether I'm interested or not. I'm a knowledge junkie. A bad one.

Years ago a friend of mine told me that he had decided to do something with his reading addiction, to make it more worthwhile. He'd simply put something worth reading in every place he was likely to land. Every chair or spot in the house. In his car, for really bad traffic. At work, for breaks. The bathroom (of course). Even in his pocket while shopping, so when he had to wait to check out, he could read *his* stuff instead of theirs. It worked. I did the same and it worked for me. I still read all kinds of other stuff when I get stuck, but I've made that into an exercise to expand myself into new areas. I sometimes read things, purposely, that I think won't have the slightest bit of interest for me. Sometimes I find out just how wrong I can be about that. It's wonderful.

How about you? Do you enjoy reading? Are you addicted? What do you like to read? Why—what do you like about it? How does it affect you? What do you think, feel or remember during and after you read? These are basic questions that all adults (who read) ought to be able to answer, given a little time for thought. The same should be true of the kids, eventually, but they probably haven't taken the time to make those observations and decisions the way an adult would. Unless the kids have fully mastered the *process* of reading, and it has become easy and natural for them, they won't be able to make those decisions at all.

This is the place to begin with your kids. First, of course, you have to know what level of reading they can handle. For example, if they can read, you'll want to find out the answers to those questions I just asked you. If not, you'll have to help them learn to read and save those questions for later. For now, let's talk about learning *from* reading.

I always like to start with kids reading something that's totally fun for them. It doesn't really matter what it is; it's the process that's important here. You should know what your kids are reading and what they like and don't like. If you don't, find out. Remember, we don't want to make judgments about their taste. If it's exactly the same as ours, there is something seriously wrong. I always encourage kids to read what they enjoy, even if it's the horrible-death-and-destruction-slasher-from-another-planet-comic-about-the-video-game-from-hell-that-all-parents-are-terrified-of . . . I, personally, don't care. They're reading, and that's a start. You, of course, will have to make your own judgments about that. But find out what they like about the things they do like; and find out if they understand it and have an easy time reading it.

Also, it's worthwhile to read together, for several reasons. First, it lets the kids know that you read and that you value it. Second, they may pick up some of the ways that you understand, just from being there with you (no guarantees about that, of course). More important, it gives you the opportunity to find out how well they are doing with their reading and help them along. This helping includes every part of the process from seeing the words, to understanding the meaning, to relating it to other things they know. Most of all, it builds in the habit of reading. I like to have people start with easy things, then progress to more difficult ones during this process. Start with comic books or the comics in the paper, especially if you don't know how your kids are doing. It's fun and non-threatening. Next, go to fun magazines, even kids' magazines if you have access to those. They're usually designed pretty well for the kids. Then go on to good newspapers, or news magazines, the ones you find you enjoy. Later you can include short stories, novels, poetry and finally their schoolwork to go over together.

With younger kids especially, start with comics or other illustrated reading, since the pictures will help them build some pictures in their minds while they read. Work up to ones without illustrations. The reading can go from easier to more difficult as you go along. One clue to the reason something may be difficult to read, besides the difficulty of the vocabulary or concepts, is the language itself. If you look at some of the things you read, for example a good novel, you'll find lots of sensory words. The author will literally tell you what to see, what to hear and what to feel. All of the sensory representations will be really clear. More difficult reading, complex textbooks, professional publications and the like will have very little of this in most cases. That's what makes these things more difficult to read. It's unfortunate that people write that way, but we all have to learn to read and understand this kind of writing in some circumstances so it's worthwhile to practice with the kids. The initial struggle pays off later.

During your practice, you want to check how well the kids do on each of the different major skills of reading that I described earlier. I can't give you effective specific exercises to do like before because I don't think that's the best way to help your kids with reading. The best way is to do it together, interactively. Asking questions and sharing your understanding, what you see, hear and feel while you're reading, seems to me the best way to help the kids. Here is what you need to do for each of the various skills:

## Seeing the Words

This sounds too obvious, but a lot of people, especially kids when they are in the learning process, don't actually look at what's on the page. Remember, I'm not talking about kids who don't know or can't recognize the words; that's a different problem. I mean the ones who *can* understand, but don't. The two biggest problems I've noticed are: 1) They go too fast; and/or 2) They get lost in what they are doing in their own minds and don't really pay attention to what's on the page. At one time or another, we've probably all done these. Each of these can become a real problem if they turn into habits during the learning stages. Each usually has a specific reason, as well, and if you can find out what the reason for the problem is it might make it easier to solve.

For the problem of going too fast, there are two very common reasons. The first is obvious: lots of kids are in a hurry to get done so that they can do something else. It doesn't matter what that something else is, but what happens is that they go so fast that they don't have time to see the distinctions that separate one word from the next (much less make the reference experiences, they need while they read). When they've been reading well enough, for enough years, this is less of a problem because our brains can really do this process like lightning. Eventually, seeing every word isn't really very important. When they are learning, though, they need to take enough time to make it work. The second common reason I've run into for going too fast is that the kids are so nervous about their performance that they just want to be done, even before they've started.

Part of the solution here, for either reason, is to remind the kids that if they take the time to really understand what they read, it will save them from having to go over it again later. Also, they should understand that the more time they spend doing this carefully now, the less and less they'll have to do it as they go on. Of course, lots of kids can't think past the next three to five minutes (seconds) into the future, so that explanation will fall flat for them. This is where practicing together comes in.

Personally, my way of helping is that I've simply made them slow down, really slow in some cases, to the point that it's easy. I tell them it isn't a race and that they should make themselves so comfortable and relaxed that they can't make any mistakes (this isn't literally true of course, but the *idea* seems very helpful).

I usually combine this with an anchor to be relaxed and comfortable while they read. This is especially important for the kids who are nervous about performing or doing it perfectly. They need to relax, and we want that calm feeling to be automatic whenever they pick something up to read. The information should get them excited, not the task.

Finally, you can set up experiments, contests and games with them that force them to pay close attention to be able to play. You can also *use* games that do that, and you may already have some that they like. If they like it, they'll focus.

The problem of getting lost in their own thoughts is one common to all of us at some time or another. We do it in conversation with people, as well, when we don't really hear what they're saying because we are focused inside our heads, instead of on the person talking. When something is coming into our minds, we need a way to process it. This includes connecting it to reference experiences that allow us to understand its meaning. But we also have to continue to pay attention while it keeps coming. The solution is to give each one its turn, the information coming in and the processing. When we're talking with someone, it's actually more polite most of the time to ask him or her to hold on for a moment, or repeat what was said, to give us time to understand and appreciate it. We can help the kids do the same when they're reading. I've often taught kids to purposely look up, away from what they're reading, while they think about what they just read. Then they can look at it again when they're ready. This can be really helpful in giving them the time to construct the images they need to make sense out of the reading. If you've done the exercises in the previous chapter—on where they should look while making images—all the better.

## Understanding What Each Word Is and What It Means

Professional educators talk about "word attack skills." That always sounded to me like I should beat up the book if I didn't like the words. What they really mean is figuring out what a word is, in some systematic way, when you see it. This process is actually two parts. The first is recognizing the word itself. Knowing that "house" is "house" and not "mouse" or "louse" (or "Kentucky" for that matter). Word recognition, as this is called, is of course the first part of learning to read. It involves recognizing the letters, and hearing the sounds that each makes, as it becomes a word. This is a whole system in itself—and not the part I want to concentrate on here—because as far as I can tell this is mostly a matter of exposure to the words and practice. Once the kids have been taught the basic skills, they can do this.

Obviously, we also have to know what the words *mean* to be able to get the meaning from what we read. We don't always take the time to do it. Most of us have learned to get the main points out of what we read even without having to know every word. This is certainly OK, but when kids are learning, they can't be quite as lax. They might not have enough experience to make the same sense out of something that we might be able to. The kids can get the meaning of words they don't know in two main ways. One is from stopping and going to the dictionary to look it up (or asking "dictionary mom"). The other is from figuring out what the word must mean from the context, the other words and sentences around it. The first is slow but sure, the second fast but risky. The more experience we have, the more we can rely on context. Finding the meaning from context means that you have overall images (part of the movie) already and can figure out what's possible from those to get the meaning of the word. Whether this is something your kids can do is a judgment call, and you'll have to read with them to find out how successful they are at it.

Personally, I always found helping kids with this to be pretty straightforward. I simply shared my understanding of what the words meant, and as long as the relationship was working, it was OK. There are books that you can get that cover certain patterns of problem words and other stuff like that, but lots of people now seem to believe that this isn't the best way to go about it.[3] Many kids seem to just get the whole idea about what they read through experience *and guidance*. Again, sharing what you actually see on the page, what you hear in your head, and how you understand the individual words usually seems to be enough. The kids will get the idea, and the skill, with some practice.

# "Translating" Each Word, or at Least the Whole Idea, into Its Reference Experience (Picture, Sound, Feeling)

This is really no more than the process I described when I was helping that little seven-year-old boy. This means taking the time, as we go through, to help the kids make the images in their minds that correspond to what's written on the page. It depends partly on understanding the words themselves, and partly on how good we, or the kids, are in making those pictures, sounds and feelings. What we were doing in the last chapter, and all through this book, helps. We just need to make sure that their reference experiences correspond to the dictionary's reference enough to make the same sense out of what they read as everyone else (or the author who wrote it, in an ideal world). This is the part where asking questions and sharing can help the most:

"What picture do you have in mind when you read that?"
"Can you hear what their voices must sound like as these two characters talk?"
"What do you say to yourself about that?"
"Doesn't that story make you feel excited (scared, disgusted, curious, etc.)?"
"What do you think that character feels (sees, hears) in this situation?"

The answers to those questions will tell you what the kids got out of the reading, in terms of their actual pictures, sounds and feelings. Then you can share yours. The more detail they can develop in each area, the more impact the reading is actually having on them. If your kids like to draw, that can be a great way to make this into a fun game. Have them make their own little cartoons about what they read. Instructional techniques aren't important here. Doing it together is.

Sometimes this is easy, for example in a story as a scene is described, or when things happen in chronological order. Sometimes, though, it's a little tougher, as in a description of a theory or method or principle of some sort in which the order is simply part of a bigger picture. In that case, sometimes this is about seeing a series of pictures and, literally, putting them together like a puzzle so that they fit into a bigger picture. Sometimes it may involve a series of definitions, where each word connects to something else and becomes more of a way of talking

215

about something than seeing it clearly in our mind's eye. So, as you read different kinds of writing, you would read each one in the same way, but you'd have to decode each one differently.

For example, here is a scene from a book by John Updike, one of the great writers, called *S*.[4]

> The roads down here are *endless*, and mostly dirt packed into ruts and ripples. It seemed to take forever to drive that forty miles, bumpety-bump-bump, trailing this enormous cloud of dust. I don't see how people in Arizona can have any secrets, because anywhere you go you leave this giant clue of dust in the air for hours. Not that there were any houses or people that I could see—not a sign of life except a few sorry-looking cattle and a lot of black-faced sheep who leave their wool snaggled all over the barbed wire. All the time, you are gradually rising, and the sagebrush, or maybe it's mesquite, getting sparser around you, and the ground rockier, and then suddenly you're overlooking this valley with tidy long fields of different shades of green, and yellow bulldozers and school buses crawling around on a system of roads below, and this big flat-roofed mall and rows of aluminum trailers, and on a shelf above them rows of A-frames being constructed on red earth scraped into shelves, and in the center of everything a sort of blue-paved space with an actual fountain, a fountain surrounded by rainbows and spray.

The following passage is from a story called "Way in the Middle of the Air" in *The Martian Chronicles*,[5] by Ray Bradbury:

> Silence.
>
> The men on the porch listened.
>
> Hearing nothing, they extended their thoughts and their imaginations out and into the surrounding meadows. In the early morning the land had been filled with its usual concoctions of sound. Here and there, with stubborn persistence to custom, there had been

voices singing, the honey laughter under the mimosa branches, the pickaninnies rushing in clear water laughter at the creek, movements and bendings in the fields, jokes and shouts of amusement from the shingle shacks covered with fresh green vine.

Now it was as if a great wind had washed the land clean of sounds. There was nothing.

This next passage is from a story called "Ernest and the Machine God" in a collection called *Deathbird Stories,*[6] by Harlan Ellison.

Blessed cool wetness cascaded over her hot face, and she opened her eyes. Stringy moist strands of auburn hair hung across her face, and she moved her head idly, shaking them back with difficulty. Then she tried using her arms. They were limp from having been in that bloodless position for so long. But agonizingly . . . she drew her left hand up onto her lap. Her dress was soaked through, on the left side . . . .

Selena rolled her body back against the seat, and a surf-crash of sickness broke over her. She pulled the door handle and barely managed to swing the door out and up, realizing the car was tilted. The door was incredibly heavy. But she threw her weight against it, and fell from the car. The slamming door barely missed her legs.

The rain helped.

In a few moments she was able to stand, leaning against the side of the car. Her knees were filthy with road mud. The storm beat against her . . . .

These are all examples of wonderfully descriptive writing and it's obvious that these authors are excellent at getting their ideas across. This is, in general, the easiest writing to understand, and when it's done well, it draws you into the story. Did you notice the difference between the three examples while you were reading? If you look back at them now, the first passage, from Updike, is extremely *visual*. He's painting a picture for us as we read it. The second, from Bradbury, is almost entirely *auditory*; it's about the sounds. The Ellison passage is extremely kinesthetic. You can almost feel each movement the character makes. Now that you know that, think back on the effect each one had on you as you read it. Was it different? Was one easier than the others? More interesting? More to your *taste*? Each of these authors is fully capable of writing in any of these ways, or any combination, whenever they want to (and they do, all the time). They *chose* to write each of these passages in this way on purpose, to create the sensations they wanted in us as we read their words.

There are, obviously lots of other kinds of writing besides fiction, and much of what kids learn in school involves these. Here are some selections that are examples of the difference. I've chosen ones much more on an adult level, so you can have the kind of experience that your kids often have in making sense out of them. This first selection is from Thomas L. Friedman, who at the time was the New York Times Foreign Affairs correspondent, from his book *The Lexus and the Olive Tree*,[7] about the politics and economics of globalization.

> As we increasingly move into a world where the Internet defines commerce, this push for common global standards is going to become hugely intensified, for one very simple reason: from the minute you decide to do business on the Internet as a retailer or service provider, from the first moment you open your Web site, you are a global company—whether you are in India, Italy or Indianapolis. To do business on the Internet is by definition to be global. Therefore, you have to think globally and you have to think about what will appeal to and attract global buyers of whatever you are selling. And you'd better be able to assure customers that you can ship your goods in a timely and safe fashion, that their credit card number will be safe in your site, that money can be transferred according to international standards, laws and best practices and that all accounting and commercial issues will be dealt with according to international norms.

The following is from an article by science writer and biologist Stephen Jay Gould, in a book called *Predictions*,[8] about advances in science and other areas of our lives.

. . . human futures are unpredictable and it is futile to think that past trends will forecast coming patterns. The trajectory of technology might offer some opportunity for predicting the future—as science moves through networks of implication, and each discovery suggests a suite of subsequent steps. But even the 'pure' history of science features unanticipated findings, and must also contend with nature's stubborn tendency to frustrate our expectations—factors that will cloud anyone's crystal ball.

Moreover any forecast about the future must consider the incendiary instability generated by interaction between technological change and the weird ways of human conduct, both individual and social. How can the accidents that shaped our past give any meaningful insight into the next millennium? Pasts can't imply futures because a pattern inherent in the structure of nature's materials and laws too often disrupts an otherwise predictable unfolding of historical sequences.

This next passage is from a little book called *The Problems of Philosophy*,[9] by the great mathematician and philosopher Bertrand Russell.

The world of existence is fleeting, vague, without sharp boundaries, without any clear plan or arrangement, but it contains all thoughts and feelings, all the data of sense, and all physical objects, everything that can do either good or harm, everything that makes any difference to the value of life and the world. According to our temperaments, we shall prefer the contemplation of the one or of the other. The one we do not prefer will probably seem to us a pale shadow of the one we prefer, and hardly worthy to be regarded as in any sense real. But the truth is that both have the same claim on our impartial attention, both are real, and both are important to the metaphysician.

In each of the above selections there is much less obvious use of pictures, sounds and feelings to convey to us a direct experience. Instead, these writers are giving us their ideas in a more *conceptual* way. We have to work a little to make our own images in our minds, to make our own sense out of what these writers, also very great ones, are trying to tell us. You may notice, if you look back over them, that the first, from Thomas Friedman, is at least filled with things we know about: the Internet, regions—even specific cities—of the world, business and economics, and how people relate to each other. This allows us to make our images of these things reasonably easily. The next selection, from Stephen Jay Gould, is more difficult because the things he talks about—science, progress, technology, history, human conduct—are much more abstract. If you're not used to reading about these ideas, it can be quite a challenge. The third passage, from Bertrand Russell is by far the most difficult, because there is very little reference to anything in our everyday lives. It is, by its nature, extremely conceptual; in fact, that's what it's about. Unless you have some background in the field of philosophy, it would be quite difficult to understand what Russell is talking about, not to mention relate it to your own ideas and experience. Yet, this is how much of what we read is written.

Even more of a challenge are writings that are *metaphorical* in nature. In those cases, the writing itself may or may not be difficult, but it's *not really about what it says it is*. Metaphors are about something else. You have to figure out what, and then relate it to your own ideas and experience. Some people seem naturally gifted in decoding symbolism and metaphor in writing, while others are much more literal, meaning they prefer (find it easier, usually) to take things on face value. In fact, we are all built to be able to do both. Teaching and practice make it work.

I could give you an unlimited number of examples of different kinds of writing, but I think you have the idea. If you spend time looking over examples of the things your kids are reading in school, it should become obvious to you what they have to do to make sense of them. Talk with them about this, and the different things they're asked to read, and they'll get the idea, as well. In time, with practice and good guidance, they'll develop various ways of reading to accommodate various kinds of writing.

## Gathering the Reference Experiences Together into a Coherent Sensible Package

As we've gone over several times, putting ideas together to form bigger ideas, conceptualization, is a skill in itself. In the case of reading, this is usually done in a sequence first. In other words, taking the ideas in the order they come, and understanding and remembering the order so that you can follow what's going on. This is what we want for the kids.

Sometimes it means having the kids be able to re-explain what they've read in their own words. The act of doing that forces them to put the ideas together. It also takes practice, and in the long run kids are usually asked to write their understanding in a paper, or on a test. If they can say it, they can write it. If they can discuss it intelligently, and answer questions and challenges, they'll make the ideas their own.

## Remembering the Package Later on When It's Important

We've talked a bit about memory already. Reading is no different from other things we need to remember. It involves (1) controlling the state we're in while we're reading, (2) planning to remember later (future-pacing, practicing as necessary), (3) and actually remembering later by calling up the images and feelings that have been stored. We'll talk more about this in the chapter on studying. If the kids can do the kind of discussion and explanation, in their own words, that we just talked about, this will set up their ability to remember nicely.

# The Punch Line

There is a movie about the game show scandal in the 60's called Quiz Show. One of the main characters in this true story is shown with his family over what is, apparently, a typical dinner in their home. Each member of the family recites a passage from one of Shakespeare's plays and the others have to name the play, the scene and the act. The amazing thing is that they *can!* This might be taking the idea of reading together a bit too far for most of us, but it's fascinating to watch truly gifted people sharing the love of reading and knowledge. Clearly, at least in the movie, this was a lot of fun for them.

I would never suggest that this be the goal. It would be ridiculous for most of us. But the idea of sharing and enjoying reading isn't ridiculous—it's smart. What will make it worthwhile is planning and sharing with the kids in a way that makes it fun for your family. The fact that it's *possible* to do the kinds of things shown in that movie should be an inspiration, even if it isn't a goal.

Regardless of what level of reading your kids can do now, eventually you want to share the love of reading with them. Sharing means both of you get to share and talk about what you read and what you get out of it. It might mean even be willing to read each other's stuff, so you can really share. It's like watching TV or going to the movies together. You don't always have to like the same things, but the sharing is good for the relationship and for the building of knowledge and experience that comes from the activity. Reading is a natural part of modern life, and it's one of the most wonderful. If you're reading this book, you probably already believe that.

## The Tie-Up

I once had an adult student in one of my professional training programs who told us he was severely learning disabled and unable to read. When we got to know him a little better, it was obvious that this wasn't really true. We gave him a number of different kinds of things to read. He read technical material, detailed instruction manuals and the like, with no difficulty. He could get through the newspaper OK. When he tried to read a novel, he froze up and got confused and scared. He had difficulty following story lines and wanted to avoid it altogether. In his mind, he couldn't read. What he *meant* was that he couldn't read everything comfortably, and he was so disappointed about it that he diagnosed himself as disabled.

The importance of reading well is obvious. However, like everything else, unless the kids enjoy it, they won't do it. You probably wouldn't either (maybe you don't, and need to do more of what's here for yourself). Perhaps you've found certain things to read that are easy and others you avoid. That's true for most people. There are successful people around the world who limit themselves to what they *have* to read. There are many I've met who have managed to manufacture their work life in such a way that there is *nothing* they have to read. For the most part, when I'm on airplanes (a lot of the time) surrounded by corporate managers, engineers, and consultants (like myself), they're reading big fat novels. Eventually, most educated adults include reading into their lives in some fundamental way. Let's give the kids free choice by making them comfortable with all kinds of reading, rather than having to settle for what they can handle (or stand).

One way to increase the kids' range of choices is to help them develop a variety of ways of reading, as they get more practice. For example, think about how you read. It may be that you read every single word of everything you see, but I doubt it. Most of us have learned to skim over things and find what we're looking for when we need to, or if we're in a hurry. We've also developed some way of getting really deep into things we especially enjoy. Maybe, for example, when reading a set of instructions, you read one, imagine doing it (or look at the thing you have to assemble, for example), then read the next instruction, until you feel ready to begin to tackle the job. Maybe you skim over some of them and only spend time on the hard ones. Or maybe you skip the hard ones and try to work it out on your own. When many people in business get a new computer program, they just boot it up and ignore the manual altogether. Often that's the best choice, since most of the manuals are awful. But the point is that all of these are just that: choices. You can only make a choice if you have a choice.

Reading, like most other things in life, will depend on our intentions. What we want from our reading will determine how we read it, how fast and how much. It will also determine how much we try to remember, while we're doing it. That's what will help us or hinder us later when we need it. There are many reading programs out there in the world, in schools, private tutoring, workshops and seminars and in books. I recommend that everyone who cares about learning look into them for themselves as well as their kids. The learning we all got in school about reading was very limited. It can be much better, but we have to go out there and find it. Of these programs, the good ones all help people read faster and with better comprehension. The better ones provide choices in how to read different kinds of material. The best can change your life and the lives of your kids.[9] See the section on recommended reading in the back of this book for more information.

# Chapter 15

# How to Communicate Effectively

I will always remember public speaking class when I was in high school. Most people who have taken a course like that in school remember it as well, usually for the utter terror that went with standing in front of the class. I had a different experience, however. I remember the very first presentation I had to give, and how afraid I was beforehand. But, because I was scared, I prepared a lot. I followed instructions and did what I was told. At the end of my talk, which was actually a reading, I looked up to a class that was totally silent, staring at me, looking a bit stunned. For a moment I wondered if my fly was unzipped, or something. But then, a girl sitting in the front row, one of the "class brains," said: "That was wonderful!" Then everyone else joined in, including the teacher. *I* was stunned.

The effect of the experience was to make it easy and comfortable for me to speak in front of groups of people, large and small. I often wonder what it would be like if we could engineer something like that for everyone. For most people, speaking in front of others is nerve wracking and, in fact, for 50% of the population in the United States it is really terrifying. Among phobias, this is the most common. What a shame. Why are we so afraid of one another? *I'm afraid* that most of that fear is learned in school. After all, it's the first place most of us are called on to talk in front of groups. I think it extends to writing, as well, for lots of people, and this is what makes it difficult for people to write clearly and confidently. I'm also convinced that it doesn't have to be that way. Communicating doesn't have to be so hard.

Effective communication is the process of getting our ideas into someone else's mind in a way that changes them. Period. This means that we have to know what pictures, sounds and words and feelings we have: our reference experiences. These are what we want to give to others, but we have to do it in a way that they can take those reference experiences and make them their own. So there is a translation process again, but as long as there is a decent relationship established, we can do it.

Ask your kids to tell you about the people, friends, relatives, teachers and others they like, trust and get along with great. Ask them to describe what makes it easy in their communication with these people. You'll get a variety of answers, but I'll bet they include things like:

"It's just easy."
"They understand me without a lot of talking."
"We see eye to eye."
"They listen to me and I listen to them."
"We feel the same way about stuff."
"We both know how the other thinks."

Next, ask them about people they don't get along with, relatives, teachers, or others. You'll hear very different descriptions, like:

"It's too hard."
"They don't understand me no matter what I do."
"We don't see things the same."
"They don't listen to me and I don't want to listen to them."
"We feel different about everything."
"I never can figure out what they think."

These are all the same kinds of things adults (yeah, you) say. In my work in consulting and training, in businesses and organizations in various countries around the world, it's the same everywhere. People complain about communication more than anything else, and they also say it's the most important thing that connects them to the people they care about. It's universal.

We will never be able to open up someone's head and get their ideas right out. We can't pour ours in either, much as we might like to. What we *can* do is ask questions about how others see and hear things, and how they feel. This goes for teachers, fellow students and everyone else in our lives.

So many of the things that happen to us in school, even the little things someone says, a compliment or an insult, can mean so much and make such a difference in our lives. I always wished that I had had some great experience with my writing as a kid, like with that little presentation in speech class. When I tried writing my first book, I went through all the fear of doing it well that many people do when they are speaking to a group. Worse, I didn't really know how to do it. It took three tries.

After the book was published I spent some time with one of my NLP students, a college writing teacher named Dixie Elise Hickman, Ph.D. She was able to show me all the reasons I had so much difficulty, and even help me figure out what was different when I was finally able to do it. With that, we were able to add some things to what writing instructors already know, and develop a new model anyone can use in writing, speaking or any other communication that's important.[1]

# The Underlying Principle

Like most of the other things we have to do in life, there are steps to follow in writing that make it work much more smoothly. We really do have to break large tasks down into smaller ones, usually, to make them easy enough to do, without scaring or overwhelming ourselves. These steps, in the form Dixie and I developed them, are called the **POWER** model:

**P**reviewing
**O**rganizing
**W**riting
**E**valuating
**R**evising

I'm going to go through all of these in just enough detail so you can help the kids. The first step, **P**reviewing, is going to be the most important in writing for school. It breaks down into five elements to consider for getting clarity about the communication context, the **SPACE** in which the communication will happen. It's this SPACE that we Preview in this first step:

> **S**elf: who you are as a person, your role and point of view in this writing
> **P**urpose: what you want to accomplish, what you want the reader to do
> **A**udience: who is reading this (usually the teacher) and what they want
> **C**ode: how it's supposed to look and sound, and what form it will take
> **E**xperience: what you know and can find out to include in the writing

> Once you've effectively finished determining the SPACE elements (which are really effective for planning *anything*), the next step is:

> **O**rganizing: putting the content, the Experience, into some useful format or order

This will be in the form of outlines, lists or other formats. It can even be a set of instructions for how to write what you've decided you need to, a step-by-step procedure for writing. The order of all the POWER steps is really important. You can't outline or organize it well if you don't know who you're doing it for, why, how it's supposed to look and sound, and what should go in it. It wastes time and energy.

The final three steps are pretty straightforward:

> **W**riting: getting what you've Previewed and Organized onto paper or the computer
> **E**valuating: looking at what you've done and deciding if you did what you planned
> **R**evising: fixing what you've done so that it looks and sounds like what you want

This whole process is designed for writing papers, but, as I said, you can use it for lots of other things as well. It certainly works exactly the same for speeches and other presentations. You can even use it just as well for taking tests:

**Self:** your role is student, demonstrating your knowledge and ability

**Purpose:** convince the teacher that you know what you're doing

**Audience:** teacher, the one who gave you the information you're giving back

**Code:** the format the teacher provides, unless you get some choice

**Experience:** what you got in class and in homework

See how this process is already built in? But it makes it more valuable to consciously think about it ahead of time. The only tasks left for the test are, in the case of essays, to **O**rganize and **W**rite it, then **E**valuate and **R**evise if you have time. I once had a professor in college who actually made us spend an hour, during our final exam, just planning and organizing the answer to our essay questions. He wouldn't give us the examination booklets we had to write the answers in until the second hour of the test. He said this would accomplish two things. First, it would help us think through our answers and get them clear so that we could write them better and more easily. Second, and probably most important to him, it would keep him from going nuts trying to decipher our disorganized mess. It seemed to work in both cases.

Just about everyone knows that different teachers are different, and they have to be treated differently, or severe hardship (the student's, not the teacher's) could result. Even in class, students can prepare for differences by being clear on what it is that teachers want and expect. We can help the kids by reminding them of that separate relationship they have with each teacher, in terms of the SPACE model, just like we do for the tests. Knowing what to say, or not say, and when, could be different in each class.

# The Set-Up

There's a really good scene in an otherwise fairly mediocre movie called *Summer School,* starring Mark Harmon. In this movie he plays a teacher who is semi-forced into teaching English class to a bunch of difficult kids, all summer long. In this scene, he's finally figured out a way to get kids to want to write. He tells them: "If you can write a letter, you can get free stuff!" The kids in the class are surprised and skeptical. But he asks them if they've ever bought anything they were disappointed in. They pretty much all have, and he teaches them how to write complaint letters to the companies. Soon, replacement items for their broken or faulty purchases start pouring in, and they see some value to this whole writing thing after all.

The idea in communication is that it's *always* for a purpose. We want something. Whether it's to make ourselves heard (or seen), to complain, to explain, to ask for help, to give or get ideas or even just to make contact with other people, there is some reason for it. This is the idea we need to get across to kids. They need to ask themselves what they really want, then how to communicate in a way that will get it.

If you can get them to think about when they communicate well, usually with those people (including teachers) they like and trust, and compare it with times they do it badly (with those other people), it's a good start. Then you can ask them:

"What are the differences?" ("One's cool, the other's an idiot" will be first, but keep going and you'll get more detail that might be helpful.)

"Can you figure the differences out?" (You may have to point them out.)

"Can you make improvements?" (You may need to suggest some.)

"Do you know what you really want?" ("For them to die" is not a good answer.)

"Is there anyone else who does well with this person?" ("Yeah, but he's a nerd" is OK for a start. You can work from there.)

The idea here is to expect emotionally charged answers. It's OK; the kids are supposed to feel bad about the people they don't get along with. If they don't feel bad, you can worry. Share your ideas and feelings about the same kinds of difficulties you've had. We've all had them. Offer hope. Then tell them you may have some formulas that they can use from now on.

At some point or another just about all parents get dragged into their kids' papers. This is, of course, especially the case when they are first learning. The kids will get stuck, confused, disorganized, despondent, and possibly homicidal. They'll need help—help that helps. Remember that wonderful story from *Bird by Bird* in Chapter 9? You might want to pick up that book for some more ideas you can give the kids. Another good choice would be Natalie Goldberg's *Writing Down the Bones*.[2]

# The Delivery

My belief is that the best way to get the kids to learn to communicate well is to ask them really good questions that get them to do it. Good questions are good communication. Each step in the process I've described to you has specific questions that you can ask that will help the kids when they have to write, or present, something. As you look over this list of questions, you'll undoubtedly notice that they can help with lots of other stuff, too. I'm sure you'll find lots of ways to use them.

For a start, you might want to wait until your kids have a paper or presentation to do, unless you think it's a good idea to create one for them (they probably won't think so). When it's time to jump in, be ready to help guide the kids with the POWER Process and the questions that go with each step. You, and the kids, will probably be writing and taking notes at each step in the process, so it will get you started into the writing from the beginning. This is a help all by itself. But answer the questions well, and the project will take form as you go along. Let's go over each one, starting with the **P**reviewing step (**SPACE**).

## Self

Here is where you have to decide your role in writing what you are working on. These are questions that the kids will eventually be asking themselves, so that's the way they are worded. At first, of course, you'll be asking the kids these.

> Why am I presenting *this* topic? Do I have a choice?
> What role am I playing in this project? Has my

teacher given me a specific role, point of view or
position to play? If not, how do I want to think
about it?

Is there a particular tone, or attitude that goes with this
role I've chosen? Is it one I really want?

What is my vantage point in this role?

Here are some examples of roles that kids can take in writing a
paper or giving a presentation. This isn't all of them, certainly, but a
sample to give you the idea and help develop a good role for the kids in
each paper or presentation.

| Role | Tone, attitude | Vantage point |
|---|---|---|
| **Researcher** | observing, learning, exploring | inside the action |
| **Reporter** | giving the facts | outside the action |
| **Peer** | sharing information | side by side with the reader |
| **Teacher** | demonstrating expertise, with ideas and opinions | above the action |

Figure 27: Examples of Roles, Tones and Vantage Points in Writing

Finally, when you've figured out which role to take:

Have I chosen a role that is *comfortable* for me? Can I use it well?

If the audience is my teacher, has he or she given me some ideas
about what my role is in this project?

Purpose

Again, eventually, the kids will ask themselves these questions.

Why am I writing this? What is my primary purpose? How many purposes do I have?

Are these personal, or about the topic?

Am I trying to impress someone (the teacher)?

Am I trying to develop or enhance a particular relationship with my reader (teacher)?

Am I trying to solve a problem by writing this?

Do I want to create a certain attitude or feeling in my reader (teacher)?

What do I want my reader (teacher) to do as a result of reading what I have written?

Am I simply trying to learn something by writing about it?

Is it possible to do all I want, or do I need to change, or narrow down, my intentions?

If the audience is my teacher, has he or she given me some ideas about what my purpose(s) should be?

Audience

This is the point at which we most strongly consider the needs of the person reading, listening to and using the paper or presentation. We also need to think about the relationship with this person (usually, but not always, the teacher).

Can I imagine seeing and hearing that person in my mind while I think about this project? How do I feel about that person? Do I really know that person well enough to write or present my work to him or her? If not, what should I do about that?

What is *my audience's* purpose in reading or listening to this? What does my audience really need or want? What can I do to make sure I give this to that person?

Does what I want, and what my audience wants, match? Can I make us both happy (educated, successful, etc.)?

If the audience is my teacher, has she or he given me
some ideas about what she wants or needs? Can I tell
from the way she teaches and explains things in class?

# Code

The **C**ode step is the point at which you decide how your work will
look, sound and feel. How it will be "packaged" so to speak, to help
get your points across. This will depend on the material, but also on the
audience because it needs to be attractive to them, in some way, to make
the impact you want to make.

What level of vocabulary is appropriate? Technical,
everyday speech, special jargon?

Have others done what I'm doing? Could I "borrow"
(not copy or steal, just get the idea from) an effective
format, design, or jargon from someone who has
already done this? What have I seen or heard that
looks and sounds good to me? Do I think it will be
appropriate for my audience, too?

Do I need any of the following?

Charts, graphs, pictures or other kinds of illustrations?

References, guides, or other helpful ideas to help the
reader or listeners?

A table of contents, index, outline?

Various (but limited) changes in type style or size, color,
or design?

If the audience is my teacher, has she given me some
ideas about how this should look or sound? Do I
have a specific format I'm required to follow?

# Experience

Here you decide what goes into the paper or presentation—which
things are relevant, which aren't, what you can use, what you can't or
shouldn't. This is the information step. Gathering research, data, ideas

and content together and figuring out how to use it depends on knowing what you want to accomplish and who your audience is.

> Have I listed everything I am aware of that could be relevant and useful in this presentation?
>
> Do I have enough information to write this? If not, where can I get what I need?
>
> Remembering more personal experiences?
>
> Library, Internet or other research?
>
> Government, association, industry, or other information sources?
>
> Personal contacts, experts, interviews or others who have written on this?
>
> Television, radio or other media sources?
>
> Are my sources of information credible? Reliable? Would my audience agree?
>
> Do I really understand my information? Do I have a sense of "ownership" of this experience? Does it work for me? Will it work for my audience?
>
> If the audience is my teacher, has she given me some ideas about what should be included, or not?
>
> Does sharing this experience or information make me uncomfortable in any way?

# Organizing

When you've answered all the questions above, and gathered all your information together, it's time to put it into some format, outline or other kind of order. There is no perfect way to do this and there are lots of good choices. If you have good ways of organizing yourself that you can share with your kids, that's great. If they already have their own, that's great too. Here are some helpful standard patterns of development.

Chronological narration (how-it-happened, in order)
Spatial description (what the scene looks like)
Illustration, example, analogy or metaphor
Compare and contrast

Classification, list or hierarchy of some kind (how-it-is-organized)
Cause-effect relationship analysis (how-it-works)
Definition or other description
Instructions (how-to-do-it)

Here are some good questions:

Is there a best method for organizing this information? If so, do I
    know what it is, and can I use it?
Do I need to get a bigger overview, the big picture point of view?
Do I need to break it down into smaller pieces?
Is there some organization that will work best for my audience?
If the audience is my teacher, has she given me some ideas about
    how this should be organized?

# Writing

This part is pretty easy, once you've done the steps that come before
it. All you have to do is follow your own directions and do what you
planned. Dump out your ideas, onto paper or the computer screen, as
quickly as you can. It doesn't have to be perfect. In fact it really shouldn't
be. It should be a bit of a mess because you should just pour it out at
this stage. You'll fix it later.

The main questions you have to ask here are:

How fast can I get this down on paper or into the computer?
Can I do it comfortably?

# Evaluating

At this step in the POWER Process, you've finished writing a first
draft. Now you have to decide if you did what you planned when you
answered all those other questions. The way to do it is simply to compare
all those notes you took while you were answering the questions, with
what you've written. We like to suggest that you lay the answers out on a

table next to the written work, or in a separate file on the computer, side by side (in whatever way this makes sense for you). As you go through, just make notes on your draft about any changes you need to make. It's best not to try to fix it as you go along, just evaluate first. Fix it later. Decide if you followed your own directions.

## Revising

This is the fixing step. Take all the notes you made on the draft, and do the fixes that need fixing. Simple. It's kind of like **W**riting again, but you're really re-**W**riting.

When you've finished that fixing process, go back and **E**valuate again, then **R**evise again. Your job is to keep going back and forth until the paper or presentation is as good as you can get it.

This process is great for all kinds of projects, but you have to do it thoroughly in most cases to get it to work well. The steps are in the order they are for a reason, and if you try to skip over any of them you can run into trouble. In fact, that's how people have been getting themselves into trouble for years, and that's why we developed this procedure in the first place. For papers it's pretty straightforward. For speeches or other kinds of presentations, it's the same, but you probably need an extra step at the end: rehearsal.

The same is true for taking tests. Kids who do really well on tests have usually figured out what the teacher wants, ahead of time. This is the **A**udience step. It helps them guess what the questions on the test will probably be. Then they can imagine what the test will be like and practice, either on paper or in their minds. I've known really good students who actually wrote out the answers to the test questions they predicted would be asked, and memorized what they'd written. It takes time, but it works, and it practically eliminates test anxiety if they guessed right on the questions.

## The Punch Line

Albert Einstein was one of the greatest geniuses of all time. He gave us a new view of the way the universe works, one that has allowed us to move forward in science and technology tremendously. Most people have seen famous pictures of him standing in front of a blackboard covered with impossible formulas, holding the chalk in his hand. He is generally considered to be history's greatest mathematician and physicist.[3] He always said that his ideas started in his head—as imagination—or what he usually called "thought experiments." Einstein knew that these "daydreams" were important but that he needed to put them in a form that was acceptable to communicate to others. In science, that form may start with words, but often has to be translated into mathematics. Math was the means (the Code) he used to verify his thoughts and communicate them in an acceptable way to his audience.[4]

# The Tie-Up

Without the ability to communicate what they know, the kids will be at a loss in school. It's a simple, maybe sad, fact that much of what is being measured in school isn't really what the kids know and can do, but actually how well they can communicate it to their teachers. That's why so many people, not just kids, have learned to get by with very little talent except their ability to convince others that they have some. Some of it is just plain confidence; some is real skill in communicating. I, of course, would like the kids to have real talent and knowledge, real confidence and real skill in getting their ideas across to others. My belief is that those things go together and that without any one of the components, the kids' education is incomplete.

*Education is that which remains, if one has forgotten everything one learned in school.*
Albert Einstein

# Chapter 16

# How to Study to Learn, Remember and Use What You've Learned

I once met an extremely interesting Tibetan Lama (a Buddhist monk from Tibet) who had spent many years living in a cave. Apparently, his group of monks truly goes on complete retreats from the world. Living in a cave, alone, with nothing but someone to bring you food once or twice a day, is common. While in this retreat they meditate, read and study. They are silent and alone the whole time. After this Lama had been in the cave for eight years, he decided he had finished what he set out to do, came out and re-joined the community. He quickly realized that he was *not* finished, so several months later he went back to the cave. Another three years. This time when he came out, he felt that he was ready, again, to join the world. Now he travels to many places sharing his thoughts and philosophy freely. When you meet him, it's obvious that he is very special: brilliant, joyful, disciplined and an immediate comfort to be around. He'll also tell you that sometimes he misses his cave and longs to go back.

Knowing when we have learned something we set out to learn can be tricky for all of us. It's like knowing, for sure, that we're ready for anything we may be faced with in life. Often kids feel like that Lama when they go into a test. They wish they could go back to their cave and study some more. Since there is always more to learn, about anything we study, it's never about knowing it all. It is, rather, about knowing enough. And that is something that changes for each different situation, whether it's a test or anything else that might be important to us. Most tests, in school and in life, require that we show more than just knowledge. They usually require *understanding*, which is something deeper. Also, it means being able to demonstrate that we understand and can use that understanding.

Studying, especially for tests, is about everything we've done in this book so far, all at once. It takes the steps in this section of the book—the skills—and uses them:

Controlling and using our best states of mind
Effectively using our senses
Reading to learn
Communicating what we've learned

So at this point, if you've helped your kids to develop the skills we've been exploring, they've got all the pieces in place. It's just a matter of developing a system for using them, one that works.

# The Underlying Principle

Think back to when you were a kid. Remember what it was like to learn spelling? I do. I had teachers who would say things like: "Write each word out ten (or ten thousand) times until you *know* them." I remember how that sometimes didn't work. I discovered that writer's cramp and learning don't always go together. Sometimes, but not always. This is a perfect example of how to study that may or may not get the information into your head in a way that you can get it back out later. That's what studying is for. If you compare writing something over and over with the detailed spelling strategy I gave you in the chapter on using your senses, you'll immediately understand the difference.

Effective studying and test taking encompass all the different skills we've been discussing, used in a systematic way. So let's look at that systematic process and figure out what it really takes to do it well. Here are the steps the kids will need to follow:

Deciding what's important to learn (to the teacher, to themselves)
Gathering the information (books, notes, other sources)
Getting into a great state to study and learn
Reading and exploring the information
Planning to remember for later, imagining the test
Getting into the right state for taking the test
Understanding the questions and tasks on the test
Communicating their understanding effectively

Getting all this into a plan, or even a habit, that makes it work smoothly is the goal. Paying attention, and taking notes, in class are as important as studying for tests, so we can't forget those skills during this process. We'll come back to this issue after the steps in the studying process.

## The Set-Up

I remember a workshop I did for kids, in Singapore, on study skills. Quite an eye-opener. The workshop was going along fine, the kids and I were having a lot of fun and getting to know each other when I asked the following question: "What's it like when you guys study together?" (They were all guys in this case.) Sixty blank stares. They didn't even understand the question. So I said: "You know, that's when you have a little trouble with your math work and you ask your friend for help. Later on he's having a hard time with his social studies, so you help him out. You know?" They began looking around at each other *dumbfounded*. Then from one of them: "You mean we can do that?" I told them that we could indeed, and I would show them how. We spent the next hour practicing. It was not only a lot of fun, it was a totally new experience for them. It reminded me that what is natural for some of us is totally alien to others.

When I was in high school, I had terrible test anxiety—especially on math tests—for a couple of years. It was awful. I would study really hard for the test, and think and feel that I really understood the material. I even remember one test in particular because a bunch of friends came over the night before to study together. I taught. I knew the stuff thoroughly and was able to help the guys pretty well. But when test time came around, I froze. I stumbled through, but most of the other guys did better than I did. They didn't understand how it could happen, and at the time, neither did I.

Many of us have had this experience at some point. If your kids have had this, they'll be plenty ready to listen if you can help. If you tell them that it simply involves things they already know how to do, in a particular order, they'll be even more ready. Even if your kids haven't had trouble like this, tell them you can make their lives easier.

# The Delivery

I think that helping your kids learn to study is the most pure teamwork experience you can have, in this context. You can tell them you wish you had had someone to teach you this when you were in school. Let them know you are going to help them develop a system that works for them, from the ground up.

By "from the ground up" I mean start with a *place* to do it in. Even before kids begin to study, you and they can make sure that it's set up properly. That means making sure they have whatever they need to be effective while they're doing it. I like to think about this like I would think about setting up an office. That's really what you're doing: it's their office. Here are some of the common issues parents ask about in terms of the setting up of this office and handling the whole homework issue, as a family.

## What would be a general description of a good study space?

Think psychogeography, like we talked about earlier. Quiet and private. Distraction free. Good light. All the materials, books, references, pens, paper, plenty of water and so forth. There are plenty of books on study skills that list all these, and more, but these are the basics. How much each of these things is important, you'll find out with a little experimenting.

## Is there an ideal place in the house to study?

Maybe. Kids are different. Personally, I've always been easily distracted, especially by outside noises, when I'm trying to concentrate. If it's something easy, or routine, it doesn't make much difference, but if I'm really trying to get something new into my brain, or really work something out, I need quiet so I can focus (maybe you're one of those people who has to turn down the car stereo to find a parking place, like me). I've known others who need to have a fairly plain room, without too much stuff around, to avoid distractions. Others need certain personal creature comforts that make them feel safe and secure. You have to determine what's best for your kids (not for you; for them). For some kids studying in the middle of a shopping mall, surrounded by seemingly overwhelming distractions and noise is just fine. If your kids are like that, let them find their own spot to land in when it's time to get to work.

## Are there good methods for handling distractions, while you're studying?

It depends on what kind of distraction you're talking about. If it's something on the outside (noise, activity), the best way is to avoid it if possible. If it can't be avoided (and ear plugs or a headset is not an option), it becomes a matter of focus and concentration. This is where anchors for focus and intense concentration are particularly useful. All of us have been in situations in which our attention was fully concentrated on what we were doing, and we didn't even notice the total chaos around us. Sure, we don't want to have to do that all the time, if we can avoid it, but we should have those anchors for when we need them. That means you'll have to spend some time with the kids building these, as we did earlier.

Lots of times, though, the real distractions are coming from inside: stray random thoughts that have nothing directly to do with what's important. There is a strategy that works very well for most people, and it's easy. First, tell the kids that instead of trying to ignore our nagging thoughts, it's better to pay attention to them for a moment. Second, make a decision about the distracting thought. If it isn't important or relevant, shift the focus back to what we were doing. If it is relevant, or might be important later, *make a quick note about it.* Make this note on a *separate* pad of paper (or *separate* computer file) than what you are working on. Then, as earlier, focus attention back on the task at hand. When you're finished studying, go back over the things you've jotted down, and put each one where it belongs. This is a very good strategy any time any of us has to do one thing and lots of other ideas keep coming up. When we are in a truly creative state, writing for example, it's natural for other thoughts to be generated and stimulated by what we're doing. This is a good thing, and keeping separate notes means those ideas aren't lost, and we can go back to them later and use them. Most writers, artists and musicians I know use some kind of system like this.

## Should we be looking over the kids' shoulders? Checking up on them?

Again, this will depend on your kids. Once they learn how to study on their own, you shouldn't have to check on them. They ought to be self-sufficient. But, as in most other things, this is generally a learning process for most kids. We don't pop out of the womb with a study skills program already in place. Most of us have to develop a program that works for us, and as far as I can tell, many of us never do. The natural progression is to do less and less checking on the kids as they go along. If you find you aren't, or they aren't doing their work without *your* motivation, it means they don't have *their own* motivation. This is a cycle you want to avoid. If you help the kids develop their own skills and motivations, they can have all the responsibility, and you won't need to take any of it. If you find yourself trapped in your kids' homework, you'll find some more tips in the next section of this book.

# How about food and drinks? My kids seem to want their own kitchen to study with.

Food is one thing, drinks another. Some of us like to snack all the time, and this is really a matter of our energy levels, mostly blood sugar. We burn a lot of blood sugar when we intensely use our brains, more than physical labor in most cases. And, as usual, we're not all the same. This is another thing to pay attention to, along with your kids, and find out what works best. Some kids just want to eat junk food, and it makes them sluggish, so it's not a good idea. But for some, they need the fuel supply or they can't last very long.

Water, on the other hand, is always a good idea. Most of us don't get nearly enough and it's important, or we can't transport the nutrients we need to be at our best. Many experts in accelerated learning insist that everyone drink a large glass of water at least every hour while they're learning. I've checked in my own classes, and it does seem to make a difference for some people. Of course I'm talking about water, not soft drinks.

# What about music? The kids want to listen while they study; are they kidding?

Lots of kids like to listen to music while they study, and lots of parents complain about it. Don't. Most research studies show that it doesn't hurt, and many show that if it's the right music, it can actually help.[1] You might challenge the kids to experiment to find out what kind of music, at what volume, for what tasks, works best for them. This, of course, isn't an excuse to just listen and not study, but for many kids it doesn't hurt, and for just as many it really helps. In fact, if the kids can play the music in their heads later on (and they usually do anyway), it can help them remember what they learned. It can be a powerful anchor, if used purposefully.

Some of this setting up of a study space, and style, as I've mentioned, will take some experimenting. It's well worth it and can solve lots of the problems that look like they have some other cause. I know that many kids, who seem to have problems learning simply haven't a clue when it comes to studying. Remember, although learning is natural, studying is not a natural thing for kids to do, or to know how to do. They have to learn it.

Once the kids have a place to work, and it's time to study, then they have to follow a program that works for them. There are a number of things that are necessary, and there are lots of different styles and methods, as well as tips and tricks, that can make it really effective and even fun. All of them usually involve the following steps.

Organizing the ideas and things to be learned
Gathering the information together, so it's handy (books, notes, other sources)
Getting into a great state to study and learn
Reading and exploring the information, taking notes as necessary
Planning to remember it all later on

Obviously each of these steps is a big chunk and takes specific skills. So we'll go over each one here. Later you might want to go through some of the recommended books to get a broader look at the subject of studying. It's a big topic. Remember, too, that we're talking about the kids doing this *in relationship to having to perform later*. Usually this means a test. So we need to have a way to *connect* the act of studying and the act of taking the test. And please understand, I don't mean that we should only be "teaching to the test" as if that's the only time information is important; that's not my intention (and I think you know that if you've gotten this far).

## Organizing the Ideas and Things to Be Learned

Assuming the kids have been paying attention in class, the first thing they need to do, when they're studying, is to decide what's really important. It's not always easy for kids to know, but if they can answer a few questions, they may be able to figure out at least what's important to the teacher. A good general rule, of course, is to keep track of what the teacher emphasizes and spends the most time on: what they keep talking about, writing on the board, giving assignments about and so on. This is usually easier after some time, or even at the end of a course, when they can look backward and find some patterns.

I think the most straightforward way to do this is to begin with these basic questions:

What are the most important topics covered in the course?
What do you think the teacher thinks are the most important?
    Which did the teacher talk about most, or spend the most time on, or simply tell you were most important?
    What were most of the assignments, or reading, about?
    What does the teacher expect you to know, or be able to do?
    How would you show the teacher that you've learned what's important?
What do you think will be on your test?

Once the kids have answered these basic questions, then they can start working with the material. To make studying efficient, the material needs to be organized in some way so that going through it can connect it to how they're supposed to know it. There are a great many strategies for organizing information, and I'm not going to go into them here; it isn't necessary. The important thing is that you and the kids find a way that works for them. So, start simple. List the main ideas or points that are most important to know on a piece of paper. Then take them, one at a time, and break them down into smaller pieces, or sub-points. If the kids can do an outline of the material, all the better, but simple lists work just fine. It's also good to make special notes about each of the following:

Most important points for the teacher (as we discussed above)
List of possible things that will be on the test
    Things the teacher has mentioned repeatedly
    Notes about past tests or quizzes that could give useful clues
    Anything the teacher may have mentioned about the test
Important skills to be learned
Specific pages, charts or pictures to be considered
Particularly difficult concepts or procedures to concentrate on
Notes on the notes, if you need them to stay organized

The point to all of this is to help the kids *make a set of instructions* for how to study what they need to learn. It really will save them time, make their studying more effective and help them stay focused. It's like making a plan for any project they might have to undertake. Good practice. If you have special knowledge or skill in this area of project management or planning, you can teach the kids these skills, to whatever level they're able to easily use. As they get more practice, they can experiment with, and learn, some of the standard methods (outlines, Pert or Gantt charts, mind maps, etc.).

# Gathering the Information Together, So It's Handy (Books, Notes, Other Sources)

The notes the kids have made up to this point are a guide to what they will need. Then they have to have all their other notes, books or other materials available. They can use their earlier notes as a guide to these other materials.

# Getting into a Great State to Study and Learn

As crucial as anything else here is to make sure that when the kids are studying, they're in a great state for learning what they need. This is what the whole section on anchoring was about. Much of the method of this book is aimed at this. States of mind are so important that I can't really overemphasize how valuable it is to make effective anchors that the kids can use whenever they study. It's also why most of the time it's a good idea to keep the study area much the same. It can be a good anchor all by itself.

Spend time finding a state that works well for the kids to study in. Take all the time you need. Next, make a specific anchor for this state and have the kids practice using it (go back to Chapter 12 for review if you need to). They should use this anchor every time they sit down to study, at this point in the process. It's important, and they'll use it again later when it's time to actually take the test. Always remember, the best way to anchor any state is to use a combination of all three primary systems—visual, auditory and kinesthetic. This means a touch, combined with a visual image and some sound or words they can say inside.

# Reading and Exploring the Information, Taking Notes as Necessary

It's really helpful to get the kids to understand that reading and studying are much easier when there is a purpose to it. That purpose is to get the specific information they've decided they want from it. Modern reading techniques usually have this decision making, and focusing step, built into them. If the kids have their notes and lists right there with them—and they're following their own instructions—they'll be thinking about, and looking for, just what they need. This will help them remember it later, as well. One reading expert says, "Read as you would shop for groceries."[2]

Next we need to apply all the skills we talked about in *reading*. The kids need to be able to read the information, understand and make meaning from it, and learn what they need. This means making those movies we talked about in their minds, based on what they need for their classes and tests. They also will probably need to take some more notes as they go through, depending on what their specific goals are.

# Planning to Remember It All Later on

As silly as this may sound, the kids need to actually *plan to remember* what they are studying. This means thinking about actually being in the testing situation, taking the test, and writing or saying what they know. If they've planned their learning, gotten into a great state for learning and studied effectively, this part is really easy. It can even be fun to pretend to go through the test, successfully. This is the future pacing process, and it will help them return to this great state, and maintain it, during the test.

This is also a great time to study with someone. The activity of asking each other questions is really helpful. You can even get the kids to practice anchoring with each other, while they go through the material. They'll also be able to share different perspectives on what's important, what they think the teacher may want and how best to express what they've learned.

# Test Taking

If the preparation has been done well, it should be fairly easy to apply it to the test. There are basically three steps in our test taking process.

Getting into the right state for taking the test
Understanding the questions and tasks on the test
Communicating their understanding effectively

For many years I've been preaching these steps to students of all ages. The test actually starts well before the kids walk into the room. Preparation on the actual day of the test really helps, too.

## Getting into the Right State for Taking the Test

Before walking into the room where the test is, the kids need to use the anchor that gets them into their great learning state. This is the same one they'll want when they take the test. The reason, of course, is because of the state-dependent learning phenomenon. If they are in the same state they were in when they learned the material, they'll have a much easier time remembering it during the test. Also, since this state is probably really comfortable, it prevents the anxiety that can go with test taking, and helps get the kids focused on doing their best. If they can also remember to use this anchor at any time they begin to feel uncomfortable—or have any kind of difficulty—it will make the test taking easier.

| Before Studying | While Studying | During the Test |
|---|---|---|
| ***Gather your materials*** together in the best place for you to work | ***Use the Anchor*** to maintain the *Learning/ Studying/ Performing State* from before | ***Get settled*** *and focused,* with all your materials for the test ready |
| ***Create a Learning/ Studying/Performing State,*** making sure you're comfortable, alert, prepared to learn and perform | ***Create full sensory*** *experiences* & memories you'll use later during the test, complete with pictures, sounds & feelings | ***Use the Anchor*** to re-create & maintain the *Learning/ Studying/ Performing State* you had while you were studying earlier |
| ***Anchor this state*** in whatever way is best for you—using all three primary systems—visual, auditory, kinesthetic | ***Future pace*** to the test —prepare to recall the specific images & memories you create | ***Recall*** the specific images you created while studying and apply them to the test material |

Figure 28: State Management Strategy for Test Taking

## Understanding the Questions and Tasks on the Test

The kids also need to apply their reading skills to the test. It's important that they understand what they're being asked, clearly. It also helps, while they're doing it, to remind themselves about what they studied in relationship to what they're being asked. Most of us have had the experience of remembering certain pages of books, pictures, charts or other information we've studied while we were taking a test. We also usually think of this as a lucky break. If we try to use this phenomenon on purpose, though, we can do it more.

## Communicating Their Understanding Effectively

Finally, it's a good strategy, especially with essay questions, to take a few moments to think through how they can best express their thoughts. As that history professor I told you about said, it really does help.

## Paying Attention in Class

I mentioned earlier that paying attention all the way through the course is a key component to knowing what to do during the studying process. Class time is for learning. Learning works best when it's goal oriented. So, the kids need to learn to have goals for learning, even while they're in class. The same questions I suggested earlier that they ask before studying are just as useful when they walk into their first day of class. They can begin the organization process that they'll need later on. If they can do it all the way through the course, it will be a lot more accurate than if they just do it at the end, from memory. It will also be a guide for them in their note taking, our next topic.

## Note Taking

About 30 years ago when I began teaching these things to people (adults, mostly) on a regular basis, I noticed something very interesting. Also, very painful. I didn't have much experience in teaching or training, so I wasn't as well prepared for getting my students to go through the learning process in a systematic way. I just did what others had done with me in my training. I also would always invite my students to call me between classes, or after the course was finished, if they needed help with anything they'd learned from me. I got plenty of calls that went something like this:

Them: Hi, Sid!
Me: Hi.
Them: I was in your course last week and guess what!
Me: What?
Them: I did just what you said!
Me: Yeah?
Them: That whole process . . . the thing you showed us . . . that technique (etc., etc.) . . .
Me: And . . .
Them: And guess what!
Me: (Again) What?
Them: It *failed* totally!! It didn't work at all!! A major mess!!

Me:     (Trying to be patient) Well, tell me exactly what you did.
Them:   I followed the procedure exactly . . . .

Then they would usually describe some of the strangest things I'd ever heard. Things they did that were so weird that I couldn't make any sense out of them at all. No wonder they got the results they got! Then the conversation would continue:

Me:     Well, why did you do that?
Them:   I learned it from you!!
Me:     I don't think so, because I don't even understand it. Tell me why you think you got it from me.
Them:   Well, it's in my notes!

After the next few classes I asked people to show me their notes. Shock. What most had actually written was so full of deletions, distortions and generalizations that I couldn't make any sense out of it. Pieces missing out of procedures. Misinterpretations. Comparisons to other training they'd had—ones that usually didn't correlate. Reminders of other things they'd learned in their lives that popped into their heads when I was talking. Then, of course, the usual grocery lists, love notes, schedules, to-do lists and some of the most beautiful artwork (doodles) I'd ever seen.

In a few cases, it was the opposite. These were the ones who got it *all* down, perfectly neatly, organized, better than I ever had it myself. Unfortunately, they couldn't remember a thing that had happened in the class because they had been in a deep "note taking trance" the whole time. That state of mind didn't allow them to think about what was going on while they were doing it. Not all of them were like that, but enough to make me take notice—and take precautions.

I now give people their notes. Lots of handouts (or more generally a complete notebook) of the most essential pieces. Students can add to it when they want to, or leave it as is. Either way, they'll have what they need. The class and the notes are integrated in a way that helps make studying easier and more systematic. It also frees them to use their brainpower more constructively in class.

Many classes, however, won't be organized in a way that integrates the notes into the learning process so systematically. So, kids have to figure out what they should be writing down, in a way that helps them. Note taking *can* take a number of different forms. Each of them works for some people, and is a waste of time, for others. Experiment.

If writing everything down helps store it in mind, great. If not, it's a waste of conscious energy and a distraction from learning. Then they have to go back over the notes to remember anything that happened in the class. Most people, I've found, just write down the things they find most interesting, or that they find complicated and want to go back to later. Again, this isn't the most efficient way to do it, but it works for some. Then there are those who make nice neat outlines of everything said in class, almost like the minutes of a meeting. This can be helpful, but again, it's lots of work.

Most experts will suggest that notes be very goal oriented to begin with, just like everything we've been talking about. They usually recommend some sort of topic headings, or main points, being clearly written down. Then, under each one, the sub-topics and major ideas covered. Only when it is especially important, do they suggest that it's a good idea to write out everything that is said. This is usually reserved for specific quotations, definitions, procedures or instructions in which the actual words are important. Remember, the words that we use, or write down, only make meaning in our minds when they turn into reference experiences. That's what we want our notes to do. This is what the kids need to learn in their note taking. It takes practice, obviously.

In my view, note taking should never be a substitute for understanding. Writing things down is not the same as learning them. Remember that class time, notes, studying and test taking all need to be part of a larger system of learning—integrated, working together.

# The Punch Line

I once helped the son of one of my professional students with his history work. Like some kids, he was great in math and science, but when it came to history, essays, names, dates, and the like, he was clueless. We spent time making sure that he read the books as we discussed earlier, making clear images in mind, so that he could see and hear the "stories" he was reading about. Then we made sure that he could control his state properly, so that he could reproduce the one he had when he was reading, during the test. Doing it this way, he could clearly remember the story, and easily talk about it. The next day he went into class a little early and announced to his friends: "Ask me anything. I know everything." They did, and he did. When they asked him how he'd suddenly become some sort of genius he said: "I'm not telling!" His mother still cracks up every time she thinks about it.

# The Tie-Up

Years ago, on the TV show Saturday Night Live, there was a great character who would appear on the "news" segment from time to time. His name was Father Guido Sarducci and he was, supposedly, the editor of the Vatican gossip newspaper. One night he did a gag about inventing "The Five Minute University." This was based on the idea that if you took everything you would normally *remember* 10-15 years after you got out of college, it would only take about five minutes to learn it in the first place.

I don't think this is a comment on *us* as much as it is on the education we get. If it's all content, without some process to help us learn it, we may only remember five minutes worth. And that isn't worth much. If, on the other hand, everything we learn of any importance becomes a part of who we are, then it changes us into better people.

# PART 4

## Troubleshooting and Getting More Help When You Need It

*Sometimes one sees in the school simply the instrument for transferring a certain maximum quantity of knowledge to the growing generation. But that is not right. Knowledge is dead; the school, however, serves the living. It should develop in the young individuals those qualities and capabilities which are of value . . . the aim must be the training of independently acting and thinking individuals . . .*
Albert Einstein

*The surest way to corrupt a young man is to teach him to esteem more highly those who think alike than those who think differently.*
Friedrich Nietzsche

# Introduction to Part 4

## Whose Problem Is This, Anyway?

Chances are, if you picked up this book, you have a specific problem you're trying to solve. Maybe some difficulty your kids are having in school, or something more general related to education. You might even be home-schooling your kids, but running into difficulties you didn't expect.

In the book on writing I co-wrote, that I mentioned earlier, we gave lots of advice on solving problems in writing. The main piece of advice was to follow the map we laid out for completing a writing project, because if you follow that plan, you prevent the most common problems from ever coming up. The same point bears repeating now. When it comes to learning, if you help your kids learn how to learn, you'll prevent most of the later problems that kids have in school, and even in their lives.

In this final section of the book I am, however, going to outline some ways to approach the various difficulties people complain about with their kids. I always start by breaking problems down into some logical types and suggesting some things to do. This is certainly not meant to be a complete list or an exhaustive set of strategies for making everything perfect. That isn't possible in any one book, or even in books at all. This is more of a discussion and outline of approaches. As in all things, you will need to be creative and adapt what's here to your own needs and the needs of your kids.

Remember this: If there were some perfect path or system to follow, that worked all the time, we'd all be following it—all the time.

# Types of Problems

When I help people solve problems, of any kind, the first two things I try to do is help them figure out (1) *what* the *real* problem is, and (2) *whose* problem it *really* is. Sometimes problems disguise themselves, as we all know. What looks like a reading problem on the surface might be an emotional one underneath. It might also be something simple that the child doesn't know how to do. Or something else. So paying attention to the real problem is important.

Also, when we're trying to help the kids solve something, we have to know who we should focus on. Sometimes the problem is primarily *ours*, as helpers. It could certainly be the kids' problem, but it might just as likely be the school's. Ultimately, of course, if there is something really wrong, it's everyone's problem, but that's not what I mean. I'm talking about what we can do to solve it, and figuring out who can best do that is a good step. This section of the book is organized to help you focus first on whose responsibility it is to tackle the problem, second on understanding the different kinds of problems that commonly come up, and third what to do about them.

Most of all: practice prevention.

# Chapter 17

# When the Problem Is Yours

A few comments are in order to begin with. First of all, we all know that kids have some basic needs that have to be met. We've talked about the Neuro-Logical Levels (environment, behavior, capability, beliefs and values, identity, spirit) and how there are needs at each of these levels. But let's not forget the obvious overriding need: safety. That's safety at each level. Safety to explore their world, try new things, have feelings and work to understand them, learn, practice, create and grow. They also need to develop their own set of beliefs and values, a sense of who they are and who else is important in their lives. Their home needs to be a safe place for all these things, just as we would like their school to be. It's up to us, the adults, to create that.

In my first book, I wrote the following, and I think it still holds:

> For most people, home is a safe refuge from the world. It should represent some stability, physically and emotionally. If children have love, respect, and a reasonable amount of freedom at home, they will generally develop a substantial level of self-worth to

take to school with them. Hopefully, the school will foster this. Sometimes it won't. If the school doesn't foster these feelings, a particularly harmful pattern can develop. The following is an example of this pattern. A child feels good at home and is doing well. Then some difficulty develops in school. The child's self-esteem suffers a blow. Too often, when the parents hear about trouble in school, they immediately react. They punish or criticize the child further: the child's safe refuge isn't so safe anymore. Self-esteem suffers at home as well as at school. The cycle builds on itself, then builds lousy anchors for the child.

Parents fall into this trap for a number of reasons. Many are concerned about school, rightfully so, but tend to jump in too fast, trying to make everything OK. It doesn't have to be OK all the time. If it were, kids wouldn't learn to take care of themselves. Some parents automatically assume that the school must know what it's doing. They forget that the *school* doesn't know anything. It's the staff and teachers that know. And they are quite human. Sometimes they know a whole lot of stuff that just isn't so.

Another kind of parent is the one who takes problems in school personally. So many times I've heard anguished parents bitterly ask, "How could my child do this to me?" It is very seldom that a child is doing a school problem *to* anyone. There are exceptions, but they are far more rare than the complaints from parents would indicate. A little less paranoia and a little more logic goes a long way.[1]

So, as a parent, you can be very supportive to your kids, helpful and empathic. You can become a role model for curiosity, motivation and a continuing desire to learn and grow. Or you can fall into the trap of being insistent or strident about what they "have to" do, or even threatening. I've known some parents who took sort of a gloating attitude toward their kids and the school work they had to do, one that said: "I hated school too! So just get with it. We all had to do it. Now it's your turn; you have to do it too." True as this might be, it's not very helpful.

If you realize you've fallen into a kind of negative view of your kids and learning, this is something for you to change. To begin to do this, I find, the easiest way is to put yourself into the shoes of your kids (this is what it means to be empathic). Remember I asked you at the beginning of the book to spend a few minutes recalling your own experiences from school, seeing the room in your mind's eye, hearing the sounds and having those feelings again. You can imagine what your kids must go through, sitting in the classroom, or even learning at home if that's what they do. You can do the same thing by imagining what their experience is when you are talking with them about their own learning. It may become quickly obvious to you that "something is wrong with this picture." If that's the case, it should also become pretty obvious what you need to do, or change, to take care of the situation.

If it isn't obvious what to do, but you know that you need to do something, then you may need to talk with your kids or other family members about it. Sometimes this is hard. It's also part of being responsible as a parent. Spend some time thinking about how things have gotten into the shape they're in, and ask others what they've seen and heard. Be willing to listen, even when you don't like what you hear. Remember, too, that everyone has a point of view, and each one is valid for that person whether you agree or not. The key here, as in any problem or conflict, is collaboration. You want to work together with your kids and family to make your home a safe and nurturing place. If it isn't, change it.

Obviously, I'm suggesting that you have the power to communicate with your family and kids, take stock of your situation, come up with a plan and make any changes that you may need to make. Look back over the sections of the book on rapport and on managing your states and, if necessary, anchor some useful ones in yourself. If you develop and use your rapport skills, and can manage your own state of mind well, you'll be able to communicate in helpful ways.

Maybe, on the other hand, you are generally in a good frame of mind about your kids' learning, and your home life reflects that. But that doesn't mean you can't still be uncomfortable working with your kids on their learning for some reason. Here are some of the most common reasons discomfort in working with kids seems to occur, and what you can do about it in each case.

## You don't have the kind of relationship you'd like with your kids.

Some parents feel that they can only do some things with their kids, and schoolwork and learning aren't among them. This, of course, is a choice. But remember that your kids learn from you whether you want them to or not. If they think you can't talk with them about some things, you're actually teaching them to have that same limitation. You might not want that. Look back over some of the things we've talked about in the area of improving relationships. Remember that you have much more in common with your kids than things that separate you. It will help.

## You don't have great self-esteem around learning.

I've known lots of parents who didn't have much education or didn't feel confident about their own abilities in that area. Remember, I'm not suggesting that you have to know all the things your kids are expected to learn. What we're talking about here is helping them with the learning process itself. And that *is* something you can do. If you don't feel confident with any of the skills I've talked about in this book, you can spend time practicing on your own. The skills are certainly just as useful for you. When you feel more confident, then you can try them out together with the kids. In some cases, even if you don't feel confident with your own skills, you can still try and see how well you do. As a best alternative, work on them together.

## You want to avoid interfering with what the kids are doing in school.

Some parents are afraid that they will get in the way of the kids' learning, or contradict something they are doing at school. This won't happen with what's in this book. This is about how to learn.

# You prefer to let your kids explore learning on their own.

This, again, is a choice, and it's a good one in many cases. If your kids seem to be doing fine, and you and they are comfortable with their learning, you might choose to leave it alone. On the other hand, if this isn't the case, you may want to try some of the things here to help them out. If you ask them, or offer to help, they'll let you know.

# This all just seems too hard.

It's not nearly as hard as most of the things adults do at work every day. It's not really as hard as most of the stuff the kids have to learn in class. It can seem that way because it's a different way of thinking about teaching and learning. It also requires you to examine what's going on inside yourself, and that isn't always easy to do. Like anything new and different, it will seem awkward at times. This won't last once you get into it. And, hopefully, the kids will just get motivated, interested and curious. When that happens, they'll take over.

My goal is to help you help your kids. It's not to burden you or challenge you beyond your means. To me, this is part of being a parent. We teach our kids, and help them with, all sorts of things. Why not one of the most basic ones: how to learn.

# Chapter 18

# When the Problem Is the Kids'

Kids have all sorts of challenges, some small, some large. We can't cover all of them here; no one could. Lots of the problems kids have are much bigger than learning, and some are really serious. Severe emotional or behavioral problems. Drugs. Illness. Though these aren't really the subjects of this book, I think it's appropriate to mention them, and offer help when I can. If any of these are the case with your kids, you'll also want to get some professional help, and I'll talk about that more in a later chapter. Even in the case of severe problems, however, some of what is in this book may help.

## Learning Problems

If your kids have been diagnosed as having some official sounding learning problem, or disability, the first thing to do is relax. It usually means someone (teacher, counselor, psychologist) hasn't yet figured out how to help them learn something. That's all. If the help they need is available in the school, and it seems to be working, great. If not, many of the exercises in this book were designed primarily for that purpose. In some cases, regardless of what you've heard from the experts, you'll be able to help your kids solve their learning problems. Once you help the kids get inside their own heads, and pay attention to what they're doing that works or doesn't work, things can change pretty quickly. All kids learn. All of them do it in whatever way seems natural to them at the time. The trouble with this, of course, is that they always have to learn new things. Some of these can be learned in their natural ways, but some require new ways (new information, new ways of learning).

All learning involves the same elements. You have to take in information, process it (think, understand), store it and remember it. All of these things are built out of pictures, sounds, feelings, tastes and smells. When the kids learn to control those, they can control all of their learning. Do the experiments with them. Repeat them as often as you feel you need to. If they run into some very specific thing they just can't do, no matter how hard you've both tried, then ask for professional help because there may actually be some other kind of problem. This, truly, will be a *very, very rare* occurrence. That means you need to really give it your best try first.

# Health Problems

If your kids have some already identified physical problem or limitation, you probably already know more about that than I ever will. Many parents become the experts on the diseases and disabilities of their children. They usually also do a great job of getting the best help they can find. Especially in the age of the Internet.

Some physical problems are not so obvious, however. Allergies or food sensitivities. Nutritional deficits. Hypoglycemia (low blood sugar). Any of these can be the real culprits behind the commonly diagnosed learning disabilities like ADD (attention deficit disorder) and ADHD (attention deficit hyperactivity disorder). I'll state my personal bias again: I don't believe learning disabilities exist.[1] I think they are always symptoms of something else. Unless someone can show you physical evidence (a picture, x-ray, CT scan, MRI, blood test, etc.) of a problem in your kids' brains, assume they just don't know, regardless of the diagnosis they give you. But, these other issues I just mentioned can cause problems in learning, and they can all be addressed effectively. Let's look at each.

## Allergies and Food Sensitivities

I've personally seen some kids who had all kinds of learning and behavioral problems that were the result of food allergies, blood sugar problems, yeast infections and other not-so-obvious physical problems. These have even included kids in psychiatric hospitals, diagnosed as schizophrenic because they couldn't connect any two thoughts together. In some cases just taking them off sugar made all the difference. In others, they had allergies to common foods, like corn, wheat or artificial sweeteners. We've had two children in my family who had these problems (one sugar, the other corn) that were the causes of severe behavior problems. The elimination of that food was the elimination of the problem in both cases. In addition, both improved simply with age.

I've read summaries of research suggesting that allergy-related learning problems are really very rare. I'm in no position to say for sure, and I don't think others are either. Until you find a specific allergy in a specific child, and can reliably connect that to a specific learning problem, you have no proof. If you've ruled out other obvious possibilities, however, it's worth checking for.

Food sensitivities are not the same as allergies and can be more subtle. Many of the tests for these seem to have some problems, but some seem reliable. Once again, this is probably not the place to start, but could be an avenue to explore if the other more obvious physical conditions that can cause learning problems have been ruled out.

In case of both allergies and food sensitivities, you'll need to consult your doctor, and possibly a specialist who works with kids in this area.

## Blood Sugar Levels

As far as I can tell, the most common health problem that affects kids' performance is one even many adults have: mild hypoglycemia. If we don't eat the right foods at the right times, and drink lots of water, our blood sugar levels can rise and fall quickly. Think about when you've seen a bunch of kids together eating lots of sweets, for example at a birthday party with gobs of cake and ice cream. The next thing you know most of them are wired and out of control from all the sugar. A while later, after you've pealed them off the ceiling, they can get cranky, whiny, argumentative and sleepy. It's easy to think that they just wore out from all the running around. More likely, though, is that they had too much sugar, which caused their bodies to produce too much insulin to counteract it. Then their blood sugar drops quickly, and the kids are no fun any more. This is the same mechanism that gets many adults to get sleepy around three in the afternoon. Then we often crave something really nutritious like a candy bar to perk ourselves back up (think about those commercials on television that show office people in the middle of the afternoon—advertisers aren't stupid). We crave sugar because it's dropped out of our blood stream. The answer is a good diet, high in complex carbohydrates (veggies, mostly) with some protein and plenty of water to transport the nutrients to our brains.

Unfortunately, we have the brains and digestive systems of cave people. In many ways, we *are* cave people. Evolution is slow. Our ancestors adapted to the food that was available, and we haven't changed much. This doesn't mean everything new is bad, but we need to consider the choices we make. Cave people didn't eat much candy or ice cream. Or white bread, cake, pizza, chips, soft drinks or the other things that make up a modern day diet. Cave people would have liked all those things, I'm sure, but that doesn't mean it would have been good for them. Or us. If you think about how much food has changed just in the last 50 years, it's amazing. But it's the food that's changed, not us: not our brains, our digestive systems or our metabolism. A candy bar (and I like them a lot) is probably a massive overdose of sugar for a human being. Add in the caffeine and other chemicals that are in the chocolate and the preservatives, colorings and texturizing agents, and think about what it does to us. We can certainly handle it, within reason, but we weren't built for it.

In summary: brain cells use only one primary fuel: glucose (blood sugar). There is only one thing that will carry adequate amounts throughout the brain, and also eliminate waste products: water. That means your brain requires you to have adequate blood sugar levels, and water, at all times to function properly. A steady dosage of the kind of sugars our brains need comes from eating complex carbohydrates (most vegetables), not refined sugars or bleached, over-processed foods (white bread, French fries, sweets, etc.). Too much of these foods cause your body to *over-react* and *lower* blood sugar levels. When that happens, thinking and learning will pretty much quit.[2]

Again, I've read research summaries that suggest that learning problems almost never have any relationship to sugar. This is not what I've been hearing from parents, teachers and other professionals working with kids, nor does it fit with my personal experience.

## A Diet Survey

Whether you suspect a problem or not, I think it's a great idea to do a survey of what you and your kids eat, and ask yourself some tough questions about how it's affecting you, and them. In this age of massive numbers of choices, we need to make good ones. We were built for certain things and not others.

Once you've found things in your family's diet that you'd like to cut down on—or cut out—I've found that it's easiest to use substitution. In other words, find something else to replace the culprit you're trying to eliminate—something that tastes good and gives the same kind of satisfaction. You could choose fruit, or sugar free stuff (some of it's awful, some is pretty good) instead of regular sweets, for example. Then make it really convenient for the kids to grab that stuff. After some time, they'll do it out of habit.

## Breathing and Exercise

This may sound silly, but most people don't breathe properly. Pay attention to your own breathing, especially when you are ill, injured, confused or under stress. It isn't the same as when you are healthy and relaxed. Watch your kids as they work on things. You may notice that when they are trying to think through something, or answer a question, they hold their breath. Try it yourself and see how long you can think that way.

This, again, is something that can be helped simply by focusing attention on it. Point it out to the kids when you notice it, and have them pay attention, as well. Anchoring relaxed states helps. I'm also a firm believer in yoga, Tai Chi and Chi Gong (Chinese exercises), breathing exercises, running and self-hypnosis for this reason.

# Reading Problems

Reading is so central to most other learning in school that I want to spend a bit more time trouble-shooting it. Remember, many reading problems are the result of something simple, even mechanical. For example, not following along the line of words, missing part of a sentence—some sort of deletion. Paying attention for these usually finds them without too much difficulty. Then, slowing down and paying close attention to these mechanics usually does the trick. Lots of times kids just don't know some of the words. Sometimes the problem is something bigger, like not decoding meaning and making personal reference experiences. These can be handled as we discussed earlier in the chapter on reading. In general, though, I do have some tips on helping you to help your kids if they are having problems in getting what they need to from their reading.

1. Speed. In reading, this comes from a combination of things:

    a) Moving your eyes across the words faster than you can say them. If you hear each word in your head, the way you were initially taught in school, you won't be able to read faster than you can talk.

    b) Being able to fill in enough of your images with fewer words, i.e. seeing whole scenes flash by quickly, without having to fill in all the details. This requires some sort of filtering out to get the nouns and verbs first, and the other words only when necessary.

    c) Having the turn of the page as a part of the strategy, rather than an interruption. Many people can speed read for two pages, and then turning the page itself *anchors in their old, slow, strategy.* Some speed-reading courses teach you to turn the pages in a different way than you used to.

d) Not having to be perfect the first time through. Many speed-readers will tell you they scan the first time just for the general idea. Then they go back for as much detail as they need. Often they will read something five or six times to get what they need. This will depend on how much they want, how technical the material is, and how well it is written. *No one* really speed reads a chemistry text full of formulas and gets it all the first time, with the exception of certain people who *really* have total "photographic" recall. Even they usually don't have the concepts, either. They just know how to get the information back from their unconscious mind so they can figure it out later.

e) Being able to speed up or slow down at will. This is a plus if you can read quickly, when you understand enough, and slow down when you need more detail. If you can do this, you can go through the material in a fewer number of passes.

2. Comprehension also means more than one activity:

a) Making your movie with enough accurate detail. This means including enough details as well as not adding your own if they change the meaning. Creative license is admissible only when reading for your own pleasure, not when reading to learn someone else's ideas.

b) Being able to relate one internal movie to another. Sometimes switching to visual *still pictures* helps in comparing images, like in our discussion of children's strategies. This can also mean holding a still shot while running the new movie alongside it as you read. For example, you've probably skimmed through something, maybe a newspaper article, looking for some specific information you already have in mind. This means you are holding some thought—a collection of images—while you read through to look for some kind of a "match." You can teach the kids how you do this.

c) Reading the words in a logical order when you have trouble. Just as with speed, start with nouns. These will give you still pictures. Verbs will add motion and relationships between the stills, bringing them together, and making it into a movie. Adjectives and other words will add in the other crucial sub-modalities (detail) for you.

3. Enjoyment comes from several things, on several levels:

   a) Physical comfort.
   b) The right sub-modalities in the internal movie, visually and auditorily. This is, of course, a personal matter, but anything on the list below can cause discomfort and anxiety. If this happens on a regular basis, reading is no fun. Avoid the following:
   Too many images in a small space (or field of vision)
   Images moving in different directions, too fast, or at different speeds
   Images that are too close
   Images that are too large or too bright
   Sounds that are too close, loud, or shrill
   Too many sounds or voices at once
   Sounds or voices of unpleasant tonalities
   In addition to these, in reading, not enough can be as bad as too much. When people don't understand something, they tend to make themselves uncomfortable. Mental pictures with "holes" in them, or lack of clarity are common when we don't quite get what we are reading. You have probably figured out by now that if we just worked on repairing those sub-modalities, it would make us more comfortable. But remember we want to fill in the gaps with accurate information. We need comfort *and* learning.

4. A sense of reading for its own sake is invaluable. This is my opinion, but I really like to learn. I also like enjoyment. I have the belief that I will get both from just about anything I read. So I automatically go into a pleasant state of consciousness whenever I read. It took me a long time to get there, though. I

had a lot of old anchors and memories that connected reading and drudgery. I had to overcome those before I could enjoy it. If you have some old anchors like those, use what you have learned to do something about them. You might do the same for the kids. At least don't give them any new unpleasant ones.

# Homework Problems

Earlier I talked about the homework cycle that some families, not just the kids, can find themselves in. This is the one in which every night there is a struggle over the homework. In some households this is a major ongoing nightmare that seems destined to go on until the kids are in their thirties, just finishing sixth grade.

This is a relationship issue, for the most part. What it needs to be replaced with is a homework system that the kids can use, on their own, to get their work done. They should be coming to Mom and Dad when they legitimately need help or guidance. Some parents like to look over their kids' homework, just to make sure it's done, or done well. That's OK as long as there is a limit to it. Otherwise, the parents become part of the homework, and the cycle kicks in.

Anyone who does counseling hears the same things: "But they'll never get it done unless we stand over them!" or "They're so far behind, that we have to help, or they won't ever get into college!" or "My parents did the same with me, and it made me the success I am today!" or "Kids are always like this. You can't expect them to take responsibility on their own; you have to make them do it!" It usually boils down to some explanation about how the parents are in school with the kids, whether they like it or not, because there just isn't any other way. Ridiculous.

Remember, when we talk about motivation, even a lot of adults complain about not being organized, motivated and self-directed because they never learned how. In my experience, the most motivated people I've known were very often the ones who took charge of, and responsibility for, their own lives at an early age. I think the key here is responsibility, or as we often say in counseling: response-ability: the ability to respond appropriately to whatever is important. Motivation, means, opportunity: great gifts for any child. Parents who are part of the homework struggle usually provide the motivation and the opportunity, sometimes all three. Almost everyone I know who counsels parents in this says the same thing: knock it off. Let them fail, or suffer whatever consequences there are. At which point, of course, the parents freak out and look at the counselors like they're some kind of maniac. It isn't true, of course, because most counselors have learned that the kids will usually pick up the slack, eventually, depending on the perceived consequences. The difficulty in many cases is that the cycle has gone on for so long that it takes the kids a long time to pick it up. Worse in many cases, they've become so unmotivated, complacent or disgusted that they no longer care. The cure is prevention.

The cure also includes a relationship with the school. Some school systems, schools or individual teachers have a philosophy that includes the parents in the homework. Remember, though, that many of these attitudes on the part of school officials are based more on their own upbringing than any real data or experience. They often point to the obvious truth that the more parents are involved and interested in their kids' education, the better the kids do. Making the parents into homework police isn't the answer, though. Involvement and interest aren't the same as taking over responsibility for the work. Homework is for learning, and the kids need to do that. The responsibility issue is one for the schools and teachers, in my opinion. If the teachers and parents want to work out an arrangement—convenient and logical for both—about devising consequences for the kids if they don't do their work, that can be a good solution. Don't allow yourself to become a prisoner of your kids or the school because of homework. It's silly.

In the event that you find yourself already stuck in this problem, go back to the chapter on study skills. If you work to help develop those skills enough so the kids can do their work efficiently and effectively, you won't have to do it for them. It might be hard in the short run, but you'll thank yourself for it later. Especially here, in the United States, there are plenty of continually available opportunities for people to get an education. Parents who tell me their kids won't amount to anything if they don't do great on their next math test have completely lost that perspective.

Finally, if there is really a serious problem, this can be a good reason to seek family counseling. This cycle is really almost always a family issue, and it's sometimes best taken care of at that level. If that's the case, everyone might need to make some changes to get things back on track. It does no good to point fingers at each other. What does help is good guidance, clearer communication and the ability of everyone in the family to be "response-able." Of course I always recommend a counselor trained in NLP, but there are plenty out there who aren't and are quite effective.

If you are interested in delving further into the homework problem area, there is a pretty good book by well-known family counseling curmudgeon John Rosemond called *Ending the Homework Hassle*[3] that has a number of good tips and plans that might help you out of the trap.

# Emotional Problems

Sometimes when people use the words "emotional problems" they just mean that someone doesn't feel the way we expect them to about whatever is going on. Maybe their attitude doesn't seem helpful. Or on some deeper level they seem to be very upset (depressed, angry, confused, frustrated). Emotions are rarely the problem. It's usually the expectations.

Remember the work we did on states of mind and anchoring? This is one good way of controlling emotions, in us as well as the kids. What we would all like is that the classroom itself, reading, studying, learning in general, become anchors for the kids to get into their very best states. Then no one has to motivate them: the learning itself becomes the motivation.

There will, of course, be plenty of times that the kids' emotions overwhelm them. When you notice this, it might be best to answer a few questions for yourself, before trying to do anything about it.

First, do you need to do anything at all? Could this be something they can get through on their own, naturally? Sometimes you just have to wait and see, unless of course they ask you for help.

On the other hand, you may decide that they do really need some help, based on your own understanding of them and what you see and hear. It can't hurt to look over the answers to those questions about who they are—as people—which I asked you to think about at the beginning of this book. Then, ask yourself about the following possible sources of their discomfort:

your relationship with them

other family relationships, or problems

their relationships with their peers

something else in the environment, or the neighborhood

some recent event, impending event, or the anniversary of an
important event

In each case, communication is going to be the key, as we've been discussing all along. If you suspect it's about your relationship, then that's the thing to work on. Once you have that, and the kids trust you, they'll be able to talk about whatever else is bothering them. Then you'll usually know what to do. If you don't, get help.

I want to mention something about family systems, as well. That was it: your family is a system. It works like one and follows the rules we talked about earlier in the book that all systems follow. If there is a problem in one part, there will likely be effects in other parts. When I was working as a family counselor years ago, we took a straw poll among ourselves to find out what effects serious marital problems had on kids. The first thing all of us noticed was that if there was a divorce in a family, the year the parents got divorced, the kids really suffered, and sometimes failed, in school. We used to call the kids the "barometer" in the family, because they responded to the "atmospheric pressure" in the house. Your family system is the weather your kids live in most of the time. Make it sunny.

# Self-Esteem

The concept of self-esteem is an important one, but I've listened to an awful lot of people throw that term around who clearly don't know what they're talking about. When you hear someone try to tell you that everything that goes wrong in people's lives is a sign of low self-esteem, walk away. We've already listed lots of other possible things that can affect kids, from their families, to their peers, to their diet. Great self-esteem won't get you through all of these challenges. By the same token, of course, a feeling of worthlessness can make it all harder.

The word "esteem" is from the same basic root as the word "estimate." Both words mean to judge or appraise something.

Self-esteem means—inside your mind—stepping outside of yourself and judging yourself as someone else might. We learn this as we're growing up. We put ourselves into other peoples' shoes and imagine how we look and sound. Then we decide if we like what we see and hear, or not. The *decision* is our estimation (judgment, appraisal). We learn how to make those sorts of decisions from other people. When kids are surrounded by people who hold them in high esteem, they tend to do the same for themselves. When they step outside of themselves, they step right into the shoes of those other people. Then they make the same judgment. That's how high self-esteem gets made. Low self-esteem is often made in the same way, but this time the shoes the kids step into belong to people who look down on them.

One of our great trainers, years ago, said that if you want to really increase your self-esteem, look at yourself through the eyes of someone who loves you.[4] It works. Teach your kids to do that. You might even want to try it yourself.

# Drugs: Legal, Useful, or Neither

Whenever I work with groups of parents or teachers, the subject of drugs comes up. They are so much a part of modern life in all their forms: over-the-counter, prescription and recreational. Some are legal that shouldn't be. Some are illegal that shouldn't be. We have major problems with drugs all over the world—but not just in the ways we usually talk about. There are reasons the problems with drugs are growing, and they mostly have to do with some things most people just don't know about, or don't think about.

First of all, the use of drugs to improve the way you feel is *natural*. I mean that literally: it occurs throughout nature, in the wild, among all sorts of animals. There are thousands of plants growing all over the world that are "psychogenic" or "psychotropic," meaning that they affect the thinking and experience (psyche) of the animal that takes them. When animals in the wild are under increased stress, many will change their diet, naturally to include plants (nuts, berries, molds and more) that relieve that stress. They find and eat different stuff. Period. Animal behaviorists have been studying this phenomenon for many years, in labs and in the wild through observation.[5] The animals somehow know—or learn—which foods will make them feel better. It's natural for us as well. Wine, hemp, coca leaves and other substances have been taken by people for *thousands* of years, usually in natural and relatively healthy useful ways. But lately, we've gone crazy.

We now have the technology to refine these substances, and make new ones, that are way beyond what nature ever came up with. People in modern societies seem to have the belief that if a little of something is good, more is better. We can chemically induce states of mind that are completely overpowering and even addictive. This is done legally, by pharmaceutical and agricultural companies, and illegally, all over the world. We don't usually pay attention to all of the effects this has, so I want to talk about some of them.

First is the meta-message that we send when we give someone a drug to control his or her thinking and behavior. The message: that person doesn't have the means (internal resources) to control themselves. The message is that there is something wrong with them—that they are different from others and defective in some way. Believe me, it doesn't matter how much we tell people nice stories about how they just need a little extra help, or they have a slight "chemical imbalance" and we can fix them right up so they'll be just as good as new. On a deep level, they won't believe it. Friends of mine did major research in this area years ago and found that if you ask almost anyone who has been diagnosed with a long-term illness or disability what he or she really wants, at some point he or she will tell you: "I just want to be like everyone else."[6]

Here is the second meta-message: "If you can't control yourself, we will." In psychiatric hospitals, strong tranquilizers are often referred to as "chemical restraints." Think about the effect that has on the relationship between the people giving the medicine and the ones taking it. The long-term effects, especially.

Another meta-message: "If you feel bad, take drugs." Some doctors complain bitterly because patients come in and ask for a magic pill to make the bad feelings go away. Some doctors willingly participate. What's worse is that it can get really tough for the ones who refuse, and would rather help the person solve their problems than just give them a drug. These doctors know that the patient might just leave and go shopping for one who'll cooperate. Kids do the same thing. They just don't always go shopping at the doctor's office.

This is a big problem in the medical profession, and doctors have to deal with it regularly. There are some countries in which the doctors actually sell the medicines they prescribe right in their offices. When we lived in Singapore, my wife taught at the National University in the Social Work and Psychology Department. During the course of her work, she consulted with a young psychiatrist who candidly told her that this is how he made the bulk of his living. It's accepted practice there, and of course, encourages doctors to prescribe more medicine than they might otherwise. They recognize this, and they know it's a problem. In the US, it's pretty much illegal, but that doesn't mean it isn't encouraged by other means. There are indirect financial incentives for doctors to prescribe drugs in addition to the many other pressures. If you haven't had a conversation about this with your own doctors, you should.[7]

A fourth problem is that there are sometimes strong *state dependent learning* effects from drugs. Remember we talked about this when we discussed states of mind and anchoring. When someone is in a particular state of mind, and they learn something, they may need to be able to reproduce that state of mind to remember it. That's what anchors do. And drugs. The difference is that it can be hard to reproduce a drug state without taking the drug. When you stop taking the drug, what happens to your ability to remember what you learned? We don't really know. Some research suggests that kids who've been on drugs for many years (such as Ritalin for hyperactivity) seem to be able to remember just fine. I've seen the opposite, in some cases. We just don't know enough.

Another built-in problem with all medicines is that the effect of any drug isn't hiding inside the tablet we swallow. The effect is the result of that combination of chemicals combining with our system, our digestion, bloodstream, metabolism, and so on. We're all a little unique, and in fact we don't stay the same from one day (hour, minute) to the next. Even a meal we eat one day that makes us feel great can make us feel lousy the next. The same is true with medicines, and that can make the effects inconsistent. If we come to rely on them over a long period of time, we're likely to be disappointed at least some of the time.

So, what does all this mean? Should we fire all our doctors and pharmacists and fend for ourselves? Of course not. I don't mean to sound like a fanatic. I do believe there is a place for drugs in modern society, when used intelligently, carefully and thoughtfully. That means we have to think about all these aspects when we use drugs. Before we ever give a drug to someone to change his or her thinking or behavior, we need to think *even longer.* Some overworked teachers would like to have all those pesky kids in their classes drugged with Ritalin to calm them down. Ritalin does calm kids down, but it does the opposite to adults: it speeds us up. So we used to challenge the teachers to take it instead of giving it to the 30 kids. That way they could keep up with all those high-energy kids, and it would be lots cheaper. One common response was: "I wouldn't take that stuff. It could be dangerous!"

We've produced, in modern society, something that has never existed until recently: addictions. We can develop addictions to all sorts of stuff, including drugs. That doesn't just come from technical progress in chemistry; it comes from a lack of coordination in our society, our educational system and our health care system. Here are some things we know about drug abuse.

1.  People under stress, or experiencing problems they have trouble coping with, will try to find relief in whatever way they think is available to them. If all they can come up with is drugs, sometimes they'll use them, legal or not.

2.  Many of the serious consequences of the use of drugs are dependent on the "set and setting" as well as the substance itself. That means the mind-set (state of mind) and the time and place (environment) that they're in when they take the drug. That means sometimes the results will be a relief from suffering, sometimes not. When it doesn't work, people sometimes just take more.

3.  People under stress, or having problems, will abstain from drugs if they have good ways to handle the stress or solve the problems—ones that work. That means the key to resolving or avoiding drug abuse problems is to give people the tools they need to feel safe, in control of themselves, and resourceful to handle their lives.

There are other things we know as well, of course, but these are the most important for what we're doing here. I would like to make one more important point about drugs before we go on to other things, though. There are a lot of people who will tell you about the wonders of some new drug to help kids (or you) behave, learn, feel better, whatever.

These new wonder drugs have been coming along at a steady rate for decades. Some of them really do make people feel better, but that might not be the whole story. When people have gotten hold of something that makes them (or their kids) feel great, it can give new hope, temporary relief, and even more. So when we hear people raving over the wonders this great new drug has done for them, we shouldn't be surprised. Read the following quote:

> Exhilaration . . . which in no way differs from the normal euphoria of the healthy person . . . You perceive an increase in self-control and possess more vitality and capacity for work . . . . In other words, you are simply normal, and it is soon hard to believe that you are under the influence of any drug . . . Long intensive mental or physical work is performed without fatigue . . . without any of the unpleasant after-affects . . . no craving for the further use . . . [8]

As you read this, you might think that it's from a person taking a new wonder drug. It is, in fact, a quote from Sigmund Freud, in the 1880's, describing one of the very first in a long line of psychiatric wonder drugs. People still use it today. It's called *cocaine*.

The next time someone tells you that any emotional problem is the result of a chemical imbalance, and that medical science has just the answer: run. Then remember that you, and your kids, have all the necessary resources, right inside. They might need a little help finding, learning about and using those resources, but they have them. Real help isn't likely to come from a pill. It may be a temporary or partial help, but the final answer comes from thinking and behaving differently because they are able to do so themselves.

# Labels

We can't avoid labels in our society. They are everywhere. We categorize things, ideas, organizations, and unfortunately, people. Sociologists have been warning us about the dangers of the labeling process, and what it does to people, for decades.[9] We just haven't learned our lesson yet.

The reason is simple. It is easy to label things and people. It is convenient to be able to put something, or someone, in a tidy little box so that we no longer have to pay attention, or think about how to deal with it, or them. But people aren't nearly so simple. We change constantly. We learn. We grow. We have different abilities and attitudes at different times. We are shaped by our experiences, and these are changing as well. It's still easier for others to simply slap a title on us, and treat us *as if we are that title*, rather than fully functioning, ever-changing individuals.

In education it has been fashionable to use the practice of medicine as a model in diagnosing children and their problems. This is part of the reason so many kids are on drugs for school problems. It isn't always a good model, though. If you have a broken leg, a doctor can give you a straightforward test—an x-ray—and then look directly at a very accurate picture of what the break looks like. When the doctor sees the image of the break, he or she will know exactly what to do to repair it. The diagnosis—the label—of "broken leg," and the determination of exactly what kind of break, gives a very specific determination about how to repair it. We say that the diagnosis, or label, is *prescriptive* of the treatment. It tells you what to do. When the disease is beyond the knowledge or skills of medical science to do this, things get a little tougher. For example, in certain kinds of immune system disorders, some chronic illnesses, chronic pain or psychiatric disorders, there are no good objective tests like an x-ray that we can give. We have the same problem in education. The tests we give for finding problems aren't advanced enough to tell us exactly what to do. We can't look directly at a picture of a reading problem, or a misunderstanding about some concept, or a difficulty relating to classmates or teachers. We can't put a cast on a "broken behavior."

And yet, we try. Rather than treating kids as individuals, with specific, sometimes personal or special needs, we diagnose them. It sometimes just makes people (teachers, parents, doctors, everyone) ignore the child's actual behavior, except when it fits the expectations suggested by the label. This can cause people to see the labeled kid as an insult ("bad kid"), a diagnosis ("hyperactive," "attention deficit disorder," "behavior problem") or a test score ("a C—student"). We don't generally appreciate it when people reduce us, as adults, to some stereotype. When we try to do it to kids, we teach them that it is OK to do it to others. In fact we encourage it.

I remember, years ago, making a discovery about working with teachers, as well as kids, that was really valuable. I worked with a child who'd been misbehaving in class, and was sent to me for help. We did some work on it, solved the problems, and I sent him back to school. In talking to his mom, however, I discovered that the teacher and he still weren't getting along. After a couple more weeks trying to figure out if I'd missed something, I got permission to call the teacher to talk about it. I asked about the child, and the teacher immediately started telling me about how awful he was. I asked for specifics and she gave them to me (basically, how horrible it was to deal with this behaviorally disturbed, hyperactive, uncontrollable, impossible nightmare of a human). I established some rapport, by being sympathetic, understanding and attentive. Then I asked: "When was the last time this child behaved this way in class?" The teacher paused for a few moments, then said, "Now that you mention it, it's been about six weeks since the last incident I can remember." I pointed out that that was exactly when the child and I had worked out the problems he was having. The teacher was really embarrassed that she just hadn't noticed the change. She had labeled this boy as bad, and the label stuck. She didn't notice that it was no longer true until I pointed it out to her. I was again sympathetic and understanding and, of course, offered to help out any way I could from then on. I enlisted the teacher's help to carefully observe the child and keep track of his progress.

I know this is how we all work, naturally. This teacher was a normal human being. She had a *reference experience* of this child, just as any of us would. He really had been quite difficult, and she associated those bad feelings to him. He became an *anchor* for her to feel frustrated every time she even thought about him. Her unpleasant experience of this boy had turned into a generalization—a label—one that just needed to be updated.

I saw this happen many times. First impressions would stay the same *regardless of what the child actually did in class*. We've already mentioned the effect expectations have, on everyone. And, of course, this is one of the biggest problems of labeling: we often don't even know when we're doing it. I finally figured out that I should tell the parents about this,

285

ahead of time, so they could enlist the help of the teachers from the start.

A second problem with labeling is that the kids hear the names we call them and they don't understand what they mean. Years ago someone suggested to me that I ask the next child diagnosed as "hyperactive" (the most popular label at the time) to tell me what it means to be hyperactive. When I did it, the response was immediate: "It means I'm bad." We did a little experiment with a number of kids and found that about 80% of them told us the same thing: "Hyperactive means I'm bad." When we told them that it really just meant that they wiggled around too much, or didn't sit still and pay attention as much as the other kids, a lot of them were shocked! Then they came up with ways they could improve. In a lot of cases they did much better on their own. We had given them a diagnosis they could deal with: *wiggling*.

The third major problem is that labels are *very sticky*. They can travel long distances, over long periods of time. School records can go with kids from school to school, year to year. The same is true with the labels that are in those records. How many of us would like to re-live every mistake or bad judgment we ever made, over and over, for the rest of our lives or careers?

My belief is that most of the labels we stick on kids are meaningless. I don't believe in any of the standard definitions of learning disabilities because I can't find the disabilities in the children. I always seem to be able to teach them whatever they're supposedly unable to learn. And they seem to be able do all the things the teachers, reports and experts say they can't do. I do occasionally find disabilities in the teachers, reports and experts . . . .

So my advice is to stay *descriptive* and *results oriented* when dealing with kids. Instead of saying they have a disability, talk about what they do and what we want them to do instead. Who we are (the label) is not what we do (the behavior). Kids are lots more capable and flexible than we give them credit for. Sometimes it's the adults around them who are really stuck, no matter how well-meaning they may be.

# Chapter 19

# When the Problem Is the School's

## Teacher Problems

In my first book I wrote the following, and it still holds:

> Understanding schools and teachers really isn't that much different from understanding kids and parents. Teachers have the same needs from their job that people in general have. To start with, though, teachers are very poorly paid. Second, they are poorly educated to perform their functions. Third, they don't get much respect. Everyone knows of the massive problems of education, but few will recognize an individual teacher who does WELL. While the job of a teacher is certainly challenging, the rewards are often quite meager. That's a generalization I am willing to make.

As a result, teachers, no matter how well meaning they are, can fall into several traps. The first is disappointment, discouragement, or both early in their careers. I have seen many first—and second-year teachers in despair over the difference between what they expected and what they have found in their profession. Those who don't or can't make the adjustments they need, stand a real risk of falling into the second trap: burnout. The symptoms include apathy on the job and/ or in other areas, poor health, seething anger or massive depression, a jaded attitude towards students, and a host of other noxious symptoms to which we don't want kids exposed. But the teacher can't be blamed any more than the social worker, doctor, nurse, policeman, and so forth. Both of these traps represent teachers' ways of rebelling against being stuck in the system, just as the children do. It's a natural response. It is also the reason we have so many good people leaving the profession. . . . There are ways that parents can help, or at least avoid aggravating, these situations when they run into them: they all boil down to effective communication skills. First, recognize the teacher(s) as a human being(s). Second, listen to them, just as you should your children. Don't jump in too quickly. I know lots of parents who have told me that allowing teachers to get stuff off their chests can help troubled situations tremendously . . . .

Third, and most important, share your experience of your child with teachers. That doesn't mean your pet theories on child development. If you know something that works or will not work with your child, share it. Give an example of a time that it has worked (or not), and make sure the teacher understands. Like everyone else, teachers are usually willing to take advice or try something new if it makes sense to them. Fourth, if you think of specific instances in which the teacher might be able to try something with your child, tell him or her. When talking with teachers, remember a couple of things. Teachers, kids, and you have similar needs as people. Both you and the teacher really have the same ultimate goal: your child's successful education. Sometimes that goal gets obscured by systemic problems or human weakness. It's OK, that's why we have each other.[1]

Remember to look back through the chapter on understanding systems (school and otherwise) and working with teachers. You especially might want to review it if you're having problems with a specific teacher, or the system in general.

# School System Problems

I live in a community with serious problems in the school system, ones that have been going on for years. The fights between the school board, several mayors, teachers and parents organizations and the city council became the subject of national debates. The system went through something like 11 Superintendents in 13 years. Almost no one in the country wanted the job. Most people who can afford to long ago took their kids out of public schools altogether, and put them in private ones. A mess that was partly solved by a hurricane.[2]

Your kids can't fight these battles. In fact, if it's a battle at all, it means it's not about them in the first place; it's about the system. While we figure out how to fix these systems, it's sometimes important for parents to focus on what they can do that will work, and at the same time keep the problems from getting bigger. That's why I've spent so much time talking about communication and relationships. There are communities in which the teachers, school administrators and parents really do work well together. From talking with people who have been involved in those systems, it's always taken real time and effort. Lots of learning, on all sides. Lots of patience. Lots of perseverance. Some of these organizations have made their approaches available, so you shouldn't have to reinvent the wheel.[3]

# Chapter 20

## Working with Consultants

The idea throughout this book is to help you develop a systematic way of working with your kids, to help them learn to learn. I've given you a number of formats you can follow, each time you want to teach your kids something new, to make the process easier. You have undoubtedly also realized that you can't do exactly the same thing each time, because of the nature of the beast. Flexibility will be your friend. As long as you make a serious effort to "stay on the path," most of the time you'll do fine.

There are times, though, when all of us need some help. It's no "failure" to admit that you have a problem and don't know what to do. Even in this, though, you can have a systematic plan when you go about looking for it.

## Clear Outcomes

First, gather your thoughts about what you want. Be as specific as you can. Be able to describe what you want in clear, behavioral terms.

There are some very good guidelines for setting up specific outcomes that I think are useful here:

1.  The outcome you want should be stated in terms of what you want—not what you don't want.

    For example, I used to have parents come to me all the time asking things like: "Can you make him stop getting distracted when he's in class?" Or: "We want her to quit feeling bad about math tests." It's much more useful to ask: "Can you help my child learn to stay focused?" Or: "Can we find a way to make tests into more of a fun challenge?" Stopping something, or making some feeling go away doesn't really make sense if you think about it. We have to know what we want to replace it with, what we want instead. Focus on that.

2.  The outcome should be something that is under your child's control.

    You must focus on what you and your child can actually do, and be responsible for, not the behavior or responsibilities of others. Even if the outcome involves other people, you can only be sure of how you or your child will behave; then maybe you can predict how that may affect what others do or think. This is especially true if there is a conflict with some other person, other kids, teachers, principal, and so on. It doesn't do any good to say: "I want to get my child to make the other kids act nice to him." Or: "I want the teacher to notice the good work she does." We can ask for things like: "Let's find a way for him to reach out to the other kids in as friendly and fun a way as possible." Or: "I'm sure we can get her to show the teacher what she's doing, in a reasonable and respectful way."

3.  The outcome should be something you can verify by directly observing for it, or at least something that is so obvious that it will be clear when you get it.

    Vague outcomes seldom lead to decisive, well-directed action. I used to spend lots of time with parents, teachers and children getting them to be specific. Requests would be things like: "We want her to be more outgoing (assertive, conscientious, motivated, etc.)." Or, "I want him to communicate better." We've spent considerable time in this book talking about what those things might actually mean. Better: "I want her to ask the teacher for help as soon as she needs it." Or: "I want her to be able to ask the other kids over to our house after school." Or: "When he asks for help, I want him to show me what he's done and tell me exactly where he gets stuck." These requests are a lot clearer.

4.  The outcome should include specific times and places where things should change, in many cases.

    Make sure you change or produce specific behavior only when and where it will have the desired effect, and not in inappropriate situations. For example, I've seen many parents and teachers try to get kids to be more assertive or outgoing with others. It works a lot better if they know who they should do this with, in what circumstances, and for what purpose. You may want your child to stand up to the other kids, but not the principal, for example. Or, in some cases, the principal and not the other kids. This is something that depends on understanding the other people and the context or situation they find themselves in.

5.  The outcome should include the continuation of whatever is already working well.

    Always check through all the possible ramifications and effects of the outcome, and the behavior leading to it. You want to insure that you don't eliminate any advantage that the kids had in the original situation. Also, we want to insure that new and unforeseen problems or unfortunate consequences aren't created as well. The kinds of behavioral changes we've been talking about are good examples. Sometimes the ability to be quiet and observe a situation is a valuable one, and I've seen many cases where kids were encouraged to speak up in situations when keeping quiet would have worked out better. Another example would be one in which a child has some very specific problem, with reading or math for example, and what the parents ask for is a complete change in the way the child studies and practices. A general rule in problem solving is to *do the least amount of change to get the goal,* so you don't upset the entire system if you don't have to.

I also think it's important to remember that there are many ways to achieve anything you're going for. Very seldom is there only one way to get some problem solved. It's important, I think, before you ask for help to focus on the solution you want, and think about the consequences of what you're asking for. Know what you're willing to do, and to spend if it might be expensive, and how much effort everyone will have to put in to get the job done. Also, find out how much others—not just the kids—will have to do. Many times you may find that you have a big role in the solution to this problem.

# Finding the Right Help

Knowing what kind of professional you might best benefit from can drive you crazy. It sometimes drives me crazy, and I'm one of them. The reason is that the label on someone's business card or office door, with a nice collection of letters behind the name, won't tell you what they think, what they do, what they believe, or most importantly, if they're any good at it. In my own case, I was supposed to be doing primarily family counseling to help children with their behavioral problems, when I began working with them on learning.

As in anything else, I think the way to proceed is to ask lots of questions. First, ask your friends, relatives, neighbors, school officials and whoever else you can find to make recommendations about who can help. The first question should be: "Did the person who went for help get what they went for?" This is much more valuable than questions like: "What are their professional credentials?" "What managed care or insurance affiliations do they have?" "How many years of experience do they have?" "Which school did they go to and what degrees do they have?" What's their reputation in the community?" These questions aren't totally irrelevant, but they are far less important than most people think. I've known brand new, fresh out of school, professionals whose attitude, caring, curiosity and passion made them wonderful as helpers. I've also known world-famous professionals I would never recommend anyone to, no matter how much I didn't like them! So ask people about what kind of work the person does, instead of what their title is. Ask about their actual effectiveness, not their reputation. Then go ask some of those same questions when you meet the professional, over the phone and in their office.

It is helpful to know what different professionals concentrate on, though. Doctors, psychologists, social workers, counselors, tutors and other consultants have some *traditional* specialties. That doesn't mean they follow tradition; I certainly never did. But they might, and it's easy to ask them. For example:

Your pediatrician can be a great start when there is any kind of problem. Good ones know the possible causes of different kinds of difficulties and may be able to make great recommendations. Some even specialize in this area. Others, though, don't know much about educational problems. They might not think about allergies or other environmental problems that could be causing a problem. They may not know, beyond medical kinds of diagnoses and treatments, what else is available. Ask.

Psychiatrists and neurologists are also doctors. If they are up-to-date on the possibilities, and are willing to try various approaches, great. Some of these also specialize in educational issues and can be wonderful. Others just prescribe drugs as a knee-jerk reaction, without exploring much. Ask, and if all the doctor talks about are potential medical problems, he or she may not be thinking broadly enough. Ask about the various possible treatment options. If the *only* ones are drugs: *run.*

Allergists can be very helpful if they are knowledgeable about the kinds of things that cause learning and behavior problems in kids. Some are, some aren't, and you should ask. Often allergists in a community know each other, so they can refer you to someone who specializes in these sorts of problems.

Nutritionists come in many flavors (sorry, I couldn't resist). They have various kinds of training and specialties, so again, ask about their work with kids having learning or behavior problems. A good one can help you improve the health of your whole family, so it's worth a little shopping to find someone you can work well with.

Psychologists, also, can be fabulous, especially if they specialize in this area. Some, though, like doctors, can get too narrow in their focus. There are psychologists who just do testing, and that's it. My experience, too often, has been that they do very expensive and elaborate tests, and then make recommendations that are impossible to follow. Not always, certainly, but enough to be scary. It's useful to ask for bottom-line possibilities, like: "What kinds of things do you typically recommend if you find a problem on one of your tests? Give me some examples." A good psychologist should be *thrilled* to answer a question like that.

Social workers, counselors, tutors and other professionals. I lump these together in one group, because there is no real way to lump them together at all . . . . These folks can have just about any kind of training you can imagine, and lots that you can't imagine. Many are just terrific, and some have no clue about how to help people except in some very narrow specialty. They usually will tell you right away what their specialty is. Ask about their typical clients. Then you can ask them specific questions about what kind of things they actually do, what they recommend, how they know when it's working (or not) and who else they might work with or refer you to if you need more help.

In all cases, here is what you can ask to give yourself an idea about whether this might be the right person for you:

"Who are your typical clients?"

"What do you actually do with people?"

"Why do you do it that way?"

"What do you think the possible causes of this kind of problem might be?"

"Do you have an idea about how long it might take?" (It's all right if they don't.)

"Can you give me an example of a time you've worked with someone on a similar problem, with some success?"

"If what you do doesn't work, what would be a next step, or someone to refer us to?"

"Do you offer any guarantees?" (Many Practitioners of NLP do, most others do not. Some professionals will be insulted by the question; just be prepared if you ask it. No answer to this one is right or wrong.)

The answers to these questions will get you talking with the person, and give you a feeling about what they would do, how well they communicate, and whether or not you feel comfortable with them. All of these things are more important than the actual answers to the questions. In fact, the answer to that last question will almost always be: "There are no guarantees. I can't make any." Many people in my field, NLP, *do* guarantee the results of our work, but we're rare. The same goes for how long it might take. This is often very difficult to predict, especially with some kinds of problems, but in some cases you may be surprised. It's worth asking. Most important, perhaps, is to pay attention to whether or not the person seems understanding and sympathetic. If not, get someone else.

# Talking with the Kids about Getting Help

One of the most common difficulties for parents is talking to their kids about the need for help. After all, you want to start off on the right foot, so that your kids are ready, willing and able to get the most out of it. Dragging them, kicking and screaming, into someone's office isn't the best way to start a new relationship. Preparation is key. Here are some steps to follow before you actually take one of your kids for help:

Make the *announcement.* Tell them what you have planned.

Give a good *reason.* Tell them why you think they need help.

*Describe* what will happen. Explain what it means and tell them as
much as you can about the consultant and what will happen
when you get there.

Give the intended *outcome.* Tell them what result you hope for.

Give the opportunity for *discussion.* Tell them about any other
meetings that may be planned (with teachers, other consultants,
whoever) to talk more about what's happening. Also, talk about
any other *chances they'll have to talk about how they feel* about the
consultation process.

If it makes sense, give a *review* date. Tell them when you can all look
at the results and decide how it's going and what to do from that
point forward.

You know your kids, and what they'll likely need to feel comfortable
getting help, and how they can get the best out of it. As in most things
like this, let the kids ask all the questions they need to and answer them
the best you can. Let them know that everyone is working together to
help them improve in whatever the problem area might be. This is a
team effort, and everyone has some responsibility to make it successful.
Certainly you may have to make the decision about getting help—even
if your child doesn't want it—but your communication should be really
clear, regardless. Most of all, consultation is about help, not punishment.
You may have to stress this, repeatedly: "Nobody did anything bad or
wrong. We all just need a little help sometimes."

# Working with Professionals

It is worth the time and thought to develop a system for consultation
with professionals. As modern societies get more and more complex,
we're all likely to need more and more help navigating. There are
different ways of thinking about how these folks help us, as well. Let's
look at medical help, as an example.

When you go to a doctor, it's usually for one of two reasons: a)
Something is wrong, or b) It's time for a checkup. Lately, though, some

of us have started using our doctors as *consultants*. That means they are working *with us*, not doing things *to us*. They are helpers, teachers and guides whose goal is the same as ours: keeping us healthy and strong. It really is a different way of using doctors than most of us grew up with. Even when we get sick, the doctor might prescribe a lifestyle change (diet, exercise, rest, or some other change) instead of medicine. This will be more and more important as our lifestyles get more complicated.

We can work the same way when there is a problem with our kids and their learning, or schoolwork. Consider the professional to be a consultant. We're all working together in this. The professional isn't likely to fix the kids—especially since they're not broken to begin with. They can help, teach and guide the kids and us. This is a much better approach. Here are some guidelines:

1.  When you ask for help, be aware that the consultant can't really give you the best answers without seeing your child. It isn't wise to ask the consultant to trust your perceptions of the problem, exclusively. In fact, be willing to recognize that your perceptions may be the problem in the first place. The consultant needs to have the child present so he or she can do his or her own observations. You wouldn't (shouldn't) ask a doctor to diagnose a serious illness without actually seeing you.

2.  The consultant should be able to demonstrate, right in front of you, what needs to be done. That way you can learn all of the skills needed to solve this type of problem in the future. Suggestions are OK, but demonstration is better.

3.  It is not fair to the child to be excluded from any solutions you decide on. It's disrespectful and risks damaging the relationship. It also risks their ability to trust professionals in the future. This makes it dangerous. Your kids deserve to express their own opinions and to be heard and considered. You may need to make hard choices, but be respectful and fair, just as you would expect others to treat you.

4.  A good consultant will help to strengthen the relationship between you and your kids, as well as solve the problem. He

or she may be able to help you in many other areas beyond the obvious ones you have asked for help with.

5.  Remember that you are not only getting help for your kids when you get consultation, but you're also *teaching them how to get help* as well. Keep this in mind and keep the kids in the loop as you work with the consultant.

I know that lots of people are reluctant to ask for help, for a variety of reasons. Some of these are valid. Some are not, but they're understandable. Think about how much little kids sometimes hate going to the dentist or doctor. They think it's going to hurt, because sometimes it does. So the thought of the doctor may have become an anchor to feel pain and get scared. The same can be true with adults. If you only ask for help when you feel bad, then the idea of help can be an anchor to feel bad, and even to remember all the other problems you've had. Realistically, though, we need to get past that. Just as treatment from dentists and doctors are far less painful than they used to be, the same is true for getting other kinds of help, like counseling and professional consultation.

I know families that regularly get consultation, because they've found that it helps them in many ways beyond what they expect. It has become part of their family life, and it works for them. I don't necessarily advocate this, but I think the idea of having help when we need it should be a natural and comfortable part of our lives. Just like reading good books to improve ourselves.

# Appendix I

# A Special Note to the Parent of a Child with a "Diagnosis"

Since the 1960's or thereabouts, in the United States we've had a strange connection between education, psychological and psychiatric treatment and medicine.[1] This seems the case in many of the countries I've worked and trained in over the past couple of decades as well. Obviously, some kids need special help, and it's only humane in this modern world for us to give them all that they need. It seems, though, that in many cases school, social services and medicine have become all one big, very confused, system with kids bouncing around from class, tutoring, counseling and the doctor's office. Often, kids who need the most help aren't getting it anyway, even though they're on medicine, in special classes and in counseling.

The belief many of us in the field have is that a lot of this is the result of "conveyer belt"[2] teaching without much thought to how kids learn and what they really need to succeed. The problem isn't in the kids; it's in what we're doing with, and to, them. That belief is at the heart of what this book is about and for. Since, often, the welfare of

301

kids depends on what happens at home, what is between these pages can help maximize the potential of your kids, regardless of what special needs someone says they may have.

Certainly there are times when counseling and special help are appropriate, and we discussed these situations in Part 4. But I believe these situations are much rarer than many people have been led to believe. I also believe that good relationships at home, and in school, along with good teaching and learning skills, can overcome just about all the difficulties kids have. Not everything, of course, but just about.

It may be that you'll find what you need in this book to help your child, regardless of what the label or diagnosis might be. It means you may have to do some work, and some learning on your own, to make it a success. It's worth it. Remember, you are not alone.

# Appendix II

# A Special Note for
# Practitioners of NLP

In 1982 or 1983, I was invited to give a day of training in the first 28-day training program held in Santa Cruz, California, by the Society of NLP. This program was a big experiment in "content free discovery method" training. Robert Dilts and Todd Epstein, primarily, designed this training, along with Richard Bandler and others. The idea was that the first 20 days of the training would be as purely process oriented as possible, meaning there was no discussion about business, therapy, education, medicine or any other kind of application. Instead, it was just exercises and experiments to build pure skills, so that participants in the program could do lots of things, but didn't really have any guidance about how to apply what they'd learned. I was invited to teach on day 21, the first content day of training, and to show applications to education (since I'd written "the book" on NLP in education, *Meta-Cation: Prescriptions for Some Ailing Educational Processes*).

I began by talking with the 60 or 70 participants about what they'd learned and how they were going to start teaching each other some things, using their new skills. Instant panic! People immediately began to say (implore, beg, plead, whine) that they had no idea how to teach anything, and that they couldn't believe I was going to ask them to. They said they'd just had 20 straight days of pure confusion, their brains were totally fried, and they didn't really know how to do *anything*, come to think of it. I told them they were wrong; they just didn't know it yet.

So I asked for a volunteer, with some specific learning difficulty (though I don't remember what it was). The idea was that we were going to help this person, or teach them in some way, depending on what the problem was. They thought I was going to show them how to do it. The volunteer came up. Then I asked them to do it, as a group. Again, they told me they didn't know how. I, again, said: "Yes, you do. You have a human being here. Find out what the problem is, how it works and how this person works. Then do whatever you think makes sense. I'll help when I think it's appropriate." They immediately started asking really good questions. Gathering information, using the Meta-Model, watching eye movements, posture and physiology and listening for representational systems. I guided them a little, but they did most of the work. They did it well, too, and solved the problem—and got the outcome everyone was hoping for.

Then I told them they were going to do the same thing with each other, helping each other to learn new things. They spent the day teaching each other everything from math problems, to music, to juggling and more. It was great fun and at the end of the day they showered me with thanks for showing them how much they already knew.

Over the years, NLP trained people have asked me all kinds of things about helping other people to learn. I'm supposed to be some sort of expert. The reality is that I think about these things more than most others, but that's about the only difference. I'm not an expert in education; I'm an expert (if there is such a thing) in NLP. I simply use what I know in an educational context, from time to time. I also do all kinds of other stuff with it, as well (medical applications, psychotherapy, sales and business consulting and training, and more), like lots of NLP Trainers. When NLP Practitioners ask me "what to do" questions, I give them NLP answers. These usually begin with: "Find out how it works, how the person works, who they really are inside, what they need, what they are aware of, or not, what they have control over, or not, and what can be changed that will make a difference." It doesn't matter if it's about learning, quitting smoking or managing a difficult business restructuring. As the late Todd Epstein loved to say: "It's all made out of the same goo."

The NLP books I've written have all shared the same basic form and set of intentions. I like to write about the basics, because I think people who haven't had the opportunity for training deserve to have the tools. I don't expect books to replace training; that would be ridiculous. But with guidance—a user friendly format, lots of stories, examples and exercises—even untrained folks can use some of our wonderful NLP ideas, skills and techniques to improve their lives and the lives of those around them. This is a pretty big book, by NLP standards, with lots of stuff in it, but it's not very advanced. If you're a well trained Practitioner in our field, you'll find much of what's here to seem obvious, though you may not have spent much time thinking about it, especially in this context, before now. I hope the book will help you to do that.

I also hope it will show you how much you already know, and how easily and successfully you can apply it. It is, and you can. I also hope that you will go way beyond what's on the page as you read, and into the depth underlying it. And that you'll do the same with your own skills, maybe taking them a lot farther than I ever have.

Though this book is aimed at parents, and presents specific things for them to do with their own kids, you certainly don't have to limit yourself in that way, or leave yourself in that specific frame. I think what's here is just as valuable for anyone in education, any of the people-helping professions and even for our own personal development as life-long learners.

To repeat something I said in one of my previous books, in a similar note to NLP Practitioners:

> When you began to learn NLP, it may have seemed overwhelming, both in the acquisition of skills and in the sheer volume of information. But when you began to chunk these down, practice techniques and play with alternative ways of thinking, you undoubtedly found it a worthwhile and fascinating journey. One with no end. My hope is that this book will widen, and even smooth, the road for you.

Keep in mind also that we can all benefit from lots of questions asked in new ways and in different sequences. Remember that NLP began with a set of questions about how experts process information. These were based on a set of presuppositions that were operationalized as well as stated. Then a model of asking even better questions, based on specific patterns in people's language. I did not include the Meta-Model, specifically, in this book for a variety of reasons, but you can certainly remember to have it active in your thinking as you go through the questions that I did include.

This book then, for the Practitioner of NLP, is an invitation and a challenge. An invitation to use your skills, within a framework that makes sense. And a challenge to use all of your other knowledge and skills to make your experience of going through this book even richer than what, I believe, is on the actual pages. Enjoy!

# Chapter Notes

## Part 1

### Chapter 1

1. This is a controversial idea people have been arguing for a long time, largely because success is difficult to define. In general, success in school seems to predict success later in school, but not too much else. Probably the most famous study of this kind began at Harvard many decades ago, following graduates and looking at their achievements. For a good summary of that study, and its director George Vaillant, see: Joshua Wolf Shenk, "What Makes Us Happy?" (*The Atlantic*. June, 2009). Also for information on this topic and the factors that do seem to influence success, see: Daniel Goleman, *Emotional Intelligence* (New York, Bantam, 1995, p. 34) and Janet Caplan and Robert Kelly, "How Bell Labs Creates Star Performers" (*Harvard Business Review*, July 1993), and K. D. Arnold, *Lives of Promise: What Becomes of High School Valedictorians: A Fourteen-year Study of Achievement and Life Choices* (San Francisco, Jossey-Bass, 1995), and Thomas J. Stanley, *The Millionaire Mind* (Kansas City, Andrews

McMeel Publishing, 2000). Finding more information on this topic is quite easy with a quick Internet search.

2.  The relationship, and differences, between a focus on task and a focus on relationship have become a rich source of discussion and exploration in recent years by people in NLP, linguists, management consultants and others. For a good discussion and a really interesting look at gender differences in this area, see Deborah Tannen's wonderful book *You Just Don't Understand: Women and Men in Conversation* (New York, Ballantine, 1990). Also, for the NLP descriptions, see Robert Dilts' The Parable of the Porpoise, in *Visionary Leadership Skills: Creating a World to Which People Want to Belong* (Cuptertino, CA., Meta Publications, 1996, pp. 220-225). Also, Robert B. Dilts and Todd A. Epstein, *Dynamic Learning* (Capitola, CA., Meta Publications, 1995, pp. 10-21), specifically applied to the learning process.

3.  The modeling process is something psychologists have been studying for about 100 years. We all know from experience that children pick up traits, attitudes and beliefs from their parents and other important people around them. It is unconscious and very pervasive and powerful. It is so commonplace that specific references seem unimportant: a discussion can be found in just about every introductory book on psychology or human development. In contrast, *formal human modeling* is, essentially, the act of doing this on purpose, in a structured, intentional and reproducible way, to gain useful knowledge and skills from experts. This is central to NLP as its methodological core. I believe this has been useful in helping shed light on the more unconscious forms that happen in everyday life. For a discussion of formal human modeling in NLP, see *The Structure of Magic* by Richard Bandler and John Grinder (Palo Alto, CA., Science and Behavior Books, 1975) and Robert Dilts et. al., *NLP Volume I: The Study of the Structure of Subjective Experience* (Cupertino, CA., Meta Publications, 1980, Introduction, pp. 1-24). Also see *Whispering in the Wind* by Carmen Bostic St. Clair and John Grinder (Scotts Valley, CA., J & C Enterprises, 2001).

# Chapter 2

1. See for example Gregory Bateson's early discussion of map and territory: "Cybernetic Explanation" in *Steps to an Ecology of Mind* (Northvale, NJ., Jason Aronson, Inc., 1972 (and the later 1987 edition), in the 1987 edition, pp. 405-416). Bateson discussed this in various spots in this book and elsewhere. He was fond of saying: "When you go into a restaurant, don't eat the menu." This basic notion appears throughout philosophy in one form or another, certainly back to the ancient Greeks. The first verse of the ancient Chinese *Tao Te Ching* expresses, probably, the same notion. The idea that "the name is not the thing named" has been wrestled with down through the ages for all the reasons discussed here.

2. The Mind/Body connection has been argued about in psychology for decades. Now we have the field of psychoneuroimmunology: the study of how our thinking, as part of our neurology, actually affects our immune systems, perhaps contributing to disease formation, or helping us to heal. The NLP volume on the subject is Robert Dilts, Tim Hallbom and Suzi Smith,. *Beliefs: Pathways to Health and Well-Being* (Portland, Oregon, Metamorphous Press, 1990).

3. For fuller discussions of the processes of deletion, distortion, generalization, again see *The Structure of Magic* by Bandler and Grinder and *NLP Volume I* by Dilts, et. al.

4. Again, see Dilts, Hallbom and Smith, *Beliefs: Pathways to Health and Well-Being*.

5. For a more thorough discussion of reference experiences, see Dilts and Epstein, *Dynamic Learning*. They also stress this as a central theme throughout their book.

6. For a thorough, professional and quite readable discussion of information processing theories, see Joseph LaDoux, *The Emotional Brain: The Mysterious Underpinnings of Emotional Life* (New York, Touchstone, 1996, especially chapters 2-4). Also, see Steven Pinker's brilliant, massively thorough, funny and engaging book, *How the Mind Works* (New York, W. W. Norton, 1997). Both these books are modern classics.

7. David Gordon does fascinating workshops about how beliefs tie themselves together in systems. He's one of the premier instructors in NLP and has written a number of good books on the subject, though not primarily aimed at education.

8. Katherine Bell, "Life's Work: Wynton Marsalis: An Interview with Wynton Marsalis" (*Harvard Business Review*, January-February, 2011). Also found on-line at: http://hbr.org/2011/01/lifes-work-wynton-marsalis/ar/1

# Chapter 3

1. Years ago Richard Bandler told me about an encounter he had with the great family therapist, Virginia Satir, who was a colleague of his at the time. He asked her why it was so difficult to get people to make changes, even in the face of truly life-threatening circumstances. She replied that the most powerful drive isn't survival, but rather it's the drive to do what's familiar. This story is also repeated in his book with John La Valle: *Persuasion Engineering* (Capitola, CA., Meta Publications, 1996, p. 70). On a basic level, that's probably a survival mechanism as well. If you think about how early man must have lived in the wild, the ability to find and maintain safe routines seems a necessity. If you eat a little of all the plants, some are bound to be poison. If you stray too far from home, you might get lost (or eaten). For a great look at how our evolution shapes our behavior even in today's world, read Steven Pinker's *How the Mind Works*.

2. The primary theorist on cognitive dissonance was social psychologist Leon Festinger. In the late 1950's he began describing how cognitive dissonance would powerfully motivate people to do almost anything to reduce its effects. He meant, primarily, the dissonance between a person's expectations of his or her role, or character, and any circumstance that strongly challenged those expectations. More broadly this is often expanded to include any situation in which expectations don't match occurrences. For our purposes, these differences in emphasis aren't important; it's the relationship between familiarity—the basis of rapport—and cognitive dissonance, its opposite, that concerns us.

3. I think most cognitive neuroscientists (who study our evolutionary/ genetic makeup and its relation to our thinking and emotional lives) would take this as given. What makes people seem so different, at times, is that the differences produce a measure of cognitive dissonance. This amplifies and focuses attention on those differences, compared to the relative deletion of similarities. Think about close relationships and all the similarities that are a part of those relationships. Any time there is stress on the relationship (anger, distrust, etc.), the differences seem much more important. When the stress is relieved, they fade into the background.

4. For a broader discussion of Rapport, see my earlier book: *Meta-Cation, Education About Education with Neuro-Linguistic Programming, Volume I* (Lincoln, NE., An Author's Guild BackInPrint. com edition, iUniverse.com, 2000). Also, see the NLP classic: *Frogs into Princes* by Richard Bandler and John Grinder (Moab, UT., Real People Press, 1979)and Dilts, et. al. *NLP, Volume I.*

5. The mirror neuron system. This internal network helps us recognize emotions from others and is involved in learning from others through observation and even in communication. This may be the key element in the brain that makes relationships possible. See Robert Dilts and Judith DeLozier, *NLP II The Next Generation: Enriching the Study of the Structure of Subjective Experience* (Capitola, CA. Meta Publications, 2010, p. 257-8), Daniel J. Siegel, *Pocket Guide to Interpersonal Neurobiology: An Integrative Handbook of the Mind* (New York. W.W. Norton. 2010, p. 19-2), and Temma Ehrenfeld, *Reflections on Mirror Neurons* (*Observer*, Vol.24, No.3 March, 2011, Association for Psychological Science).

# Chapter 4

1. The basic communication model is easy to find in introductory communication books. An old classic, and still very good book to read on this and similar subjects is Paul Watzlawick, *Pragmatics of Human Communication* (New York, W.W. Norton, 1967).

2. I recently saw a commercial on television that quoted the famous 7% words, 38% tonal qualities, 55% face and body language statistics. As you might guess, there is much more to this story than a few numbers haphazardly thrown around by just about everyone

in the communication field. The numbers, and the ideas behind them, come from very involved, enormously detailed research primarily conducted by Ray Birdwhistell, Albert Mehrabian and their respective colleagues over a period of decades. These percentages relate primarily to the "connectedness" the speaker has to his or her message. In other words, they are an indication of which parts of a communication a listener can pay attention to, to judge the importance and reliance the speaker has on the content of the message. This is especially useful during times when the speaker is sending inconsistent messages (incongruent communication). The easiest to read of the explanations of the 7/38/55 research seems to me to be Chapter 3, "The Double-Edged Message," in Mehrabian's book *Silent Messages* (Belmont, CA., Wadsworth, 1971). A much fuller description of Mehrabian's research is Chapter 6, "Inconsistent Messages and Sarcasm," in his book *Nonverbal Communication* (Chicago, Alpine-Atherton, Inc., 1972). Similar ideas were explored by him and others in the fields of kinesics and paralanguage. This was early "body-language" research and there are lots of books on it today. Also, the related field of proxemics, developed by Edward T. Hall is worth a look that goes beyond individual communication, the use of space and time, and an added cultural dimension. See especially *The Hidden Dimension* (New York, Anchor Book Editions, 1966) and *The Silent Language* (New York, Anchor Book Editions, 1973).

3. For a fuller discussion of filters and noise in communication, see: Sid Jacobson and Dixie Elise Hickman, Ph.D., *The POWER Process: An NLP Approach to Writing* (Bancyfelin, Carmarthen, Wales, The Anglo American Book Company, 1998, pp. 13-17).

4. Most professionals in persuasion, for example salespeople, have found their professional training to be largely in these two areas. For many, the name of the game is establishing rapport and minimizing or overcoming objections. That's what getting past resistance is about. That isn't, certainly, all there is to sales, but it's a big part.

# Chapter 5

1. Research on teachers' expectations, and how they affect student performance has been going on for many years. Some of the results

are unclear, but some studies have shown significant effects. Some of this research is the source of the so-called "Pygmalion effect," and the original research is described in Robert Rosenthal and Lenore F. Jacobson, "Teacher Expectations for the Disadvantaged" (*Scientific American,* April 1968, vol. 218, no. 4).

2.  For Bateson's original description see "The Logical Categories of Learning and Communication," in *Steps to an Ecology of Mind,* pp. 279-308. For Dilts' description of his Neuro-Logical Levels applied to education, based on Bateson's work, see: *Dynamic Learning,* Dilts and Epstein, pp. 2-9, and also Appendix A.

3.  The study of identity is fairly new in our field. It's related to the philosophical field of ontology. There are some good recent books that cover these ideas in some depth. See Dilts and DeLozier and Robert Dilts and Stephen Gilligan, *The Hero's Journey: A Voyage of Self Discovery* (Bethel, CT, Crown House Publishing, 2009) and Joseph Riggio, *The State of Perfection: Your Hidden Code to Unleashing Personal Mastery* (New York, Smashwords, 2012).

# Chapter 6

1.  Teachers unions are a force in education. No matter what your beliefs are about them and the politics surrounding them, there are interesting issues of testing, teaching to tests, protecting troubled teachers, trying to evolve the systems, etc. See the award winning documentary: *Waiting for Superman.* Regardless of how you come down on any sides in the issues presented in this film, they are clearly stated in the documentary, and the view of systems, their struggles to change and adapt, are well presented. See also Wendy Kopp, *A Chance to Make History: What Works and What Doesn't in Providing an Excellent Education for All* (New York, PublicAffairs (Perseus), 2011). Kopp is the founder of Teach for America and also explores these issues well, using specific examples of several school systems.

2.  This is one of the most common topics of conversation among parents I talk with all over Asia. A recent article in the magazine *The Economist* quotes the Prime Minister in Singapore, Lee Hsien Loong, imploring parents to: "Please let your children have their childhood . . . Instead of growing up balanced and happy, he grows

up narrow and neurotic. No homework is not a bad thing. It's good for young children to play, and to learn through play." ("Tiger mothers in Singapore; Losing her stripes? The prime minister goes into battle against pushy parents." *The Economist*. Sep 22, 2012).

3. Einstein repeated this, in a variety of ways. Often he's quoted as saying: "You cannot solve a problem at the same level of awareness that created it." I believe the point is, essentially, the same. Robert Dilts wrote a wonderful book on Einstein: *Strategies of Genius, Vol. II* (Capitola, CA., Meta Publications, 1994). It is filled with quotations from Einstein and describes the thinking strategies that seem to underlie them. Einstein's technical work, of course, can be quite difficult reading, but much of his other work is quite readable, fascinating and enjoyable. For those who have not read Einstein, I recommend two volumes of papers, essays, addresses, articles and quotes of his: *Ideas and Opinions* (New York, Dell, 1973) and *Out of My Later years* (Secaucus, NJ., 1956).

# Part 2

## Introduction

1. Discussions about messages and meta-messages are pretty standard in communication theory now. The most important contributions were probably first in *Steps to an Ecology of Mind*, by Gregory Bateson, in Part V, "Epistemology and Ecology." For an easier and more recent look, see Tannen's *You Just Don't Understand*, pp. 31-32 and Dilts' *Visionary Leadership Skills*, pp. 178-180.
2. Congruence is discussed most thoroughly in Richard Bandler and John Grinder's book: *The Structure of Magic, Vol. II* (Palo Alto, CA., Science and Behavior Books, 1976, Part II, "Incongruity").
3. Again, see Dilts and DeLozier.

## Chapter 8

1. These categories were developed by Robert Dilts and Todd Epstein in relation to the development of testing materials designed

to measure the different types of skills necessary for effective Practitioners of NLP. This work was done in the early 1990's for meetings of the Academy of Behavioral Technology, which they founded.

2.  I'm indebted, again, to Robert Dilts for the Bandura curve and many of the ideas in this discussion. Bandura discussed this originally in the context of his research into "self-efficacy," which is essentially how people perceive their own abilities and competence in specific situations. It, like many other seemingly simple formats, is quite involved. For the most readable discussion by Bandura himself, see Albert Bandura, *Social Learning Theory* (Englewood Cliffs, NJ., Prentice Hall, 1977). For his most thorough description of his work and ideas, see his later *Social Foundations of Thought and Action: A Social Cognitive Theory* (Englewood Cliffs, NJ., Prentice Hall, 1985). See also The Encyclopedia of Systemic NLP and NLP New Coding, by Robert Dilts and Judith DeLozier. Scotts Valley, CA, NLP University Press, 2000, pages 82-90.

# Chapter 9

1.  There are two books that thoroughly examine the Sorting principles and Meta-Programs: Wyatt Woodsmall and Tad James, *Time Line Therapy and the Basis of Personality* (Cupertino, CA., Meta Publications, 1988) and Shelle Rose Charvet, *Words That Change Minds: Mastering the Language of Influence* (Dubuque, IA., Kendall/Hunt Publishing Company, 1997).

2.  For a broad look at the various learning style formats, see Eric Jensen, *Super Teaching* (San Diego, CA., The Brain Store, Inc., 1995), especially Chapter 3, "Learning Styles Made Easy," pp. 31-42.

3.  Anne Lamott, *Bird by Bird: Some Instructions on Writing and Life* (New York, Anchor Books, 1994, pp. 18-19).

4.  "A journey of a thousand miles begins with a single step." This is from verse 64, from the *Tao Te Ching*. If you are not familiar with this ancient Chinese text, it was, arguably, written by Lao Tzu, and is probably between 2500 and 3000 years old. Like many ancient works, even the existence of the author, or even a single author, is impossible to verify. The many translations into English vary, as well.

# Chapter 10

1. That the sensory basis to learning is central is very old and generally accepted. In the field of education, Maria Montessori, an Italian psychiatrist, stressed the importance in her two great works written just about 100 years ago. See either of these two works, in any of their many editions: *The Montessori Method* (1912) or *The Absorbent Mind* (originally about 1902). The psychology literature is even older.
2. We have observed this repeatedly for many years. Again, with our understanding of rapport, and our new understanding of the mirror neuron system, we now believe we know better why this is true.
3. The notion of task analysis is much more commonly discussed in relationship to adult training and development in industry, than in childhood education. A shame, in my view.

# Chapter 11

1. You can ask your librarian or staff at a good bookstore for help, and the following books may help to lead you toward what you might want to try: Marcia L. Tate, *Worksheets Don't Grow Dendrites: 20 Instructional Strategies That Engage the Brain* (Thousand Oaks, CA, Corwin Press, 2003). Kathy Hirsh-Pasek, Ph.D., Roberta Michnick Golinkoff, Ph.D. with Diane Eyer, Ph.D., *Einstein Never Used Flash Cards: How Our Children REALLY Learn—And Why They Need to Play More and Memorize Less* (New York, Rodale, 2003), and Robert J. Marzano, Debra Pickering, and Jane E. Pollock, *Classroom Instruction That Works: Research-Based Strategies for Increasing Student Achievement* (Alexandria, VA, ASCD Association for Supervision and Curriculum Development. 2001).
2. Meta-Cation, Vol. II, pp. 38-39. Originally quoted in "Liv Ullman: Making Choices," by Leonie Caldecott (*New Age Journal*, July, 1985, p. 30).
3. Hirsh-Pasek, et. al.
4. The use of metaphor as a therapeutic and teaching tool came to prominence because of the work of Milton Erickson. For the best description and instruction in its use, see David Gordon's classic NLP book *Therapeutic Metaphors* (Cupertino, CA., Meta

Publications, 1978). Another book, from the outdoor adventure learning community is useful: *The Conscious Use of Metaphor in Outward Bound*, by Stephen Bacon (Denver, CO., Colorado Outward Bound School, 1983). Also, most of the better books describing Erickson's work, including all those mentioned in previous notes, have some explanation of the value and use of metaphor.

# Chapter 12

1. We learn more about the neurological basis for memory all the time. For a really succinct, very recent description, see Siegel, 2012, 30-1 to 30-7.
2. Obviously this is much more crucial for some things than others. Also, it can be difficult to get from some states directly to some others. That's the point of this chapter.
3. Anchoring is probably not be the same as Pavlovian Conditioning, but it does seem to follow the same rules. Regardless of the underlying physiological mechanism, it's extremely valuable and easy to use.
4. In psychology the word "learning" can have some pretty broad uses. Learning Theory, as a branch of psychology, is quite elaborate and complex. Also, lots of what is known is based on studies with animals, which cannot always be compared to humans. Sometimes the rules work the same, sometimes they don't, but even when they do (as in the case of Pavlov's work), it still doesn't mean they are the same thing.
5. Bedtime is special because right before we go to sleep is a great time to learn anything. As we are falling asleep, the first stage of sleep (there are four) is called the hypnogogic state: a natural hypnotic state in which we are more suggestible than normal. Think of falling asleep in front of the television and waking later to find that your dreams were a mix of the TV program and your own thoughts. This can be used to advantage in studying. Right before bed seems to work well because the last thoughts in mind are the ones from the schoolwork. They can blend right into sleep and seem to consolidate quite well for many people.

6.  Sid Jacobson, *Solution States: A Course in Solving Problems in Business with the Power of NLP* (Bancyfelin, Carmarthen, Wales, The Anglo American Book Company, 1996).

# Part 3

## Chapter 13

1.  Judy Kearins has done some fascinating work in comparing thinking styles and strategies of people from various cultures. I first saw the work here described in an eight part PBS series on the brain: "The Two Brains" (from *The Brain*. Educational Broadcasting Corporation, 1984). It intrigued me to look up her research: Judith M. Kearins, "Visual Spatial Memory in Australian Aboriginal Children of Desert Regions" (in *Cognitive Psychology*, Vol. 13, pp. 434-460, 1981).
2.  Michelle Deck and Lori Backer, *Presenter's E-Z Graphics Kit: A Guide for the Artistically Challenged* (Mosby Year Book, 1997). Michelle has told me that she's experimented with, and read of others using, different numbers of window panes, six or nine, depending on the task. The idea of a six pane version may go back as far as 20 years, or more, in the training field.
3.  For some good solid psychological information on memory, start with *Searching for Memory* by Daniel L. Schachter (New York, Basic Books, 1996). Also see *The Emotional Brain* by Joseph LeDoux (New York, Touchstone, 1996., Chapter 7, "Remembrance of Emotions Past," pp. 179-224). To learn more about the memory techniques, my favorites are the following classic books: *The Memory Book* by Harry Lorayne and Jerry Lucas (New York, Ballantine, 1974), *Use Your Perfect Memory*, by Tony Buzan (New York, Plume, 1991), and my personal favorite, *Total Memory Workout: 8 Steps to Maximum Memory Fitness* by Cynthia R. Green (New York, Bantam, 1999). Green gives a wide-ranging practical look at the things you can do to improve your memory, as well as a look at the standard techniques and how to use them.
4.  This notion comes from a classic article by George Miller, "TheMagical Number Seven, Plus or Minus Two: Some Limits on Our Capacity for Processing Information" (*Psychological Review*,

Volume 63, 1956, pp. 81-96). *Dynamic Learning* by Dilts and Epstein has more experiments, some similar to the ones here, plus some additional ideas and worksheets.

5. Tim Murphey, *Language Hungry!* (Tokyo, MacMillan Languagehouse LTD., 1998, pp. 56-60). This book is full of practical learning tips, easy for anyone to use: highly recommended.

6. One thing generally agreed on by all memory experts is that the more sensory information you can connect to any new idea, the easier it will be to remember. This is also the basis of most of the memory-enhancing techniques that exist.

7. Again, see Dilts and DeLozier.

8. See Schachter, pp. 212-217, or LaDoux, pp. 206-211.

9. Robert Dilts developed the NLP spelling strategy in the late 1970's by modeling people who were effective spellers. It has become a standard in the repertoire of most NLP Practitioners. This and the math strategy he developed were also the first two educational computer programs published and sold by Apple® Computer, for the Apple II. The strategy can also be found in *Meta-Cation, Vol. I,* pp. 153-154.

# Chapter 14

1. This case is in (Example 14) one of Erickson's most famous papers: "Further Techniques of Hypnosis—Utilization Techniques" (which originally appeared in the *American Journal of Clinical Hypnosis,* (2) 1959, 3-21). It can also be found in *The Collected Papers of Milton H. Erickson on Hypnosis,* edited by Ernest Rossi (Volume I) and in *Advanced Techniques of Hypnosis and Psychotherapy,* edited by Jay Haley. For those interested in learning more about this amazing person, the most easy to read introduction to Erickson is Jay Haley's *Uncommon Therapy: The Psychiatric Techniques of Milton H. Erickson, M.D.* (New York, Norton, 1973). There is a vast literature devoted to Erickson and his therapeutic techniques.

2. Diane McGuinness, *Why Our Children Can't Read and What We Can Do about It* (New York, The Free Press, 1997). See also the more recent book by Susan L. Hall and Louisa C. Moats, Ed.D., *Parenting a Struggling Reader* (New York, Broadway Books, 2002). Also, the

U.S. Department of Education has several excellent publications available that can be downloaded from their web site. For parents, there is a publication titled *Put Reading First: Helping Your Child Learn to Read, A Parent Guide, Preschool Through Grade 3*. This was developed by The Partnership for Reading, a collaborative effort of the National Institute for Literacy (NIFL), the National Institute of Child Health and Human Development (NICHD), and the U.S. Department of Education. For those interested in the research basis of their recommendations, see *Put Reading First: The Research Building Blocks for Teaching Children to Read, Kindergarten Through Grade 3* (2001). This was put together by the Center for the Improvement of Early Reading Achievement (CIERA) and was funded by the National Institute for Literacy (NIFL) through the Educational Research and Development Centers Program. There are a number of other useful publications available in the same section of the Department of Education web site, currently collected under the title Reading Excellence Program, found under Reading Resources. The web site is pretty easy to navigate and well worth a visit if you are the parent of a child struggling with learning to read.

3. Personally, I always found helping kids with this to be pretty straightforward. I simply shared my understanding of what the words meant, and as long as the relationship was working, it was OK. There are books that you can get that cover certain patterns of problem words and other stuff like that, but lots of people now seem to believe that this isn't the best way to go about it.

4. John Updike, *S.* (New York, Alfred A. Knopf, p. 36).

5. Ray Bradbury, "Way in the Middle of the Air"(in *The Martian Chronicles.* New York, Bantam, 1954, p. 96).

6. Harlan Ellison, "Ernest and the Machine God" (in *Deathbird Stories.* New York, Macmillan, 1983, p. 204).

7. Thomas L. Friedman, *The Lexus and the Olive Tree* (New York, Farrar, Strauss Giroux, 1999 p. 149).

8. Stephen Jay Gould, "Unpredictable Patterns" (in *Predictions.* Edited by Griffiths, Sian. Oxford, Oxford University Press, 1999, p. 145). By permission of Oxford University Press.

9. Bertrand Russell, *The Problems of Philosophy* (London, Oxford University Press, 1959, p. 100). By permission of Oxford University Press.

10. Paul Scheele, *The PhotoReading Whole Mind System* (Wayzata, MN., Learning Strategies Corporation, 1993).

## Chapter 15

1.  Dixie Elise Hickman, Ph.D. and Sid Jacobson. *The POWER Process: An NLP Approach to Writing* (Bancyfelin, Carmarthen, Wales, The Anglo American Book Company, 1998).
2.  Natalie Goldberg, *Writing Down the Bones* (Boston, Shambhala, 1986).
3.  At various times, however, Einstein referred to himself primarily as an *epistemologist*. That's a person who studies the origin and nature of knowledge itself. Some of the books on Einstein, including some collections of his thoughts, have entire sections on his epistemology. The central question of epistemology is: "How do we know what we know?" Many of Einstein's addresses and essays are specifically on this study of knowledge. See his essays on knowledge and science in *Ideas and Opinions* or *Out of My Later Years*. Robert Dilts discusses this thoroughly in *Strategies of Genius, Vol. II*.
4.  Einstein clearly described his thinking processes in many of his essays and addresses. He generally began with visual images that then created specific feelings. He connected series of these images to complete his understanding of a concept and only then began to mentally describe them in words. These he could subsequently test mathematically. Math would be acceptable to scientists. See the references above, as well.

## Chapter 16

1.  Though there is a lot of anecdotal evidence suggesting listening to music while studying, or even test taking, can be helpful, there isn't very much research on the link between learning and music, in the sense we're talking about here. See Eric Jensen, *Student Success Secrets* (Hauppage, NY, Barrons, 1996, p. 61-2).
2.  Scheele, *PhotoReading*, page 4-4.

# Part 4

## Chapter 17

1. *Meta-Cation, Vol. I*, pp. 126-127.

## Chapter 18

1. My teachers, the developers of NLP, Richard Bandler and John Grinder were quite vocal about their disbelief regarding learning disabilities, when I trained under them in the late 1970's. I came to agree as soon as I began working with kids. I also thank my friend Lynn Pearlmutter for introducing me, also in the late 1970's, to a book by Peter Schrag and Diane Divoky called *The Myth of the Hyperactive Child and Other Means of Child Control* (New York, Dell, 1975). This book seems as relevant to me today as it did then. Since that time, of course, the battle has raged on, and many books have been written about learning disabilities that also doubt that they really exist as defined and described by mainstream education/medicine. Certainly kids can have every kind of difficulty with energy level (too high, too low), attention (lack of focus on anything, too much focus on one thing), and just about anything else we can imagine. Creating a disease, or a label, doesn't seem a useful way of solving those individual difficulties, especially when you end up having to slap the label on a significant percentage of the kids out there. This creates a social disease in addition to the medical one, and I think that is what we now have, at least in the US and a few other countries.

2. You local bookstore or health food store will have dozens of books on low blood sugar and its causes and effects. Also, they'll have just as many diet, alternative medicine and natural healing books with information on this. Rather than suggesting titles, I think it's wiser to suggest that you browse a bit, then find a nutritionist if you suspect that this might be something useful for you to explore. In addition, if you think one of your kids may actually have a problem in this area, your pediatrician should be able to advise you. Eventually, you and your kids will have to do some experimenting to see what effects high glycemic foods (ones that break down to large doses of sugar) have on you.

3. John Rosemond, *Ending the Homework Hassle: Understanding, Preventing, and Solving School Performance Problems* (Kansas City, Andrews and McMeel, 1990).
4. Leslie Cameron-Bandler is one of the great NLP trainers and contributed much to the early development of the field. See her book *The Emotional Hostage* (San Rafael, CA., FuturePace, 1986).
5. A classic in the psychopharmacology field is Ronald K. Siegel, Ph.D., *Intoxication: Life In Pursuit of Artificial Paradise* (New York, E. P. Dutton, 1989). Another book that looks at addiction and its treatments, including a political perspective, is Stanton Peale, *Diseasing of America: Addiction Treatment Out of Control* (Lexington, MA., Lexington Books, 1989). Though each of these books is a couple decades old, they still provide, to my way of thinking, a better perspective on drugs in society than anything I've seen since.
6. My friend, the late Todd Epstein did research on addictions in several populations and repeatedly found this to be the case (Personal communication).
7. See: Peter R. Breggin, M.D., *Talking Back to Prozac: What Doctors Aren't Telling You about Today's Most Controversial Drug* (New York, St. Martin's Press, 1994) and his earlier book with Ginger Ross Breggin, *The War Against Children: How the Drugs, Programs and Theories of the Psychiatric Establishment Are Threatening America's Children with a Medical "Cure" for Violence* (New York, St. Martin's Press, 1994). Dr. Breggin has been writing on issues of the dangers of drugs and other treatments in psychiatry for many years. A useful perspective.
8. In Breggin, *Talking Back to Prozac*, p. 102.
9. The issue of labeling has been of major importance in sociology for over a half century. Two classic texts: Erving Goffman, *Stigma: Notes on the Management of a Spoiled Identity* (Englewood Cliffs, NJ., Prentice Hall, 1964) and Edwin M. Shur, *Labeling Deviant Behavior: Its Sociological Implications* (New York, Harper & Row, 1971).

# Chapter 19

1. *Meta-Cation, Vol. I*, pp. 127-128.
2. New Orleans. After Hurricane Katrina, the State of Louisiana actually stepped in and took over the majority of the school system,

leaving the then existing school board with only eight schools, the ones deemed functional, under its control. The entire public school system is still being re-designed as of this writing.

3.  Several years ago I participated in a meeting on this issue at an international conference of training and development specialists. The discussion was around the work most of them had been doing as volunteers to help their local school systems and the lessons they learned and wished to share. One of the people at the meeting had written a book on the subject: *The Eden Conspiracy: Educating for Accomplished Citizenship* by Joe Harless (Guild V Publications, 1998). See also Peter M. Senge's (ed.) book: *Schools That Learn: A Fifth Discipline Fieldbook for Educators, Parents, and Everyone Who Cares About Education* (New York, Doubleday, 2000).

# Appendix I

1.  Divoky, *The Myth of the Hyperactive Child.*
2.  See Michael Grinder, *Righting the Educational Conveyer Belt* (Portland, OR., Metamorphous Press, 1989).

# Recommended Books for Further Study

Note: These are my favorites, and I've divided them into useful categories. They do not include all the NLP books on learning and teaching, just my current recommendations. I chose to omit some good ones that are simply older, harder to find or out of print. The same, of course, goes for each of the other categories with the additional note that I have only included books meant for general audiences here; no texts aimed strictly at professional audiences are listed. Finally, keep in mind that many of the authors in this listing have written other books that may also be of interest.

## NLP Primarily for Classroom Teachers

Grinder, Michael. *Righting the Educational Conveyer Belt.* Portland, OR., Metamorphous Press, 1989.

Grinder, Michael. *Envoy: Your Personal Guide to Classroom Management.* MGA Publishing, 1996.

# NLP Primarily about Learning Problems and Special Education

Hartmann, Thom. *Attention Deficit Disorder: A Different Perspective*. Grass Valley, CA., Underwood Books, 1997.

Hartmann, Thom. *Healing ADD: Simple Exercises That Will Change Your Daily Life*. Grass Valley, CA., Underwood Books, 1998.

Jacobson, Sid. *Meta-Cation, Education About Education with Neuro-Linguistic Programming, Volume I*. Lincoln, NE., An Author's Guild BackInPrint. com edition, iUniverse.com, 2000.

# NLP and Learning in General

Beaver, Diana. *NLP for Lazy Learning: Superlearning Strategies for Business and Personal Development*. Boston, MA., Element, 1998.

Blackerby, Don, Ph.D. *Re-Discover the Joy of Learning*. Oklahoma City, OK., Success Skills, Inc., 1996.

Dilts, Robert B., and Todd A. Epstein. *Dynamic Learning*. Capitola, CA., Meta Publications, 1995.

Dilts, Robert, and Judith DeLozier. *NLP II The Next Generation: Enriching the Study of the Structure of Subjective Experience*. Capitola, CA. Meta Publications, 2010

# Related Books Primarily for Teachers

Jensen, Eric. *Super Teaching*. San Diego, CA., The Brain Store, Inc., 1995.

Jensen, Eric. *Teaching with the Brain in Mind*. Alexandria, VA., Association for Supervision and Curriculum Development, 1998.

# Related Books for Teachers and Parents

Levine, Mel, M.D. *A Mind at a Time*. New York, Simon and Schuster, 2002.

Markova, Dawna, Ph.D., with Anne R. Powell. *How Your Child Is Smart: A Life-Changing Approach to Learning*. Berkeley, Conari Press, 1992.

# Study Skills, Homework and Activity Guides

Farber, Barbara, M.Ed. *The Parents' and Teachers' Guide to Helping Young Children Learn: Creative Ideas from 35 Respected Experts.* Cutchogue, NY., Preschool Publications, Inc., 1997.

Hirsh-Pasek, Kathy, Ph.D., Roberta Michnick Golinkoff, Ph.D., with Diane Eyer, Ph.D.
*Einstein Never Used Flash Cards: How Our Children REALLY Learn—And Why They Need to Play More and Memorize Less.* New York, Rodale, 2003.

Jensen, Eric. *Student Success Secrets.* New York, Barron's, 1996.

Jensen, Eric. *B's and A's in 30 Days: Strategies for Better Grades in College.* New York, Barron's, 1997.

Markova, Dawna, Ph.D., and Anne R. Powell. *Learning Unlimited: Using Homework to Engage Your Child's Natural Style of Intelligence.* Berkeley, Conari Press, 1998.

Murphey, Tim. *Language Hungry!* Tokyo, MacMillan Languagehouse LTD., 1998.

Rosemond, John. *Ending the Homework Hassle: Understanding, Preventing, and Solving School Performance Problems.* Kansas City, Andrews and McMeel, 1990.

# On Memory

Buzan, Tony. *Use Your Perfect Memory.* New York, Plume, 1991.

Green, Cynthia R. *Total Memory Workout: 8 Steps to Maximum Memory Fitness.* New York, Bantam, 1999.

Lorayne, Harry, and Jerry Lucas. *The Memory Book.* New York, Ballantine, 1974.

Schachter, Daniel L. *Searching For Memory: The Brain, the Mind and the Past.* New York, Basic Books, 1996.

# On Reading

Hall, Susan L., and Louisa C. Moats, Ed.D., *Parenting a Struggling Reader.* New York, Broadway Books, 2002.

McGuinness, Diane. *Why Our Children Can't Read And What We Can Do About It*. New York, The Free Press, 1997.

Scheele, Paul. *The PhotoReading Whole Mind System*. Wayzata, MN., Learning Strategies Corporation, 1993.


## On Writing

Goldberg, Natalie. *Writing Down the Bones*. Boston, Shambhala, 1986.

Hickman, Dixie Elise, Ph.D., and Sid Jacobson. *The POWER Process: An NLP Approach to Writing*. Bancyfelin, Carmarthen, Wales, The Anglo American Book Company, 1998.

Lamott, Anne. *Bird by Bird: Some Instructions on Writing and Life*. New York, Anchor Books (Doubleday), 1994.


## Cognitive Neuroscience and Brain Functioning

Aamodt, Sandra, Ph.D., and Sam Wang, Ph.D. *Welcome to Your Child's Brain: How the Mind Grows from Conception to College*. New York, Bloomsbury, 2011.

Calvin, William H. *How Brains Think*. New York, Basic Books, 1996.

Calvin, William H. *The Cerebral Code: Thinking a Thought in the Mosaics of the Mind*. Cambridge, MA., Bradford, (The MIT Press), 1996.

Dehaene, Stanislas. *Reading in the Brain: The Science and Evolution of a Human Invention*. New York, Viking, 2009.

Gazzaniga, Michael S. *The Mind's Past*. Berkeley, The University of California Press, 1998.

Gazzaniga, Michael S. (ed.). *Conversations in the Cognitive Neurosciences*. Cambridge, MA., Bradford, (The MIT Press), 1997.

LeDoux, Joseph. *The Emotional Brain*. New York, Touchstone, 1996.

Pinker, Steven. *How the Mind Works*. New York, W. W. Norton, 1997.

Siegel, Daniel J. *Pocket Guide to Interpersonal Neurobiology: An Integrative Handbook of the Mind*. New York. W.W. Norton. 2010.

Siegel, Daniel J., M.D., and Tina Payne Bryson, Ph.D. *The Whole-Brain Child*. New York, Delacorte, 2011.

Siegel, Daniel J., M.D. *The Developing Mind, Second Edition: How Relationships and the Brain Interact to Shape Who We Are*. New York, Guilford, 2012.

# Linguistics and Language

Pinker, Steven. *The Language Instinct: How the Mind Creates Language*. New York, William Morrow and Company, 1994.
Pinker, Steven. *Words and Rules: The Ingredients of Language*. New York, Perennial, 2000.

# Other Books for Parents

DeBecker, Gavin. *Protecting the Gift: Keeping Children and Teenagers Safe (And Parents Sane)*. New York, Dell, 1999.
Shore, Milton F., Patrick J. Brice and Barbara G. Love. *When Your Child Needs Testing: What Parents, Teachers and Other Helpers Need to Know About Psychological Testing*. N.Y., The Crossroad Publishing Company, 1992.

# Index

## A

ability  xx, 5, 11, 32, 36, 55, 86-7, 120-1, 162-3, 170-1, 179, 221, 229, 238, 275

allergy  269

analytical  86, 121, 127

anchor  143-4, 148-50, 154, 156-8, 213, 245, 248, 250, 263, 285, 300, 312, 315, 328

associate  141, 175-6

assumptions  16, 45

attention  35-6, 41-3, 60-1, 79-81, 89-95, 97-8, 104-5, 145-6, 179-80, 186-7, 189-93, 195-7, 212-13, 243-6, 271-2

attitude  iii, 61, 65, 232-3, 262, 277, 288, 294

audience  115, 119, 228-9, 232-8

auditory  95, 107-10, 115, 160-3, 171, 178-9, 182, 200, 217, 248

## B

Backer  318

Bacon  317

Bandler  xvi, 41, 303, 308-11, 314, 322-3

Bandura  88-9, 315

Bateson  49, 309, 313-14

behavior  xvi, xx, 17-19, 42, 51-2, 55, 57, 88, 90, 122, 261, 269, 284, 292-3, 295-6

belief  22-4, 45-6, 55, 57, 88, 122, 162, 168, 231, 238, 274, 280, 286, 301

believe  xviii, xx, 4-5, 15, 17-18, 23-5, 34-5, 46, 53-5, 57-8, 71, 96-7, 122, 280-1, 302

Birdwhistell  312

blood sugar  245, 268-71, 322

body  8, 19, 35, 38-9, 49, 73, 78-9, 81-2, 114, 123, 161, 186-7, 190, 197, 311-12

Bradbury  216-17, 320

brain  23, 34-5, 91, 107, 111, 167, 170, 173, 197, 243, 270, 309, 315-16, 318, 326-8

breathing  46, 80, 83, 271-2

Breggin  323

Buzan  176, 318, 327

## C

Caldecott  316

capability  52-3, 55, 57, 88, 122, 139, 261

category  86-7

Charvet  315

eye   34, 77, 162, 165, 167, 169-71,
181-2, 200-1, 207, 216, 226, 241,
263, 304

**F**

familiar   32, 36-7, 48, 79, 95, 97, 112,
129, 141, 174, 310, 315
family   xvi, xix-xx, 22, 33, 53, 56, 59,
81, 102, 128, 221-2, 242, 263,
269, 276-8
feedback   24, 40-1, 60-1, 114, 127,
150
feel   13, 20-2, 27-8, 31-6, 63-7, 74-5,
94-7, 105, 114-16, 135-8, 151-4,
156-7, 185-93, 264, 279-83
Festinger   310
flexible   43, 55, 77, 151, 160, 286
focus   60, 82, 104, 121, 132, 157, 180,
187-8, 213, 243-4, 260, 289, 292,
308, 322
format   228-9, 234-5, 305
Foster   16, 262
Freud   283
Friedman   218, 220, 320
future-pacing   130, 155, 221

**G**

generalization   21, 285, 287, 309
goal   57, 61, 82-3, 90, 162, 167-9,
199, 201, 222, 241, 252, 254, 265,
289, 294
Goffman   323
Goldberg   231, 321, 328
Gordon   25, 310, 316
Gould   218, 220, 320
Green   200, 216-17, 318, 327

Grinder   xvi, 308-9, 311, 314, 322, 324-5
gustatory   163

**H**

habit   211, 241, 271
Haley   319
Hall   163, 312, 315, 319, 323, 327
Hallbom   309
Harless   324
Harmon   229
health   iii, vi, 19, 268-9, 282, 288, 296,
309, 320, 322
hearing   10, 20, 42, 48, 77, 105, 115, 140,
149, 154, 186, 190, 214, 216, 233
Hickman   iv, xvi, 227, 312, 321, 328
homework   13, 163, 229, 242, 244,
275-7, 314, 323, 327
hypoglycemia   268-9

**I**

identity   54-6, 88, 123, 261, 313, 323
imagination   138, 142, 238
incompetence   89-91
incongruent   73, 312
information   vi, 21-5, 60, 74-6, 94-7,
105-7, 161, 176-7, 182, 234-6,
240-1, 246-9, 273-4, 304-9, 318-19
intention   1, 18, 65, 71-4, 76, 128, 246
interactive   86-7, 121
internal resources   20, 280

**J**

Jacobson   ii-iv, vi, xi, xvi, xviii, xx, 4,
6, 8, 10, 312-14, 318, 320-2, 326,
328